CAMBRIDGE LIBRARY COLLECTION

Books of enduring scholarly value

Literary studies

This series provides a high-quality selection of early printings of literary works, textual editions, anthologies and literary criticism which are of lasting scholarly interest. Ranging from Old English to Shakespeare to early twentieth-century work from around the world, these books offer a valuable resource for scholars in reception history, textual editing, and literary studies.

Shakespeare and the Nature of Man

Analysing Shakespeare's historical background and craft, Spencer's 1943 study investigates the intellectual debates of Shakespeare's age, and the effect these had on the drama of the time. The book outlines the key conflict present in the sixteenth century – the optimistic ideal of man's place in the universe, as presented by the theorists of the time, set against the indisputable and ever-present fact of original sin. This conflict about the nature of man, argues Spencer, is perhaps the deepest underlying cause for the emergence of great Renaissance drama. With detailed reference to Shakespeare's great tragedies, the book demonstrates how Shakespeare presents the fact of evil masked by the appearance of good. Shakespeare's last plays, especially The Winter's Tale and The Tempest, are also analysed in detail to show how they embody a different view from the tragedies, and the discussion is related to the larger perspective of general human experience.

Cambridge University Press has long been a pioneer in the reissuing of out-of-print titles from its own backlist, producing digital reprints of books that are still sought after by scholars and students but could not be reprinted economically using traditional technology. The Cambridge Library Collection extends this activity to a wider range of books which are still of importance to researchers and professionals, either for the source material they contain, or as landmarks in the history of their academic discipline.

Drawing from the world-renowned collections in the Cambridge University Library, and guided by the advice of experts in each subject area, Cambridge University Press is using state-of-the-art scanning machines in its own Printing House to capture the content of each book selected for inclusion. The files are processed to give a consistently clear, crisp image, and the books finished to the high quality standard for which the Press is recognised around the world. The latest print-on-demand technology ensures that the books will remain available indefinitely, and that orders for single or multiple copies can quickly be supplied.

The Cambridge Library Collection will bring back to life books of enduring scholarly value across a wide range of disciplines in the humanities and social sciences and in science and technology.

Shakespeare and the Nature of Man

THEODORE SPENCER

CAMBRIDGE
UNIVERSITY PRESS

CAMBRIDGE UNIVERSITY PRESS

Cambridge New York Melbourne Madrid Cape Town Singapore São Paolo Delhi

Published in the United States of America by Cambridge University Press, New York

www.cambridge.org
Information on this title: www.cambridge.org/9781108003773

© in this compilation Cambridge University Press 2009

This edition first published 1943
This digitally printed version 2009

ISBN 978-1-108-00377-3

This book reproduces the text of the original edition. The content and language reflect
the beliefs, practices and terminology of their time, and have not been updated.

SHAKESPEARE

and

THE NATURE OF MAN

CAMBRIDGE
UNIVERSITY PRESS
LONDON: BENTLEY HOUSE

Copyrighted in the United
States of America by The
Macmillan Company

SHAKESPEARE

AND

THE NATURE OF MAN

By THEODORE SPENCER

Lowell Lectures, 1942

CAMBRIDGE: AT THE UNIVERSITY PRESS

1943

PRINTED IN THE UNITED STATES OF AMERICA

To

F. O. MATTHIESSEN

PREFACE

There are three main ways in which we can study the expression of human experience in the arts. We can study the historical—the intellectual and emotional—background which the artist was able to use; we can study the craft, the artistic medium, which he employed; and we can try to analyze and judge the final product in relation to what we believe to be true of human experience as a whole.

To study a great artist, such as Shakespeare, in all of these three ways may seem to be a presumptuous undertaking. Yet that is what I want to do in this book. And as a basis for this study I have taken the widest possible topic: "Shakespeare and the Nature of Man."

Such a topic obviously needs definition before we can say anything sensible about it, for if we are to accomplish our threefold aim of understanding the past, analyzing a craft, and judging the truth of what is expressed in that craft, we must have as clear as possible a picture of what we are doing, and of what we are leaving aside. Though the topic is vast, and fundamental, it does not include everything, and what we are looking for is not a complete picture of Shakespeare. We shall not have much to say about the sources of Shakespeare's plots, nor about the texture of his poetry, and we shall have to leave out any full discussion of his use of primarily literary fashions and technical dramatic devices. Frequently our account of his characters will seem incomplete. But this is inevitable; our aim is to describe the point of view that underlies all these things, the framework that gave Shakespeare his terms and his values. It is Shakespeare's vision of life we are after, its dependence on contemporary thought, its development through dramatic form, and its universal truth.

The first chapter, therefore, will be devoted to a description of the ideal picture of man that Shakespeare's age supplied. According to every creditable theorist of the time man had a definite place in the universe, in nature, and in the state, and his relations to God, to the rest of creation, and to society, were, broadly speaking, universally agreed upon. The picture was quite different from any picture that we have at the present time; a man living in Shakespeare's day was living in almost the last generation that could unquestioningly accept, with all the available evidence before him, the old over-orderly scheme, the scheme which Galileo and Newton in one way, and Bacon and Locke in another, were to re-arrange so that its basic assumptions (to our ultimate confusion) could eventually be destroyed. In theory the picture was highly optimistic, and I shall begin by emphasizing its optimism, and the exalted position it gave to man in the scheme of things.

But it could be looked at in another way. Though man was essential in the scheme, he had, through original sin, betrayed his trust, and therefore his position, when seen realistically, was as dark and miserable as it was, theoretically, bright and noble. The second chapter will describe this pessimistic picture in order to bring out as clearly as possible the "Renaissance Conflict" about man's nature which is so important a part of Shakespeare's background. Yet there was a second element in the conflict which also needs emphasis, for in the sixteenth century the very basis of common agreement about man and his place in the world was being questioned. Was it really true that the earth on which man lived was the center of the universe and man himself the end for which the universe had been made? Did man show, in practice, that he was a proper member of an ordered

state? Was he, after all, even a rational animal? These were
the questions that were being asked, towards the end of the
sixteenth century, with increasing anxiety and intensity, and they
immensely re-inforced and brought into the open the more
traditional conflict between the optimistic, ideal picture and the
picture which emphasized the wretchedness of the human situation. The contrast between the theoretical good and the evil fact
goes very deep into the thought and feeling of Shakespeare's
age, and it was expressed by Shakespeare, among others, with
great force and grandeur. To a large extent it was expressed in
drama, the form of literature to which conflict is essential, and
one of the assumptions I shall make throughout this book is
that the existence at the end of the sixteenth century of this basic
conflict about the nature of man is perhaps the deepest underlying cause for the emergence of great drama at that time.

For there are periods in recorded human history when the
essential problems that concern human nature come to the surface with more than usual urgency and are expressed with more
than usual vigor. We are living in such a period ourselves;
Shakespeare lived in another: the difference between them may
perhaps be summed up by saying that Shakespeare's age was
breaking into chaos, while our age is trying to turn chaos into
order. Shakespeare's age produced a new set of terms and ref-
erences in the light of which the old problems—the problem
of good and evil, of the dignity or worthlessness of man, the
problem of reality—were being considered with a fresh vital-
ity. These problems were so alive, so much a part of the age,
that they became available for a popular form of literature, and
I shall try to describe, in the main part of this study, how
Shakespeare, through a growing realization of what a play could
be about, was able to use them. When he did so he was not, of
course, fully conscious of what he was doing (what artist ever
is?), but there can be no doubt that they formed an important

part of the atmosphere or texture of his greatest tragedies, and that they profoundly affected his view of human nature and his way of presenting it on the stage.

I do not suggest however—and this is a point I should like to emphasize as clearly as possible at the outset—that Shakespeare made deliberate use of any of the particular authors or books which are quoted from or referred to in the first two chapters. We are in no way concerned with Shakespeare's specific knowledge of Ptolemy or Copernicus, Sabunde or Montaigne, Cicero or Machiavelli. Whether he knew them or not is of no importance to our argument. These writers are discussed because they give the clearest articulation to what Shakespeare's age was thinking and feeling; Shakespeare absorbed and used that thought and feeling in his own way, the way of the playwright who has a particular job to get done, who is sensitive to the temper of his time and who wants to use it in his work. In order to express his time, and the general truths with which its best minds, like himself, were concerned, Shakespeare did not have to spend his days turning pages in a library. That is the task of the critic and scholar who would try to understand him three hundred years later, and I trust that no reader of this book will shrink his mind into assuming that we are concerned, in any essential fashion, with the merely literal sources of what Shakespeare had so magnificently to say.

Shakespeare began his dramatic career with the dramatization of conflict on a relatively superficial level of action and character, and, as I shall point out in the third chapter, the traditional views of man are merely a part of the background. In the great tragedies the conflict goes deeper, taking on, as it were, another dimension, and in *Hamlet* and *Troilus and Cressida*, in *Othello* and *King Lear*, in *Macbeth* and *Antony and Cleopatra*, the Renaissance conflict about the nature of man finds its culminating expression as Shakespeare presents the discovery of the evil actuality under the good appearance, and describes the individual passion or weakness which has to be destroyed before order can prevail once more. The conflict between individuals is enlarged to include, in the kind of fusion which only poetry can manage, the conflict about man's nature which was so crucial in Shakespeare's age. In the fourth, fifth, and sixth chapters I shall discuss the great tragedies in some detail, and in the seventh I shall turn to the last plays, especially *The Winter's Tale* and *The Tempest*, and show how they embody a different view, one exactly the reverse, in many respects, from that expressed in the tragedies. I shall conclude by trying to relate the discussion to literature as a whole, so that we may be able to see Shakespeare's work not merely against the background of his own time, but in the larger perspective of general human experience.

2

This book was originally planned as a series of lectures which the Lowell Institute of Boston asked me to deliver in the spring of 1942. To the Trustee of the Institute I should like to express my gratitude for honoring me by the invitation, and I should like to express my gratitude to my original audiences for their appreciative understanding of what I tried to say. The material has been somewhat revised for publication.

In quoting Shakespeare, I have used, except where otherwise specified, the text of the Oxford Edition, edited by W. J. Craig. I have followed Sir Edmund Chambers' chronology of the plays. The spelling of all quotations from sixteenth and seventeenth century authors has been modernized. At certain points I have repeated or rephrased statements and interpretations which I have elsewhere expressed in published articles on individual plays and problems.

Anyone who writes about Shakespeare is bound to be conscious of his debt to those who have written about Shakespeare before. The debt is so large that complete acknowledgment of it

is impossible, and the reader of these pages will soon discover
that they owe much to both previous and contemporary Shakespearean criticism and scholarship. Some of my debts are explicitly acknowledged in the notes; others are not, since I did
not know how to acknowledge them. Who can tell where orig-
inality begins?

One of the rewards of the academic life under the right circumstances is that any book a man writes is never the work of
the writer alone. His colleagues are always on hand for information, correction and criticism. In this respect I have been unusually fortunate. Mr. Harry Levin, Professor F. O. Matthiessen, Professor Perry Miller, Dr. I. A. Richards, and the late
Dr. W. E. Sedgwick have all been interested in the kind of
problem which is treated here, and they have all spent more
time than they should have spent in discussing with me this
particular example of it. The sharing of knowledge and wisdom
which they have given me sharpens the intelligence and warms
the heart, and I am grateful, not only to them, but to the circumstances which have allowed us, in the past and in the present, to be colleagues in a great university.

I should like to thank Miss Helen Jones of Harvard for her
invaluable assistance in putting my words into readable shape.
And I should also like to express my gratitude to those members
of the staff of the Harvard College Library and to those members of the staff of the Library of Cambridge University who
have so kindly enabled me to use the resources at their disposal.

But to Miss Victoria Schrager, who has helped me to collect,
order and express the material and ideas set forth in the following pages, I owe a greater debt than I owe to anyone else.

T. S.

Eliot House
Cambridge, Mass.
September 1, 1942

CONTENTS

SHAKESPEARE
and
THE NATURE OF MAN

CHAPTER I

MAN IN NATURE: THE OPTIMISTIC THEORY

I

The first thing that impresses anyone living in the twentieth century who tries to put himself into Shakespeare's intellectual background is the remarkable unanimity with which all serious thinkers, at least on the popular level, express themselves about man's nature and his place in the world. In the sixteenth century the combined elements of Aristotelianism, Platonism, Neo-Platonism, Stoicism, and Christianity were almost indistinguishably woven into a pattern which was universally agreed upon, and which, in its main outlines, was the same as that of the Middle Ages. New ideas, such as those which the men of the early Renaissance discovered through their reading of Plato, were treated either as additions to the accepted picture or as fresh ways of interpreting the one universal truth about which there was no question. If there was dispute, as of course there was, it was about details; people were concerned as to *how* Christ manifested himself through the Eucharist; they did not ask whether or not he did so at all. They did not doubt the importance of reason in the process of knowledge; they discussed *what* specific functions reason could perform. They did not question the existence of kingship, though they might be violently anxious about *who* should be king. There was an eternal law, a general order—in the universe, in the ranks of created beings, in the institution of government—and it was the business of thoughtful men to discover it and describe it so that through knowledge of it they could fulfill the end for which God had made them.

That end—no matter how often it might be forgotten in the

pursuit of ambition or the dazzle of earthly pleasure—was also universally agreed upon: man was made in order to know and love God. "The soul was made for an end, and good, and therefore for a better than itself, therefore for God, therefore to enjoy union with him." [1] To enjoy this union man must, as far as his ability goes, have knowledge of God, and for this purpose God has given man two books, the Bible, and the book "of the universal order of things or nature." [2] Sir Walter Raleigh begins his *History of the World* by saying that though God cannot be corporeally perceived, yet "by His own word, and by this visible world, is God perceived of men; which is also the understood language of the almighty, vouchsafed to all his creatures, whose hieroglyphical characters are the unnumbered stars, the sun and moon, written on the large volumes of the firmament: written also on the earth and the seas, by the letters of all those living creatures, and plants, which inhabit and reside therein. Therefore said that learned Cusanus, *Mundus universus nihil aliud est, quam Deus explicatus.*" [3] "The universal world is nothing but the setting forth of God," and if, to use Marlowe's words, our souls

---

[1] Thomas Hooker, quoted Perry Miller, *The New England Mind*, New York, 1939, p. 3. Hooker was preaching in Connecticut, in the next century, but his words are merely echoes of the whole tradition, from Augustine and Aquinas down.

[2] Montaigne, Preface to his translation (1569) of Ramón Sabunde's *Natural Theology* (circa 1425), ed. A. Armaingaud, 1932, p. ix. Since Sabunde's explains the second of these books, says Montaigne, his work is more important than the Bible. Dante also speaks of the universe as a book, which, in his final vision, he at last comprehends (*Par.*, xxxiii, 85–86). La Primaudaye, *French Academy*, English trans., 1618 (6th ed.), p. 333, writes of the book of nature as a witness of God, and du Bartas begins his *Divine Weeks* with the same image (Sylvester's trans., ed. 1613, p. 6):

> The World's a Book in Folio, printed all
> With God's great works in letters Capital:
> Each Creature is a Page; and each Effect
> A fair Character, void of all defect.

Cf. *Antony and Cleopatra*, i, 2, 10: *Soothsayer:* In nature's infinite book of secrecy/A little I can read.

[3] *Works*, ed. Oldys and Birch, London, 1829, ch. i, sect. i, vol. II, p. 3.

can comprehend
The wondrous architecture of the world,

we may then have some knowledge of the divine architect who planned so marvelous a structure.[4]

Nearly every sixteenth-century writer speaks in the same fashion; to know God one must know His works; by knowing His works one learns the nature of man, for whom those works were made; by learning the nature of man one learns the end for which man was made, which is the knowledge of God. This universal belief is well expressed by a French writer named Pierre de la Primaudaye who in 1577 (his work was translated into English in 1586 and went through several editions) wrote a huge book—a kind of summary of universal knowledge—which goes by the name of *The French Academy*. La Primaudaye begins as follows: "When I direct my sight . . . unto the heavens, and with the wings of contemplation behold their wonderful greatness, their terrible motions, being contrary and without ceasing, the lively brightness, rare beauty and incomparable force of the Sun and Moon, their unchangeable course, one while cause of light, and by and by after of darkness, the infinite number of goodly stars, and of so many other celestial signs: and from this excellent and constant order of all these things, as one ravished and amazed, when I withdraw my spirit lower into the elementary region, to admire and wonder at the situation and spreading of the earth amidst the waters, both of them making one round mass or lump, which in the midst of this great firmament occupieth the room but of a prick or tittle

[4] Marlowe, *I Tamburlaine*, ii, 7. The image of God as an architect is extremely common. Sabunde uses it (ch. 3, Montaigne's trans.); it is frequent in du Bartas, *op. cit.*, pp. 7, 102, 156, etc.; it is used by Romei, *Courtier's Academy*, trans. I. K., 1598, p. 26, and by many other writers who describe what Danaeus calls *The Wonderful Workmanship of the World* (trans. T. T., 1578). Danaeus is interesting as belonging to the tradition which tries to combine the two books and describe, as he says on his title-page, the "Form, knowledge, and use of all things created" from evidence "specially gathered out of the Fountains of holy Scripture."

in respect thereof: besides, when I acknowledge in this earth and water as many sundry and most beautiful plants, and kinds of earthy and watery creatures, as there are grains of sand on the sea banks: and when I delight myself in the variety of minerals and precious stones, considering the form, quality, and virtue of each of these things: briefly, when I admire . . . so many wonderful works under the cope of heaven I cannot marvel enough at the excellency of Man, for whom all these things were created, and are maintained and preserved in their being and moving, by one and the same divine providence always like unto itself." [5]

Writers under the influence of Neo-Platonism emphasized the same thing, in even more glowing language. Annibale Romei, in his *Courtier's Academy* (1546—translated into English in 1598), speaks of man in the most exalted terms: "This heavenly creature whom we call man, was compounded of soul and body, the which body, having to be the harbor of a most fair and immortal soul, was created . . . most exquisite, with his eyes toward heaven, and was placed in the midst of the world to the end that as in an ample theater, he might behold and contemplate the works of the great God, and the Beauty of the whole world: as also there was granted unto him a perfect tongue and speech, that enflamed with love divine, and replenished with admiration, he might praise, and with words extol divine beauty." [6]

[5] Ed. cit., bk. i, ch. 1. The sixteenth-century writers on these matters are never tired of exclaiming, as Cicero had exclaimed (*De Nat. Deor.*, II, xxxix, 98 ff.) over the beauty of the world, and particularly of the heavens. Robert Recorde, for example, speaks of the heavens as "the chief spectacle of all [God's] divine works," and urges his reader to "look upward to the heavens, as nature hath taught him, and not like a beast go poring on the ground." (*Castle of Knowledge*, 1556, preface to the reader.)

[6] English trans. (1598), p. 16. The Renaissance writers were fond of pointing out that man was the only animal who stood erect, and was therefore formed to look at the heavens. They derived the idea from Plato, *Timaeus*, 90A, though no doubt it became embedded in the tradition partly because of its use by Ovid, *Met.* I,

Passages like these embody certain fundamental assumptions which every thoughtful Elizabethan took for granted. The first is this: man is not something by himself; he is, as Ramón Sabunde says, "a piece of the order of things," [7] he is the *nexus et naturae vinculum*,[8] the knot and chain of nature; it is impossible to think of him apart from the rest of creation, for just as man was made for the service of God, so was the rest of creation, including the heavens, made for the service of man,[9] provided man fulfilled his own proper function. Thus, even though the earth he lives on is no bigger than a point, and—as one astronomer says—"in comparison to the whole world beareth no greater view, than a mustard corn on Malvern Hills, or a drop of water in the Ocean sea," [10] nevertheless man's role is the most important in the universe. To play it properly he must know both himself and the environment apart from which he cannot

76–86, and by Macrobius, *Com. in Somn. Scip.*, I, xiv. It is also mentioned by Lactantius, *Divine Institutes*, bk. ii. See the dedicatory letter to the King by Louis Le Roy in his French translation of the *Phaedo* and the tenth book of the *Republic* (1553): he repeats the tradition by saying that the immortal soul was placed in the head, the highest part of the body, thus raising man toward the heavens, "son semblable."

[7] Montaigne's trans., ed. cit., ch. 3.

[8] Godfrey Goodman, *The Fall of Man, or the Corruption of Nature, etc.*, 1616, p. 17.

[9] *Ibid.* The belief that the world was made for man was a commonplace even in classical times; see Xenophon, *Memorabilia*, I, iv, 11, and IV, iii, 3 ff., Cicero, *Tusc. Disp.*, I, 28, 68–70, *De Nat. Deor.*, II, 39, 98 ff., and II, 62, 154 ff. The sixteenth-century repetitions of the idea are too numerous to list. But see Richard Hooker, *Laws of Eccl. Pol.*, I, ii, 2; du Bartas, *op. cit.*, p. 156 (God, as an architect, says du Bartas, built this "All-theater" for him who can "admire with due respect Th' admired Art of such an Architect"); Sir Thomas Elyot, *The Book Named the Governor*, I, i, London, 1907, p. 6, etc., etc.

[10] Robert Recorde, *op. cit.*, p. 5. As Professor Lovejoy and others have pointed out, we are inclined to forget that the relatively minute size of the earth was a commonplace of Ptolemaic cosmology. See Macrobius, *op. cit.*, I, xvi ("The earth, of which the entirety is hardly a point, if compared with the vastness of heaven."), Chaucer, *Troilus*, v, 1815; *House of Fame*, 906; du Bartas, *op. cit.*, p. 72; Cardinal Bellarmine, *Ascent of the Mind to God*, tr. J. B., gent., Douai, 1616, II, i, etc.

properly be conceived. In other words—and this is the second assumption—he must understand the universal *order* of which he is so essential a part, and which makes the structure of the world, of living beings, and of society, a single unity created by the hand of God.

For order is behind everything. It is order, says Sir Thomas Elyot, "which in things as well natural as supernatural hath ever had such a pre-eminence, that thereby the incomprehensible majesty of God, as it were by a bright leme [gleam] of a torch or candle, is declared to the blind inhabitants of this world." [11] And Elyot continues, in a famous panegyric, to praise the order in the heavens, the order in the four elements, the order in plants, the order in animals, and finally, the order in the "estate of mankind, for whose use all the said creatures were ordained of God." This order reveals the interdependence of everything, the essential unity of creation. As Richard Hooker says, "We see the whole world and each part thereof so compacted, that as long as each thing performeth only that work which is natural unto it, it thereby preserveth both other things and also itself." [12]

Over this order, this unity, rules Nature. To quote Hooker again, "Obedience of creatures unto the law of Nature is the stay of the whole world." [13] Nature is God's deputy,[14] just as, according to Spenser, order is Nature's sergeant; [15] and Nature's law can be discovered in both of the books, the book of the Scriptures, and the book of the world, which God has given to man.[16]

Nature rules over three domains, each of which is a reflection

[11] *Op. cit.,* I, i.
[12] *Laws of Eccl. Pol.,* I, ix, 1.
[13] *Ibid.,* I, iii, 2.
[14] *Ibid.,* I, iii, 4.
[15] *Faerie Queene,* VII, vii, 4.
[16] For an account of Scripture as natural law see Hooker, *op. cit.,* I, xii, 1 (quoting Gratian); cf. A. J. Carlyle, *History of Medieval Political Theory in the West,* London, 1928, II, ii, 3, p. 103.

of the others, since they are all parts of the same ordered unity. She rules over the cosmos—the universal world; she rules over the world of created objects on earth; and she rules over the world of human government, of man in society. It is only necessary to learn what her rules are—"Those rules of old discovered, not devis'd"—in order to lead a wise and rational life.

The first domain, that of the created universe, is an enormous sphere, containing the vast area of the heavens with the point-sized earth as their center—as Aristotle and Ptolemy had described it. This domain is divided into two highly unequal parts. In the middle, stationary and fixed, is the relatively minute, if extremely important, world of the four elements—earth, water, air and fire, and the various mixtures of them which, in the form of minerals, plants, animals and men, inhabit the round and stationary globe. Earth is the lowest of the elements—water comes next; surrounding them both is air, and above air is fire, the most refined of the four.[17] This is the sublunary world, the world beneath the moon, on which the second or celestial part of the universe exercises a considerable influence, and for whose chief creation, man, it had in fact been made. This celestial part consists of eight concentric spheres above the element of fire: that of the moon, Mercury, Venus, the Sun, Mars, Jupiter, Saturn, and the fixed stars.[18] These spheres are bodies, with definite edges, and since their circumferences are of different sizes,

---

[17] Medieval and Renaissance cosmographers always seem rather embarrassed about the element of fire. It had, as an element, to have a separate place; it could not be under the earth, because it was lighter than earth, and only heavy things fell to the center; so there was only one place for it, above the air, even though it could not be seen. Few writers try to explain it; even Dante, who explains everything else, has practically nothing to say about the element of fire. Bacon denies that there is any such thing. The second failing of the human mind, he says, is to see more "equality and uniformity" in nature than there really is: men have "feigned an element of fire, to keep square with earth, water, and air." (*Advancement of Learning*, bk. ii.)

[18] Sometimes another sphere, the crystalline, was added. See Milton, *Par. Lost*, iii, 481–85.

getting larger the further away they are from the earth, they move at different speeds as they revolve from east to west around it. Hence they rub against one another, and the friction between each produces a musical note—the music of the spheres.[19]

Each one of the spheres is governed by an angelic intelligence, just as the human body is governed by the soul, but since these intelligences are immaterial, and the stuff of which the spheres are made is superior to anything constructed out of the four elements, the celestial domain of the cosmos is of a higher quality than that of the first which is below it. That is why it is so profitable for man to contemplate it, for, as we shall see, there is an element in man himself which has an affinity with its purity and with the immaterial intelligences by which it is controlled.

The heavens are bounded by the Primum Mobile, the first mover, the outer rim of the created universe. It makes a complete revolution every twenty-four hours from west to east, and by doing so, sets the eight spheres below it whirling in the opposite direction. It is the direct cause of all heavenly movement, and—since the planetary spheres have so great an influence on the earth—the indirect cause of all earthly movement as well; it is the circumference of the circle of which the earth is the center.

Outside it is a third realm, with which Nature has nothing to do. This is the Empyrean heaven, eternal and infinite, the abode of God, and, after the Last Judgment, the dwelling of the blessed.[20]

---

[19] Not all authorities agreed on this, for though the music was generally supposed to exist, there were various theories about its production. Some writers denied it entirely. For example, Palingenius, in his popular handbook, *The Zodiac of Life* (circa 1528; trans. Barnaby Googe, 1588 [3rd ed.], p. 212), says that since the spheres are solid bodies, "most thick and great," they all revolve in the same direction, perfectly smoothly, so that there is no cause for friction, and hence there is no music.

[20] Many Renaissance writers, largely under the influence of Neo-Platonism, ar-

The world of Nature had been created, according to general opinion, at no very great distance in the past: in fact the six days of its creation had started one Sunday in August or September, 5284 years before the birth of Shakespeare.[21] Nor was it to last very long after that event. Life on earth, it was widely believed, had been planned to exist (as a result of Adam's fall) for only six thousand years, and it was to be exterminated, at the end of that period, by the fires of the Last Judgment. The souls of the damned were to be bound thereafter eternally in hell, in the center of the globe, and the souls of the saved were to be in eternal bliss in the Empyrean heaven. The structure of Nature —the earth and the planets—was to remain, but purified and cleansed. For throughout eternity the surface of the earth was to be as smooth as a crystal ball, the spheres were to stop revolving, and the stationary planets were to shine seven times more brightly on the lifeless earth than they had shone on sinful man. The whole marvelous mechanism was to be fixed forever as a monument to its creator, brilliant, empty, and alone.[22]

For the time being, however, the world was neither empty

---

ranged the Empyrean heaven into various hierarchies of intellectual beings. Spenser, in his usual dreamy fashion, gives an account of these hierarchies in his *Hymn to Heavenly Beauty*, an account that is similar to those given by Ficino, Pico, and others. (See Josephine W. Bennett, "Spenser's Venus and the Goddess Nature of the Cantos of Mutabilitie," *Studies in Philology*, XXX [1933], 160–193. Also Miss L. Winstanley's edition of the *Foure Hymnes*, Cambridge, 1907.) But these somewhat rarefied speculations did not affect the average man, like Shakespeare, and they did not become part of the general belief.

[21] Danaeus, *op. cit.*, ch. 34. He argues that the world was created in the autumn equinox, since autumn is a fruitful and productive time. There was not yet complete agreement on this matter. That had to wait for Bishop Ussher in the next century. Lipsius (*De Constantia*, I, xvi), writing in 1584, says that the world was then 5500 years old. Shakespeare writing, presumably, ten years later, knew about all this. He says of Cupid that he "hath been five thousand years a boy" (*Love's Labour's Lost*, v, 2, 11); that is, Cupid had existed since the creation of the world.

[22] See *Cursor Mundi* (xiv cent.), ed. R. Morris, E. E. T. S., 1877, vv. 23654 ff. Also Sir David Lyndsay, "Ane Dialog betuix Experience and ane Courtier," *Works*, ed. D. Laing, Edinburgh, 1879, iii, 132 ff.

nor motionless. It was a vast theater in which man could sit to contemplate what the divine architect had made for him. In it everything had its function, from the humblest mineral and plant to the most splendid constellation, and for each created thing the function was the same; it existed to work for man. Aristotle's statement that "God and nature create nothing that has not its use," [23] had been a commonplace for centuries, and had been applied to the accepted position of man in the universe. Hence the importance, for example, of astrology. "I'll ne'er believe," says Sylvester, translating du Bartas' *Divine Weeks* (the popularity of which in Shakespeare's day it is difficult to over-estimate):

> I'll ne'er believe that the Arch-Architect
> With all these Fires the Heav'nly Arches deck't
> Only for Show, and with these glistering shields
> T'amaze poor Shepherds watching in the fields.
> I'll ne'er believe that the least Flower that pranks
> Our garden borders, or the Common banks,
> And the least stone that in her warming Lap
> Our kind Nurse Earth doth covetously wrap,
> Hath some peculiar virtue of its own;
> And that the glorious Stars of Heav'n have none.[24]

The entire structure was knit together for a single purpose.

2

From one point of view, Nature's second domain, the sublunary world of the elements, may be considered, as we have seen, as part of the cosmological picture, but it has such obvious rules of its own that it may more properly be thought of by itself. It is the domain of living creatures, and it is arranged in what the sixteenth century, following Aristotle and the Middle Ages, thought of as a hierarchy of souls. At the bottom are objects

---

[23] *De Caelo*, Oxford trans. (J. L. Stocks), i, 4.
[24] Ed. cit., pp. 102–103.

which have no soul at all, like stones; they have merely being, but not life. In the next rank are plants, which possess the most rudimentary kind of soul, the vegetative or nutritive soul which takes care of growth and reproduction; in the rank above plants are animals, which in addition to possessing a nutritive soul or faculty, also possess a sensitive soul or faculty; they can not only grow, they can also feel, and hence they have the power of motion and, to some extent, the faculty of imagination. Above the animals comes man, who in addition to possessing a nutritive and sensitive soul, possesses also a rational soul. Above man come the angels, who are pure intellect, and who are able to apprehend universal truth without the medium of the senses. Above the angels is God, who—in Aristotelian terms—is pure actuality.

A moment's reflection on this scheme will show how crucial to it man's position is. For the hierarchy of souls is closely parallel to the hierarchy of the cosmos, and just as in the cosmos there is a sublunary and a celestial region, so in the psychological hierarchy there is a physical and a spiritual region—a world of sense, and a world of intellect. Man is the essential link between them. He is the highest of the animals, and the lowest of the intellectual beings. He is superior to the animals in that he can know universal truths, but he is inferior to the angels in that he can arrive at such knowledge only by abstracting it from images presented to him by his senses—a handicap of which the angels know nothing. "Man is made of two natures," says the Italian humanist, G.-B. Gelli, "one corporeal and terrestrial, the other divine and celestial; in the one he resembles beasts, in the other those immaterial substances which turn the heavens." [25]

There is a further reason for giving special attention to man; his position is not only crucial, it is precarious;—*ni ange, ni*

[25] *La Circe* (1549), bk. vii. The psychological hierarchy can be taken in at a glance if described as follows:

bête, he must strive as much as possible to be one rather than the other. Many sixteenth-century writers, especially those under Neo-Platonic influence, were extremely hopeful. For man has more than reason to work with; in fact reason is merely the lowest of his three intellectual powers. It is reason's relatively humble job to work on the sense-data which sensation, memory and imagination place on the "white paper," [26] the *tabula rasa,* of his mind, and to abstract from those sense-data the immaterial forms which they contain. These forms are then apprehended intuitively by the understanding or intellect, which is akin to the pure intellect of the angels, and which is therefore a higher power than the "discourse of reason." [27] And finally there is will—"which we use," says Sir Walter Raleigh, "to stir us up to seek God and . . . heavenly things, by which

---

> God—pure actuality
> angels—pure intellect
> man—reason
> animals—sense
> plants—growth
> stones—being

Naturally the working out of the whole matter is far more complicated than this simple outline implies. The full system was many times described in the sixteenth century, by La Primaudaye, *French Academy,* by Sir John Davies, *Nosce Teipsum* (1599)—in fact by nearly everyone who concerned himself with philosophical matters. One of the most elaborate of these discussions is that of Jean Bodin, *Théâtre de la Nature* (1596-7); Bodin produces a set of very full diagrams to illustrate the divisions inside the different ranks in the hierarchy.

[26] La Primaudaye, *op. cit.,* bk. ii, ch. 30.

[27] Milton describes this difference with his usual clear firmness. In *Paradise Lost,* bk. v, 469 ff., the Angel Raphael explains to Adam the "scale of Nature," ending with reason, which is the "being" of the soul. It is of two kinds, "discursive or intuitive"; "discourse," the angel says,

> Is oftest yours, the latter most is ours,
> Differing but in degree, of kind the same.

Milton, however, does not use the term "understanding" to mean intuitive reason, as certain other writers do; he couples understanding with imagination, thus making it the equivalent of what was elsewhere often described as the "common sense." In this he was following a common practice; the word is the most ambiguous of all those in the traditional psychology.

we rest also in these things, and are delighted and satisfied in them. . . . This is one point by which we are men, and do excel all other creatures living upon the earth." [28] Reason works *downward* on the material of sense; understanding or intellect works *upward* toward the immaterial world, and, as Cardinal Bembo says in Castiglione's *Courtier*, "from understanding, by the which man may be partner with Angels, ariseth will." [29]

This description of man's higher powers is, to be sure, somewhat eclectic: there is a good deal of disagreement, for example, as to whether reason and understanding are two different faculties, or merely different names for the same thing. The Neo-Platonic writers, who continually emphasize the fact that man's true home is with the angels, in the enjoyment of unstained intellectual apprehension, nearly always separate the two. But, no matter how various or how complicated the details might be, it was generally clear enough what man should do if he were to follow the law that Nature, under God, had laid down for him. He must begin with the senses, for that is the condition of his being, but he must rise above them to find the truth. By the proper use of her faculties, through the right kind of love, says Castiglione's Cardinal Bembo, the soul "ariseth to the noblest part of her (which is the understanding)," and then from her own and particular understanding she may rise to the "universal understanding"; there the soul, at last finding her true home, "fleeth to couple herself with the nature of Angels, and not only clean forsaketh sense, but hath no more need of the discourse of reason, for being changed into an Angel, she understandeth all things that may be understood: and without any veil or cloud, she seeth the main sea of the pure heavenly beauty and receiveth it into her, and enjoyeth

[28] *A Treatise of the Soul,* in *Works,* ed. Oldys and Birch, London, 1829, VIII, p. 586.
[29] Bk. iv, Hoby's translation.

the sovereign happiness, that cannot be comprehended of the senses.[30]

Nor is it only man's soul that is so admirable; the body which clothes it is equally magnificent—as is fitting for a creature who had been made in the image of God. In fact, the first way to recognize the beauty of the soul is to admire the beauty of the body, for the body reflects the soul, and, ideally, the outward appearance and the inner reality are the same.

> But outward beauty inward love procures, because
> It argues th'inward beauty of the mind,

says John Davies of Hereford—as Spenser and many other writers had said before him.[31]

Thus man, for whom all the rest of the world was created, stands in the center of the second of Nature's domains, the world of living beings, his head erect to contemplate the heavens, his soul able to rise from the realm of sense to apprehend the God who made him. But man has a further function to perform: "This is certain and sure—that man by nature far excelleth in dignity all other creatures in earth, where he is by the high providence of God set to govern and rule, order and temper all to his pleasure by wisdom and policy, none otherwise than God himself doth in heaven govern and rule all celestial things." [32] In other words, man must do more than contemplate the world that was created for him, he must govern it; he is a member of

---

[30] *Ibid.*, Cardinal Bembo has similar things to say in his own work, *Gli Asolani*, and they can likewise be found in G.-B. Gelli, *Circe*, bk. x; in Romei, *Courtier's Academy* (Eng. trans., 1598), bk. i; in Spenser's "Hymn to Heavenly Beauty," and in other Neo-Platonic writings.

[31] *Microcosmos* (1603), in *Works*, ed. Grosart, 1878, I, p. 65. Spenser, "Hymn to Beauty," Castiglione, *Courtier*, bk. iv, etc. This concept, which is not necessarily Platonic, though it is usually called so, is illustrated in the medieval belief that Jesus was the only man who was exactly six feet high, since six feet is the perfect height for a man, and the perfect soul of Jesus must be reflected in a perfect body.

[32] Thomas Starkey, *A Dialogue between Cardinal Pole and Thomas Lupset* (1598), ed. J. M. Cowper, E. E. T. S., 1871, p. 11.

society. Here too, in this third of her inter-related domains, Nature has her rules, which were discovered of old; in the state, as in the universe and in the world of living creatures, Nature's order is manifested in a hierarchy.

There are, roughly speaking, three kinds of temporal law for the government of men; there is the law of Nature itself, there is the law of Nations which derives from it and which is generally applicable to all countries, and there is civil law, which applies to the customs of particular communities. The first two were described by Sir John Hayward in 1603 as follows: "God in the creation of man, imprinted certain rules within his soul, to direct him in all the actions of his life; which rules, because we took them when we took our being, are commonly called the primary law of Nature: of which sort the canons account these precepts following. To worship God: to obey parents and governors, and thereby to conserve common society: lawful conjunction of man and woman: succession of children: education of children: acquisition of things which pertain to no man: equal liberty of all: to communicate commodities: to repel force: to hurt no man: and generally, to do to another as he would be done unto. . . . Out of these precepts are formed certain customs, generally observed in all parts of the world; which, because they were not from the beginning, but brought in afterward . . . are called the secondary law of nature, and by many also the law of nations." [33]

Under these laws the third law, the civil law, operates to establish and maintain in different countries the form of government best suited to each. Though other systems were possible elsewhere, custom and tradition had made kingship the only proper government for England, and it is the king's duty to act as the servant of the law of Nature which is above him,

[33] *An Answer to the First Part of a Certain Conference concerning Succession,* 1603, sig. A3v. See also Carlyle, *op. cit.,* II, 28 ff., 102–103, and F. Le V. Baumer, *The Early Tudor Theory of Kingship,* New Haven, 1940, *passim.*

and whose precepts he exists to carry out. The king is not a despot, who can independently do as he wants; he represents a universal principle of justice, as firmly established as the order of the heavens.[34]

And just as the heavenly spheres are clearly distinguished and arranged in a hierarchy, so is society, as in the Middle Ages, made up of clearly defined classes. "We in England," says Sir Thomas Smith (1583), in his *De Republica Anglorum*, "divide our men commonly into four sorts, gentlemen, citizens, yeomen artificers, and laborers,"[35] and that division reflects the order which Sir Thomas Elyot, in the book he wrote for the instruction of administrators, so eloquently emphasizes. The whole matter is summed up in the definition of a commonwealth which Elyot gives as a compendium of all that he has read on the subject. "A public weal," he says, "is a body living, compact or made of sundry estates and degrees of men, which is disposed by the order of equity and governed by the rule and moderation of reason."[36]

3

Such, all too briefly described, are the three chief domains of Nature, the three chapters—to change the metaphor—in Nature's book, which by the exercise of reason, and the application of art, it is man's business to understand. Art—and by the term is meant all the techniques by which man interprets Nature's rules and so finds out the truth; the art of cosmography, of astronomy, of government, of logic, of rhetoric, of poetry, of painting, and of the practical crafts—art is the interpreter of Nature's rules, and in the exercise of art, itself the product of

[34] See Hooker, *op. cit.*, I, xvi, 2, "There can be no doubt but that laws apparently good are (as it were) things copied out of the very tables of that high everlasting law; even as the book of that law hath said concerning itself, 'By me kings reign, and by me princes decree justice.'" See also Baumer, *op. cit.*, pp. 6 ff.

[35] Ed. L. Alston, Cambridge, 1906, p. 31.

[36] *Op. cit.*, I, i.

Nature, man helps to fulfill his natural function. Shakespeare's Perdita, in *The Winter's Tale*, has been so taught; "For I have heard it said," she observes to Polixenes, "that there is an art which . . . shares With great creating nature," and Polixenes develops the idea:

> Say there be;
> Yet nature is made better by no mean
> But nature makes that mean: so, over that art,
> Which you say adds to nature, is an art
> That nature makes.[87]

Nature rules over all; her order is manifest in the heavens, in created beings, in the state, and it is man's business, not only to comprehend it, but to see that it is maintained.

One of the chief ways in which he can achieve this comprehension is by realizing that since all three domains form a single unity and are interdependent, the best way to grasp any one of them is to compare it with one or both of the others. Nothing is more striking in serious sixteenth-century literature than the universal use of analogy: the cosmos is explained by the body, and the body is explained by the state; all three hierarchies are parallel—as they had been for centuries. "Therefore let the king recognize," says St. Thomas Aquinas, "that such is the office which he undertakes, namely, that he is to be in the kingdom what the soul is in the body, and what God is in the world," [38] and consequently, St. Thomas concludes, the state not only becomes subject to the same laws which govern the

---

[87] iv, 3, 88.

[38] *De Regimine Principium*, bk. i, ch. 13. See John of Salisbury (*Policraticus,* quot. George P. Conger, *Theories of Macrocosms and Microcosms in the History of Philosophy,* New York, 1922, pp. 35–36), who says that the prince is the head of the state and the image of the deity, and that in obeying the prince we follow the rule of nature which has placed all the senses of man in the head and subjected the other members to it. The senate is the heart of state, the provincial guards are the eyes, ears, and tongue, the army and judiciary are the hands, the menial workers are the feet.

other two hierarchies, it also becomes responsible to both of
them for upholding these laws. Such views are to be found
everywhere: the king, says du Bartas, is placed in the center of
his realm, just as the sun, with three planets on either side of
him, is set in the middle of the heavens, and as man's heart is
placed in the middle of his body.[39]

Shakespeare's Menenius, in *Coriolanus,* is not alone in drawing parallels between man's bodily structure and the state; the
same thing had been done already, not only by Plutarch but,
among others, by Ramón Sabunde, Castiglione, Sir Thomas
Elyot and King James I—as it was to be done again by Hobbes
in the opening pages of his *Leviathan.* In fact, just before Shakespeare wrote *Coriolanus,* a whole book had been written on the
subject—*A Comparative Discourse of the Bodies Natural and
Politic,* by one Edward Forset (1606), in which he states that
though the commonwealth may be set forth in various resem-
blances—to architecture, to bees, to a ship—yet no comparison
is more proper than "either . . . the universal mass of the
whole world . . . or . . . the body of man, being the lesser
world, even the diminutive and model of that wide extending
universal." [40] And in his heavy and leaden prose he develops
the latter comparison for a hundred pages. Other writers prefer
to compare the state to the universe; in 1588, for example, John
Case wrote his *De Sphaera Civitatis,* the Sphere of the State,
which is prefaced by a diagram showing Queen Elizabeth as the

[39] *Op. cit.,* pp. 106 ff.

[40] "To the Reader." See Ramón Sabunde, *Natural Theology,* Montaigne's
trans., chs. 99, 105; Sir John Fortescue, *De Laudibus Legum Angliae,* trans.
Robert Mulcaster, ch. 13, London, 1765, p. 32; Castiglione, *Courtier,* trans. Hoby,
bk. iv; Thomas Starkey, *A Dialogue between Cardinal Pole and Thomas Lupset,*
ed. cit., pp. 45–46; Sir Thomas Elyot, *The Governor,* I, i, ed. cit., p. 1, pp. 3–7;
La Primaudaye, *The French Academy,* ed. cit., p. 417; King James I, *The True
Law of Free Monarchies,* ed. Charles H. McIlwain, *The Political Works of James I,*
Cambridge (Mass.), 1918, pp. 64–65; John Davies of Hereford, *Microcosmos,*
Works, ed. Grosart, 1878, I, pp. 26, 49.

Primum Mobile, and Justice, like the earth, as the immovable center around which the other spheres revolve.

But the commonest of all comparisons was that between man and the universe, between the microcosm and the macrocosm. First mentioned in classical times, it became a medieval platitude, and as we look back on the sixteenth century it seems the most universal and most revealing symbol for the whole concept of Nature's order and unity, and for the glorification of man's place in the universal scheme. If, as Romei says, "the body of man is no other but a little model of the sensible world, and his soul an image of the world intelligible," [41] it becomes all the more important to understand man's nature and the essential role which speculation assigned to him.

For man, says Sir Walter Raleigh in his *History of the World*—and, considering his time, it was inevitable that he should make the comparison—"Man, thus compounded and formed by God, was an abstract or model, or brief story of the universal, in whom God concluded the creation, and work of the world, and whom he made the last and most excellent of his creatures, being internally endued with a divine understanding, by which he might contemplate and serve his Creator, after whose image he was formed, and endued with the powers and faculties of reason and other abilities, that thereby also he might govern and rule the world, and all other God's creatures therein. And whereas God created three sorts of living natures, to wit, angelical, rational, and brutal, giving to angels an intellectual, and to beasts a sensual nature, he vouchsafed unto man both the intellectual of angels, the sensitive of beasts, and the proper rational belonging unto man; and therefore . . . 'man is the bond and chain which tieth together both natures': and because, in the little frame of man's body, there is a representation of the universal, and (by allusion) a kind of participation

[41] *Op. cit.*, p. 17.

of all the parts thereof, therefore was man called *microcosmos,* or, the little world." [42] Raleigh develops the comparison at length, relating the various parts of the human body to their appropriate natural phenomena; he compares "our pure understanding . . . to those intellectual natures, which are always present with God"; and he ends with the final comparison of all: "our immortal souls (while they are righteous)" are "by God himself beautified with the title of his own image and similitude."

4

Thus the whole universe, which was made for man, found in man its reflection and its epitome; man was the center of the ideal picture which optimistic theory delighted to portray. Nature's order was shown in the elements, in the stars, in the hierarchy of souls, in the ranks of society. Everything in the world was part of the same unified scheme, and the body and soul of man, each a reflection of the other, and both an image of the universal plan, were the culmination and the final end of God's design. "Homo est perfectio et finis omnium creaturarum in mundo"—man is the perfection and the end of all the creatures in the world. [43]

[42] Bk. i, ch. 2, sect. 5; ed. cit., II, 58.
[43] Robert Fludd, *Utriusque Cosmi Maioris,* etc., 1617; prefatory diagram.

CHAPTER II

MAN IN NATURE: THE RENAISSANCE CONFLICT

I

I have so far emphasized as strongly as I could the essential unity of the three inter-related hierarchies which made up the optimistic sixteenth-century picture of man's nature. Each one of them reflected the order of Nature's rule, and to think of one was almost automatically to think of the others. No one expressed this fact better than Shakespeare: Ulysses' famous speech on order, in *Troilus and Cressida,* sums up nearly everything the Elizabethans felt about the matter. Ulysses is explaining why the Greeks have been so unsuccessful in their war against Troy. The trouble is, he says, that "the specialty of rule [the particular function of government] hath been neglected," and there has not been enough order in the administration of the Greek army. He first draws a parallel with the heavens, then with civil law, then with the four elements, then with natural and moral law, and finally with psychological law. Everything is inter-related and seen as part of the same scheme, obeying the same rules:

> The heavens themselves, the planets, and this centre
> Observe degree, priority, and place,
> Insisture, course, proportion, season, form,
> Office, and custom, in all line of order:
> And therefore is the glorious planet Sol
> In noble eminence enthron'd and spher'd
> Amidst the other; whose med'cinable eye
> Corrects the ill aspects of planets evil
> And posts, like the commandment of a king,

Sans check, to good and bad: but when the planets
In evil mixture to disorder wander,
What plagues, and what portents, what mutiny,
What raging of the sea, shaking of earth,
Commotion in the winds, frights, changes, horrors,
Divert and crack, rend and deracinate
The unity and married calm of states
Quite from their fixure! O! when degree is shak'd,
Which is the ladder to all high designs,
The enterprise is sick. How could communities,
Degrees in schools, and brotherhoods in cities,
Peaceful commerce from dividable shores,
The primogenitive and due of birth,
Prerogative of age, crowns, sceptres, laurels,
But by degree, stand in authentic place?
Take but degree away, untune that string,
And, hark! what discord follows; each thing meets
In mere oppugnancy: the bounded waters
Should lift their bosoms higher than the shores,
And make a sop of all this solid globe:
Strength should be lord of imbecility,
And the rude son should strike his father dead:
Force should be right; or rather, right and wrong—
Between whose endless jar justice resides—
Should lose their names, and so should justice too.
Then everything includes itself in power,
Power into will, will into appetite;
And appetite, a universal wolf,
So doubly seconded with will and power,
Must make perforce a universal prey,
And last eat up himself.

I hope to show later how important the speech is in the dramatic structure of Shakespeare's play; what I am now concerned with is to demonstrate how Shakespeare, in characteristic Elizabethan fashion, when considering the order of the state, illustrates it—as did so many of his contemporaries—by the order of the heavens, and—at the end—by the order in the faculties of man.

But that order, as Shakespeare so eloquently describes, could all too easily collapse. There is a further, and important, corollary to the unity of the inter-related hierarchies; not merely, as in Ulysses' speech, can the downfall of one of them be *illustrated* by the downfall of the others, it can actually *cause* that downfall. As Richard Hooker says, "Let any principal thing, as the sun, the moon, any one of the heavens or elements, but once cease or fail, or swerve, and who doth not easily conceive that the sequel thereof would be ruin both to itself and whatsoever dependeth on it?" [1] And what if man, "who was principally ordained for God's service, as all other creatures for man" —what if man, "being *nexus et naturae vinculum*," should break "his own bonds"? Would it not follow, as Godfrey Goodman states, "that all the rest of the creatures, which were bound and knit together in man, should likewise be inordinate, and overflow their own banks"? [2] It would; in fact it had, and the results had been disastrous for both man and the other creatures depending on him.

For to man, as a result of Adam's sin, was left only a small glimmer of the reason which had been his original birthright. His fall had been intellectual as well as moral, and though reason, since it was a natural gift, could not be entirely destroyed, yet of its original vigor, as Calvin says, "being partly weakened and partly corrupted, a shapeless ruin is all that remains." Though there are still some sparks which show that man is a rational animal and hence differs from brutes, yet "this light is so smothered by clouds of darkness that it cannot shine forth to any good effect. In like manner, the will, because inseparable from the nature of man, did not perish, but was so enslaved by depraved lusts as to be incapable of one righteous desire." [3] Man, instead of fitting into the order of Nature, now turns it

---

[1] *Laws of Eccl. Pol.*, I, ix, 1.

[2] Godfrey Goodman, *The Fall of Man*, 1616, p. 17.

[3] *Institutes*, trans. H. Beveridge, Edinburgh, 1845, bk. II, ch. ii, sec. 12.

upside down; the body rules the soul, instead of the soul's ruling the body; man is like good wine miserably turned to vine-
gar; [4] reason is virtually paralyzed, and

> Unhallowed sense, drown'd in that damnèd juice
> (Sin's cider) from Eve's fatal Apple bruis'd,
> Being deadly drunk, makes still the worser choice,
> Wherein (like Sow in mire) it doth rejoice.[5]

Consequently something occurs in the functioning of man's
powers which can best be described as a short circuit. Ideally
speaking, before a man performs an act of any kind, an elaborate process takes place. Through the working of the animal
spirits, the outward senses perceive an object, an impression of
it is conveyed to the imagination, the imagination refers this
impression to the affections as pleasing or displeasing, reason
debates the matter and presents its verdict to the will, the Queen
of the soul, who finally dictates back to the sensitive appetite
(the function which desires), telling it to act or to refrain from
action, according as the object is seen as good or evil.[6] This was
the way Adam invariably behaved before Eve gave him the
apple, and consequently his actions were invariably rational
and orderly. But once he had disobeyed God's command, Adam,
and all his descendants after him, could follow this practice only
with the greatest difficulty. The higher powers, reason and will,
had become so feeble that, as I have said, a short circuit occurred
which usually left them out, and what happened was that action
was dictated by imagination, a power which was lawless, and
much lower than reason—one shared, in fact, by the beasts.
Hence man is enslaved by passions, which are "sensual mo-

---

[4] Ramón Sabunde, *Natural Theology* (Montaigne's trans.), chs. 223, 231.

[5] John Davies of Hereford, *Microcosmos*, in *Works*, ed. Grosart, 1878, I, 23.

[6] For a full account of this process see Ruth L. Anderson, *Elizabethan Psychology and Shakespeare's Plays*, Iowa City, 1927, pp. 23–24.

tions of our appetitive faculty" aroused through imagination.[7] "Amongst the innumerable evils," says La Primaudaye, "which the desire of pleasure and fear of grief, engraven in the most secret parts of our soul by our first corruption, bring to man, this is the greatest and most pernicious, that they make sensible things more evident and plain unto him than things intelligible, and constrain the understanding to judge more by passion than by reason." [8]

This "transgressing the Law of his Nature," in Hooker's phrase, has drawn all "manner of harm after it:" it has brought "tribulation and anguish unto every soul that doeth evil," since man is the only creature subject to reward and punishment.[9] It has also corrupted the rest of creation, for when Adam fell, Nature fell too, and though, according to Danaeus, man's transgression could not take away the essential qualities of things, it produced, "as it were a sickness in the natural powers . . . and disagreement among things for lack of order. . . . In so much, that the strength and plentifulness of the earth, and of all other things, decreaseth daily, and are nothing now in respect as God first created them, which cometh to pass by reason of man's transgression." [10] If man had not fallen, Nature would have been friendly to him, but as it is, serpents and poisons attack him in punishment and revenge, and, says Robert Burton, things are so changed since the fall of our first parent Adam, that the earth is "accursed, the influence of stars altered, the four elements, beasts, birds, plants are now ready to offend us. . . .

---

[7] Thomas Wright, *The Passions of the Mind in General*, 1604, p. 8. For a good account of the Elizabethan view of the passions, see Lily B. Campbell, *Shakespeare's Tragic Heroes*, Cambridge, 1930. I cannot, however, completely follow Miss Campbell in her description of how Shakespeare used the passions for drama, since it seems to me likely that he was interested in doing more than the writing of case-histories.

[8] *French Academy*, trans. 1618, bk. i, ch. 3, p. 12.

[9] Hooker, *op. cit.*, I, ix, 1. Hooker is quoting *Rom.*, ii, 9.

[10] *Wonderful Workmanship of the World*, trans. T. T., 1578, ch. 41.

The heavens threaten us with their comets, stars, planets, with their great conjunctions, eclipses, oppositions . . . and such unfriendly aspects; the air with his meteors, thunder and lightning, intemperate heat and cold, mighty winds, tempests, unseasonable weather; from which proceed dearth, famine, plague, and all sorts of epidemical diseases, consuming infinite myriads of men." [11]

Furthermore the earth, on which man, this disgraced and unhappy creature, lives, could be regarded—and often *was* regarded—not as the center and most important part of the universe, but, to use Professor Lovejoy's words, as "the place farthest removed from the Empyrean, the bottom of the creation, to which its dregs and baser elements sank." [12] It could be seen, in the more Elizabethan language of the playwright John Marston, as "the only grave and Golgotha wherein all things that live must rot; 'tis but the draught wherein the heavenly bodies discharge their corruption; the very muckhill on which the sublunary orbs cast their excrements." [18] Viewed in "the light of our natural reason," as the gloomy Goodman viewed it, the entire system of Nature was running hopelessly down. "When I consider the diseases of these times, together with all the signs, tokens and symptoms: alas, alas, I fear a relapse, I fear a relapse," he cries. Nature is incurably corrupted, the elements are engaged in civil war; human art, like a cobbler or tinker, can only "piece up the walls and repair the ruins of nature"; all the faculties of man are "in an uproar"; man's miseries are greater than his joys, any animal is happier than a man; there is no human occupation that is not full of suffering; our laws take our corruption for granted; "the whole world is turned bankrupt"—corruption even infests the material heav-

---

[11] *Anatomy of Melancholy*, Part I, sect. i, memb. i, subs. i.

[12] A. O. Lovejoy, *The Great Chain of Being*, Cambridge (Mass.), 1936, pp. 101–102.

[18] *The Malcontent*, iv, 2.

ens (have not "perspective glasses" recently discovered spots in the moon?). In the light of all this Goodman could reach only one conclusion: the Last Judgment was about to take place. "When the hangings and furniture are taken down," he says, "it is a token that the king and the court are removing"; nature now beginning to decay, it is clear enough, "according to natural reason," that the end of the world is at hand.[14]

Burton and Goodman, to be sure, were writing in the early seventeenth century (one in 1621 and the other in 1616), at a time when pessimism about man's situation had reached a kind of climax. But what they said was only a re-iteration, in unusually strong language, of an opinion that the sixteenth century had continually had in mind. The miseries of the human situation, so frequently emphasized in medieval literature, were never forgotten by the writers of the Renaissance. Underneath the gilt brocade of the prince was the corruptible flesh, and many courtiers who talked of how their souls could be united with the angels through Platonic love had their bones racked with syphilis. Both experience and doctrine re-inforced the familiar fact of man's general wretchedness. For example George Gascoigne—one of the most typical of all Elizabethans—published in 1576 a book which he called *The Drum of Dooms Day, Wherein the frailties and miseries of man's life are lively portrayed and learnedly set forth*, and which describes with energy and detail the sordidness and suffering which man is forced to endure from birth to death. The first part of it was a translation, Gascoigne tells us, of an old Latin book he had found (it had no title page, so he did not know the author's name) as, with a guilty conscience for his misspent life, he "was tossing and retossing in his small library." The original author, as a matter of fact, was Pope Innocent III, who had written the work about the year 1200, under the title of *De Contemptu Mundi*. But its being more than 350 years old would not have

[14] *The Fall of Man*, pp. 383 ff.

troubled Gascoigne; no matter when it was set down, an account of the wretchedness of man's condition was always profitable for "the reformation of manners," and should be published "for a general commodity." It was still true, as Innocent's text said, that both the universal and human worlds "do now wax old. That is to say macrocosmos and microscosmos, the greater world and the lesser world. And the longer that life doth linger in either of them, so much the worse is nature in each of them troubled and vexed." [15]

2

Thus in the inherited, the universally accepted, Christian view of man and his universe there was a basic conflict between man's dignity and his wretchedness. Every Elizabethan would have agreed with Sir John Davies who says, in his *Nosce Teipsum* (1599),—the poem is one of the finest of all the accounts of traditional psychology:—

> I know my body's of so frail a kind,
> As force without, fevers within can kill;
> I know the heavenly nature of my mind,
> But 'tis corrupted both in wit and will.

> I know my Soul hath power to know all things,
> Yet is she blind and ignorant in all;
> I know I am one of Nature's little kings,
> Yet to the least and vilest things am thrall.

> I know my life's a pain and but a span,
> I know my Sense is mock'd with everything:
> And to conclude, I know myself a MAN,
> Which is a proud, and yet a wretched thing.

But the conflict, as Davies suggests, was also a complement. For instance, Pierre Boaistuau, in 1577 (the work was trans-

[15] George Gascoigne, *Works*, Cambridge, 1910, ii, 213, 234.

lated into English in 1603), wrote a treatise called *Le Théâtre du Monde, où il est fait un ample discours des misères humaines,* which is immediately followed, bound in the same volume, by *un brief discours sur l'excellence et dignité de l'homme.* The two views were opposite sides of the same coin, for man's wretched condition did not at all decrease his immense importance to the universe. He was, in fact, so necessary that God himself, after man's fall, had taken on man's shape in order to set things right again. Through the incarnation of Christ man could be restored to his original position in a Paradise regained.

The basic conflict, therefore, no matter how deep it went and no matter how many aspects it presented, could—by the doctrines of grace and redemption—theoretically be solved. But there was another conflict, more particular to the sixteenth century—and, since it was new, perhaps more intellectually and emotionally disturbing—for which a solution was more difficult. The conflict was this: belief in each one of the interrelated orders—cosmological, natural, and political—which as we have seen were the frame, the basic pattern of all Elizabethan thinking, was being punctured by a doubt. Copernicus had questioned the cosmological order, Montaigne had questioned the natural order, Machiavelli had questioned the political order. The consequences were enormous.

Upon the structure of the Ptolemaic system, with the earth in the center, everything had been built; the order of creation, the influence of the heavens on man, the parallels between the universe and the state, the theory of the macrocosm and the microcosm. But when the sun was put at the center, and the earth set between Mars and Venus as a mobile and subsidiary planet, the whole elaborate structure, with all its interdependencies, so easy to visualize, so convenient for metaphor and allusion, lost its meaning. "If the celestial spheres," said Hooker, "should forget their wonted motions, and by irregular volubility turn themselves any way . . . what would become of man himself, whom all these things do now serve?" [16]

We must, however, as Miss Marjorie Nicolson and others have shown,[17] be on guard against over-emphasizing the effects of the Copernican theory on the popular mind. It was confronted at first, considering its implications, with remarkably little opposition. For though Luther and Melanchthon attacked his views (they contradicted certain phrases of Scripture), perhaps because Copernicus' book was published in 1543 by the cautious Osiander with an apologetic preface and the word "hypothesis" on the title page, the Roman church took no official steps against it until 1616, when, because Galileo supported it, it was finally put on the Index. Even then the censure was mild; it could be read if nine sentences were changed so that they were turned from statements of fact into matters of conjecture.

The reason for this mildness is clear enough.[18] For the Copernican system could be looked at in two ways: as a mathematical theory and as a description of physical fact. Being simpler than the elaborate Ptolemaic system, it was welcomed by mathematicians as an easier means of making astronomical calculations, and it was well known as a hypothesis by the English reading public before the end of the sixteenth century. But it was not until Galileo perfected the telescope that the hypothesis could be proved to be a true description of reality. Only in 1610, with the publication of Galileo's *Siderius Nuncius,* which announced the discovery of four new planets, and various other phenomena, such as the true cause of the Milky Way, the irregular surface of the moon, and many new stars, was it clear that the old system was seriously upset. On the day the book was

[16] Quoted J. B. Black, *The Reign of Elizabeth*, Oxford, 1936, p. 261.

[17] Marjorie Nicolson, "The 'New Astronomy' and English Literary Imagination," *Studies in Philology*, XXXII (1935), 428–462; "The Telescope and Imagination," *Modern Philology*, XXXII (1935), 233–260.

[18] See Francis R. Johnson, *Astronomical Thought in Renaissance England*, Baltimore, 1937.

published, Sir Henry Wotton, the English ambassador at Venice, sent a copy of it to King James, as "the strangest piece of news that he hath ever yet received from any part of the world." Galileo, says Wotton, "hath first overthrown all former astronomy—for we must have a new sphere to save the appearances—and next all astrology." [19]

Wotton's phrase about the new sphere shows that he was still thinking in terms of the Ptolemaic system and that he saw how disastrous to its familiar pattern the new discoveries were. His friend John Donne, who always saw the implications of everything, went further, and in his *First Anniversary* (1611) described how the destruction of the old cosmology brought ruin to the related orders of the state and the individual as well. Nature's three domains were so closely connected that to destroy one was to destroy all. The "new philosophy," he said, "calls *all* in doubt"—the element of fire has been put out; the world, now that so many new worlds have been discovered, is, as everybody admits, crumbled to atoms; order in the state and the family is gone, and everybody thinks himself a unique individual, with no relation to anything else.

> 'Tis all in pieces, all coherence gone,
> All just supply, and all relation.
> Prince, subject, father, son, are things forgot,
> For every man alone thinks he hath got
> To be a phoenix, and that then can be
> None of that kind of which he is but he.[20]

Galileo's discoveries, of course, came too late to have any influence on Shakespeare. But they were merely a culmination of a kind of astronomical uneasiness and excitement, the kind

---

[19] Quoted Marjorie Nicolson, "The 'New Astronomy' and English Literary Imagination," *loc. cit.*

[20] Ll. 205 ff. Donne's *Anniversaries* are extremely interesting as an example of how the familiar ideas of the decay of the world could be used as poetic material. There is nothing new in any of the ideas which Donne expresses; what is new is the relation they bear to each other after Donne's wit has fused them together.

of uneasiness and excitement which makes new explorations and destroys old concepts, which was part of the temper of the late sixteenth century, and which was to haunt the century following. Giordano Bruno, a believer in Copernicus, and a man filled with an almost visionary enthusiasm about his own new picture of the world, had spent two years in England in the early 1580's, and though his influence seems impossible to trace, he must have left some impression on the distinguished Englishmen, like Sir Philip Sidney, with whom he conversed. There were both technical treatises and semi-popular handbooks which described the new theories—one of them, Thomas Digges' *Perfect Description of the Celestial Orbs* (1576), went through six editions before 1600.[21] The disruptive effect of Galileo's discoveries had been prepared for, even though, in most minds, the Ptolemaic heavens still rolled about the stationary earth and shed their influence on men's lives.

3

But if the Copernican theory did not at once seem to be as destructive of the cosmological hierarchy as it later became, there can be no question about the force with which the natural hierarchy was attacked. In his "Apology for Raymond Sebond" Montaigne gave the accepted view of the second of Nature's domains such a series of blows that it was almost entirely demolished; one by one the cards were knocked down until the whole house lay flat on the ground. Not that he was entirely original; there had been earlier theoretical attacks, particularly in Italy, on the familiar psychological structure. Bernardino Telesio, for example, in his *De Rerum Natura,* had made sense the basis of all knowledge, had stated that the difference between the knowledge possible to man and the knowledge possible to animals was merely a difference of degree and not a difference of kind, and that what we call reason is but a refinement of sense, so that

[21] See Francis R. Johnson, *op. cit.,* and below, p. 97, note 2.

"the perceptive faculty, which seems to be proper to the human soul and is called rational, we think has manifestly been bestowed upon the souls of all other animals." [22] This is radical doctrine, and it is an expression of what was a general feeling among the advanced thinkers of the time: the old rigid order no longer gave a satisfactory explanation of nature, just as the Ptolemaic cosmology no longer gave a satisfactory picture of the heavens. But no one expressed this so strongly, or in such popular terms, as Montaigne. In fact his demolition of the old scheme was so thorough, and its implications so far-reaching, that we must describe it in some detail.

In 1569 Montaigne published his translation of Sabunde's *Natural Theology*. Sabunde had written the work about a hundred and thirty years earlier, and it had been so much admired by Montaigne's father that he had asked his son to turn its bad Latin into French. Thus the translation was an act of filial piety, and in no way a reflection of Montaigne's own interests. For what Sabunde had to say was sympathetic to the older generation, the earlier and more optimistic generation, of the sixteenth century, and nothing shows more clearly the close dependence of the Renaissance on the ideas of the Middle Ages than the fact that a work like the *Natural Theology*, a product of late scholasticism, should have appealed so strongly to the father of Montaigne. What Sabunde sets out to do is to show that man can know himself by understanding the book of Nature which God has made for him; he can achieve this understanding by the use of his reason (Sabunde is so optimistic about man's capacity for achieving knowledge, even of God, through unaided reason, as to be almost heretical); the use of his reason shows man that he is the most important creature in the orderly ranks

[22] *De Rerum Natura*, viii, ch. 15. The first two parts of this work were published in 1565 and 1570; the third part, from which my quotation is taken, did not appear until 1586, several years after Montaigne had written the *Apology*. But the thesis is clear throughout. I cannot find any evidence that the work was known to Montaigne.

of creation—in fact it would be difficult to find a work more typical of the conventional picture of man's central place in the universe than the *Natural Theology* of Sabunde.

But Montaigne's pretended defense of it smashes the whole structure to pieces. Stimulated by his recent reading of skeptical philosophy, and irritated, perhaps, by the boredom of translating the naif and monotonous ideas of Sabunde, he proceeds to demolish Sabunde by launching an elaborate attack on the arrogance and vanity of man. Although on the surface he seems to be repeating merely the traditional platitudes about the misery of the human condition, Montaigne in fact goes very much deeper, and strikes at the entire inherited concept of what it means to be a human being. His purpose in writing the essay, he says, is to make people "sensible of the inanity, the vanity and insignificance of man; to wrest out of their fists the miserable weapons of their reason; to make them bow the head and bite the dust under the authority and reverence of the divine majesty." [23] How sincere Montaigne was in wanting to exalt the divine majesty, we shall probably never know; but there can be no doubt that he took a lively and ironic delight in describing the insignificance of man. "Let us then for the nonce consider man alone," he says, "without outside assistance, armed only with his own weapons, and destitute of the divine grace and knowledge, which comprise all his honor, his strength and the foundation of his being. Let us see how he will hold out in this fine equipment. Let him explain to me, by the force of his reason, on what foundation he has built those great advantages he thinks he has over the other creatures. What has induced him to believe that that wonderful motion of the heavenly vault, the eternal light of those torches rolling so proudly over his head, the awe-inspiring agitations of that infinite sea, were established, and endure through so many centuries, for his service and convenience? Is it possible to imagine anything more

[23] *Essays,* ii, 2, trans. E. J. Trechmann, Oxford, 1927, I, 439–440.

ridiculous than that this miserable and puny creature, who is not so much as master of himself, exposed to shocks on all sides, should call himself Master and Emperor of the universe, of which it is not in his power to know the smallest part, much less to command it?" [24]

"The frailest and most vulnerable of all creatures is man," Montaigne continues, "and at the same time the most arrogant. He sees and feels himself lodged here in the mud and filth of the world, nailed and riveted to the worst, the deadest and most stagnant part of the universe, at the lowest story of the house and the most remote from the vault of heaven, with the animals of the worst condition of the three; and he goes and sets himself in imagination above the circle of the moon, and brings heaven under his feet." [25]

In order, therefore, to see man as he really is and to crush his unjustified presumption, Montaigne begins by making a detailed comparison between man and animals. This, to be sure, was nothing new; plenty of people, from the Greeks down, had pointed out that Nature looked after animals better than she looked after men, and that the animal condition was happier than the human.[26] But they had done so, at least in Christian writings, in order to make man more aware of his inner potentialities, and to show, through a description of his physical wretchedness, that he could rise above anything he might share with the animals into a state of rational or spiritual blessedness. A typical and popular work of this kind is the *Circe* of Giovanni-

[24] *Ibid.*, p. 441.

[25] *Ibid.*, p. 443. The three orders of animals are those on the earth, those in the water, and those in the air. Montaigne's argument is that since man lives on the lowest element, earth, he is in the worst condition.

[26] See George Boas and A. O. Lovejoy, *Primitivism and Related Ideas*, Baltimore, 1935. The two stock passages in classical literature which describe the superiority of the animals and which were most quoted in the sixteenth century were Plutarch's essay, the "Gryllus," and the opening of the seventh book of Pliny's *Natural History*.

Battista Gelli (1549). Gelli tells us that when Ulysses was on Circe's island, Circe made an agreement with him. She would restore to his human shape any one of Ulysses' followers whom she had transformed into an animal, on one condition: Ulysses must persuade him that he will be better off as a man than as a beast. This seems to Ulysses an easy task, but, to his astonishment and chagrin, he finds, after talking with an oyster, a serpent, a hare, a goat, a hind, a lion, a horse, a dog and an ox, that not one of them will think for a moment of giving up his happy animal state to resume the miseries of the human condition. Not until Ulysses meets an elephant, who had been a philosopher before his transformation, does he find anyone who is willing to risk the change. The elephant, however, makes up for all the rest; Ulysses convinces him of the glories of being rational, and the former elephant, now a man once more, ends the book by chanting a hymn of praise to the Creator who has formed the world for man, the glorious possessor of reason, and the only sensible being who can understand the God who made him.

Such is the conclusion of Renaissance humanism. But such is not the conclusion of Montaigne. To Montaigne—the Montaigne of the *Apology*—man himself is only another animal, "he is subjected to the same obligation as the other creatures of his order, and is of a very mediocre condition, without any real and essential prerogative and pre-eminence." [27] "I could easily make out a case for my general contention," he says, "that there is a greater difference between many a man and many another man, than between many a man and many an animal." [28] And he gives example after example of the intelligence, rationality, and high

[27] *Essays*, I, 451.

[28] *Ibid.*, p. 458. This is going one step farther than Plutarch, on whose essay (*Moralia*, trans. Goodwin, v, 218), "That Brute Beasts make Use of Reason," Montaigne considerably depends. Plutarch had merely said, "I do not believe there is such a difference between beast and beast, in point of understanding and memory, as between man and man."

moral qualities of animals; they have ways of communicating
with one another that we cannot understand; they share with
us a kind of religion (as he proves by an example taken from
the behavior of elephants), and, since they do so much that we
cannot comprehend, it is clear not merely that they are our
equals, but that there is "some pre-eminent faculty in them
which is hidden from us." [29] In moral virtues they are particularly superior; unlike man, the animals do not make war on
each other; they are both more faithful and more magnanimous
than human beings. And, finally, to pursue, in Montaigne's
words, "a little further this equality and correspondence between men and animals, the privilege that our soul glories in,"
the privilege hitherto attributed to man's soul alone, of abstracting from sensible phenomena their essential characteristics, "in
order to make them conform to her [the soul's] own immortal
and spiritual condition . . . this same privilege, I say, seems
very evidently to be shared by the beasts." [30]

From the orthodox view, nothing could be more destructive
than this. The orthodox view was that because man was able to
abstract from sensible objects their essential forms, he could
therefore rise to a knowledge of forms in general and hence
to a knowledge of God, which was the goal of his existence. But
Montaigne implies that animals could do the same thing. It is

---

[29] *Ibid.*, p. 462.

[30] *Ibid.*, p. 475. Montaigne over-reaches himself here. As an examination of
the text will show, he cannot give any examples of the way animals "abstract"—
the particular function of reason—except those which an orthodox sixteenth-century
psychologist would have attributed to the function of imagination: "For when we
see a horse," he says, trying to support his argument, "accustomed to trumpets and
battles and the rattle of musketry, shaking and trembling in his sleep while stretched
on his litter, as if he were in the fray, it is certain that in his soul he imagines the
beat of the drum without noise, an army without body and without arms." This,
however, cannot be called "abstraction"—it is merely the functioning of imagination or memory, faculties which belong to any creature with, like an animal, a sensitive soul. But the fact that Montaigne could not find a good illustration to prove
his point does not matter; what does matter is that he wanted to make the point.

surprising that when the authorities in Rome examined the *Essais* in 1581, they said nothing about this point, but limited themselves to suggesting minor alterations: the *Essais* were not put on the Index until 1676. For St. Thomas Aquinas, who, only eighteen years before, at the Council of Trent, had been made the patron of Catholic theology, had said that if man, "who is led by faith to God as his last end, through ignoring the natures of things, and consequently the order of his place in the universe, thinks himself to be beneath certain creatures above whom he is placed," thereby derogating the natural dignity of his position, he is worthy of the same punishment that the Scriptures promise to heretics.[31] Yet this was just what Montaigne had alleged; he had said that there was no real difference between man and the other animals, and he thereby knocked man out of his crucial position in the natural hierarchy. If he was right, the whole traditional structure, so elaborately expounded by Sabunde, fell in ruins.

Once he has established this point to his satisfaction, it is easy for Montaigne to develop further his theme of man's ignorance and feebleness, and, as he says, to "strip him to his shirt." At his best, as exemplified by the philosophers, man can only come to the conclusion that he knows nothing. In the first place he knows nothing of God, and his presumption in thinking that God is made like him and that his affairs are the center of God's interest is entirely unfounded: "Therefore it was that Xenophanes wittily remarked, that if the animals create any gods, . . . as it is likely they do, they will certainly frame them in their own image, and glorify themselves as we do. For why should not a gosling say thus: 'All things in the world concentrate upon me; the earth serves me to walk upon, the sun to give me light, the stars to communicate to me their influence; the winds benefit me in this way, the waters in that. There is nothing the vault of heaven looks upon so favorably as my-

[31] *Summa contra Gentiles*, II, iii.

self. I am the darling of Nature. Does not man keep me, house me, and wait upon me? For me he sows and grinds. If he eats me, so he does his fellow-man; and so do I the worms that kill and eat him." [32]

In the same fashion Montaigne ridicules the familiar arguments about man's knowledge of Nature. We presume to understand the architecture of the heavens by attributing to them "our own material, clumsy, terrestrial contrivances," and we have divided the Microcosmos, "this poor creature man," into a fantastic set of "offices and vocations" which bear no more relation to the facts than do our attempts to describe the movements of the planets. And if we know nothing of Nature, neither do we know anything about Reason and the soul. Only revelation can give us any knowledge, and as for the soul's being immortal, "let us ingenuously confess that God alone, and faith, have told us so; for it is not a lesson we have learned of Nature or of our reason. . . . Whoever will consider man without flattery, will see in him neither efficacy nor faculty that savors of anything but death and earth." [33]

Nor do we know anything of our bodies, nor of our desires. There are no standards—nothing is universally agreed upon. "Those people amuse me who, to give some certainty to laws, say that there are some that are fixed, perpetual and immutable, which they call laws of Nature," for, says Montaigne, there is not one of these laws "that is not rejected and disowned, not by one nation, but by many." [34] There may be laws of Nature in other creatures, "but in us they have vanished, this fine human reason of ours thrusting itself into everything, commanding and domineering, confusing and distorting the face of things, in its vanity and inconsistency." [35]

[32] *Essays*, I, 533.
[33] *Ibid.*, p. 556.
[34] Vol. II, p. 26.
[35] *Ibid.*, p. 27.

And, in conclusion, since nothing can be known of God or of the world or of the soul, since experience everywhere refutes any possibility of the existence of universal standards of belief or behavior, what of the senses? The rational soul of man has been proved completely useless; has he not at least a sensitive soul, like the other animals, on which he can rely? Certainly not, Montaigne answers. In the first place our senses are insufficient—we have too few of them. "We have built up a truth through the consultation and concurrence of our five senses; but it would perhaps need the agreement and contribution of eight or ten to perceive it with certainty, and in its essence." [36] And the five we have are notoriously inferior to those of other animals, being deceptive in every possible way. Therefore since "nothing comes to us that is not altered and falsified by our senses," any knowledge of reality is hopeless. "To judge the appearances we receive of things, we should need a judicatory instrument; to verify this instrument, we should need demonstration; to rectify this demonstration we should need an instrument: so here we are arguing in a circle!" [37] "Finally," he adds, "there is no permanent existence, either of our being or that of the objects. And we, and our judgment, and all mortal things, incessantly go flowing and rolling on." And he ends his long skeptical orgy by saying that since man can do nothing by himself he must, if he is to rise from his miserable condition, abandon and renounce all his own powers by putting himself into the hands of God.

Thus Montaigne, by destroying the psychological order, destroys everything else; a human being who is indistinguishable from animals is not a human being who can comprehend the order of the universe or discover any Laws of Nature in society. Once more, in Donne's words, " 'Tis all in pieces, all coherence gone."

[36] *Ibid.*, p. 38.
[37] *Ibid.*, p. 49.

4

The ideas of Machiavelli, which were more practical and less speculative than those of the new astronomers or of Montaigne, naturally received more attention. Equally subversive of all the old ideas of order and law, they had an immediate application to man's life in society which made their author seem a far more formidable menace. The reasons for this can perhaps best be realized by comparing *The Prince* and the *Discourses on Livy* with the *De Officiis* of Cicero, just as the effect of the Copernican system can best be seen by comparing it with the Ptolemaic, and the views of Montaigne in the *Apology* can most clearly be understood by contrasting them with those of the work he was apparently setting out to defend. For the *De Officiis* represents the official sixteenth-century doctrine concerning the behavior of man as a governor. It was universally read; apart from many editions in Latin, there were at least eleven editions of the work in English between 1534 and 1616, and no sixteenth-century treatise on government was without some indebtedness to it.

According to Cicero, if a man is to control his fellow men and himself, justice is the essential virtue, and moral right is the basis of action. "When the Stoics," he says approvingly, "speak of the supreme good as 'living conformably to nature,' they mean, as I take it, something like this: that we are always to be in accord with virtue, and from all other things that may be in harmony with nature to choose only such as are not incompatible with virtue." [38] "It is," he observes, "no mean manifestation of Nature and Reason that man is the only animal that has a feeling for order, for propriety, for moderation in word and deed. And so no other animal has a sense of beauty, loveliness, harmony in the visible world." [39] It is man's busi-

---

[38] *De Officiis*, III, iii, 13, trans. Walter Miller, Loeb Classics.
[39] I, iv, 14.

ness to develop this capacity through cultivation of the moral virtues, and so lead a tempered and rational life. All medieval thought, when describing a ruler, said the same thing; it was the basis of political theory, and like the other inherited views of man's nature, by presenting an ideal picture for him to live up to, it made man, and especially the prince, a responsible and moral being.

But Machiavelli took exactly the opposite view. He was fundamentally practical. He thought of the state, in the words of J. W. Allen, "as a morally isolated thing." [40] He regarded human history divorced from revelation, and human nature divorced from grace; he looked at man, as Bacon said, not as he should be, but as he is, and he found that man was naturally evil and that the best way to govern him for his own good was by fear and by force. Even in details Machiavelli directly contradicts the traditional view, as represented by Cicero. Cicero had written: "There are two ways of settling a dispute: first, by discussion; second by physical force; and since the former is characteristic of man, the latter of the brute, we must resort to force only in case we may not avail ourselves of discussion." And again: "While wrong may be done . . . in either of two ways, that is, by force or by fraud, both are bestial: fraud seems to belong to the cunning fox, force to the lion; both are wholly unworthy of man, but fraud is the more contemptible." [41]

But Machiavelli, with Cicero's words obviously in mind, has very different things to say. In the famous eighteenth chapter of *The Prince* he writes as follows: "You must know, then, that there are two methods of fighting, the one by law, the other by force: the first method is that of men, the second of beasts; but as the first method is often insufficient, one must have recourse to the second. It is therefore necessary for a

[40] *History of Political Thought in the Sixteenth Century*, New York, 1928, p. 477.
[41] *De Officiis*, I, xi, 34; I, xiii, 41.

prince to know well how to use both the beast and the man . . . the one without the other is not durable."

"A prince," he continues, "being thus obliged to know well how to act as a beast, must imitate the fox and the lion, for the lion cannot protect himself from traps, and the fox cannot defend himself from wolves. One must therefore be a fox to recognize traps, and a lion to frighten wolves . . . therefore a prudent ruler ought not to keep faith when by doing so it would be against his interest. . . . If men were all good, this precept would not be a good one, but as they are bad, and would not observe their faith with you, so you are not bound to keep faith with them." [42]

To Machiavelli any concept of universal justice, of the Laws of Nature or of Nations, is quite irrelevant. Instead of thinking of human government as a reflection of the government of God, he suggests, as we have seen, that his prince take on the characteristics of animals, and where Montaigne had thought of man as incapable of knowledge, since he is intellectually ignorant, Machiavelli takes it for granted that he is incapable of good action, since he is morally evil. "Whoever desires to found a state and give it laws," he says in the *Discourses,* "must start with assuming that all men are bad and ever ready to display their vicious nature, whenever they may find occasion for it." [43]

It was because Machiavelli based his instructions on views like these that he so outraged sixteenth-century sensibilities. Not realizing that he had, after all, a desirable end in view—the unification of Italy—and perverting his views and character into a figure of diabolic significance, the later sixteenth century regarded him with mixed feelings of fascination and horror. Though for about half a generation after *The Prince* was written in 1513 (it was printed in 1532), its views attracted no

[42] Trans. L. Ricci, Modern Library ed., New York, 1940, p. 64.

[43] Trans. C. E. Detmold, Modern Library ed., New York, 1940, bk. i, ch. 3, p. 117.

very remarkable degree of attention, once they were seriously considered, the storm broke with what now seems extraordinary violence. No term of abuse was too strong for Machiavelli's principles, works and character. The Jesuits of Ingoldstadt burnt him in effigy; to Cardinal Pole he was obviously inspired by the devil; he was put on the Index as soon as that institution was established (1557); the Protestants considered his ideas directly responsible for the massacre of St. Bartholomew. He was universally described as an atheist and an unscrupulous fiend; he was referred to no fewer than 395 times in Elizabethan drama as the embodiment of human villainy; he became, in Signor Praz's words, "a rallying point for whatever was most loathsome in statecraft, and indeed in human nature at large." [44]

When we reflect upon the matter, this violence does not, after all, seem so extraordinary. For Machiavelli's realistic view of how things actually work, his statement that the ends justify the means, the deadly practicality of his unscrupulous precepts —all these violated the idealistic order which the men of the sixteenth century had been trained to believe in from childhood. "I want to write," said Machiavelli, "something that may be useful to the understanding man; it seems better for me to go behind to the real truth of things, rather than to a fancy picture." [45] And the real truth of things, as Machiavelli saw it, had no connection with the elaborate structure of inter-related hierarchies or with the responsibility of man to the universe. For him the real truth of things concerned practical matters and particular necessities; it had no bearing on morals or ideals. If Machiavelli was right all the inherited doctrines went for nothing, and man in society could no longer reflect the order of the

[44] Mario Praz, "Machiavelli and the Elizabethans," *Proceedings of the British Academy*, xiii (1928), 8. See also E. Meyer, *Machiavelli and the Elizabethan Drama*, Weimar, 1897, and Lord Acton's introduction to Burd's great edition of *Il Principe*.
[45] Quoted John Morley, *Machiavelli*, London, 1897, p. 20.

cosmos or the order of created beings. No wonder he was called an atheist; by abandoning the conventional belief in the law of Nature, and by thinking entirely in terms of immediate practical necessity regardless of universal truth, he denied God's government of the world: once more the destruction of one hierarchy implied the destruction of the others as well. The sixteenth-century attacks on Machiavelli were in fact a defense, sometimes in hysterical terms, of the traditional dogma, and the hysteria may be taken as an indication that, below the surface, men realized—with a fascinated conviction which they were afraid to admit—that the ideas of Machiavelli might after all be true.

5

Thus, in the immediate intellectual background of the late sixteenth century, two main attacks were being made on the idealistic picture of the nobility and dignity of man. There was the traditional attack, which described man's wretchedness since the fall, but which was still based on a firm belief in man's crucial place in the center of things; and there was the newer attack, which in a threefold way, threatened to destroy that belief itself. At the time when Shakespeare's development as a craftsman reached its climax, this conflict also reached its climax, and we shall soon attempt to discover how Shakespeare, practising the type of writing which relies on conflict, was able to use it.

But the causes which made the conflict seem so sharp at the end of the sixteenth century are more complicated than those which I have described. So far I have regarded the situation from the long-range view of intellectual history alone, and in doing so I have perhaps over-simplified it. If we come closer for a moment to the actual scene, and try to imagine ourselves breathing the emotional and intellectual atmosphere of the time, we shall have to be aware of many other considerations than those which I have outlined. For to explain why it was that the opposing views of man's nature seemed, at that time, so violently to clash, and why the gloomy view seemed more and more to be the true one, we shall have to think of local circumstances, local fashions, local impulses, which no doubt appeared more important at the moment than either the ancient conflict or the new iconoclasms which reinforced it. For one thing there was the religious situation. By discarding her allegiance to the organization of Rome, England had, as it were, broken the mould in which the old ideas had been formed, and Protestantism, as Richard Hooker realized, had to re-shape them with new purposes in mind. They had been moved—to change the metaphor—from one house to another, and they had been shaken up in the process. Hence it was natural to ask that if the medium, the Roman church and its organization, through which those ideas had for centuries been expressed, could be questioned and finally discarded as a system of lies and frauds, why could not the inherited ideas themselves be questioned and discarded too?

Furthermore Protestantism, in spite of the doctrine of predestination, put a new and greater emphasis on individual choice: it was a harder and tougher kind of moral life than the Roman one; the soul was no longer guarded from God's wrath by a series of shock-absorbers or saintly intermediaries; it stood face to face with the Almighty. As we look back on the period we are tempted to ask whether Protestantism, like the earlier Platonic glorification of man's capacity to raise himself to an angelic level, did not put more responsibility on human nature than it could stand, so that, for the time being, a reaction was bound to set in. Perhaps it did: at any rate the religious changes of the age made many sensitive minds doubtful about their religious allegiance, and skepticism went hand in hand with uncertainty. As Donne writes in his *Third Satire:*

> To adore, or scorn an image, or protest,
> May all be bad; doubt wisely; . . .

On a huge hill,
Cragged and steep, Truth stands, and he that will
Reach her, about must, and about must go;
And what the hill's suddenness resists, win so.

These are not sentiments which lead to over-confidence, and it is interesting to observe that though at the time he wrote this satire—about 1594—Donne is merely anxious about the *form* of his belief, later on, when he wrote the *Anniversaries*, in 1611 and 1612, he questions its whole philosophic content.

If the religious situation seemed uncertain and insecure, so did the political situation. By the end of the 1590's Queen Elizabeth's reign was obviously coming to a close: that particular *primum mobile* could not turn the sphere of the state for very much longer. But it was by no means assured who should take her place; and without her, and the kind of courtiership which her glorious if uncertain imperiousness involved, no one knew what might happen. There were rumblings in the economic order—too many monopolies and too many enclosures of land were causing dissatisfaction among those who found their hereditary privileges or their ambition cut down or thwarted. When popular literature (outside of the drama) turned away from romance to realism, and in the early 'nineties Robert Greene found it more profitable to describe the trickeries of pick-pockets than the love affairs of princesses, a different feeling was in the air from that which had inspired Spenser, in the 'eighties, to plan a huge poem which was to form a Christian gentleman in noble and virtuous discipline. In fact (though political events lay behind it) Spenser's death in the last year of the century—as a result, it was said, of starvation—can be seen by the symbolically-minded as a microcosmic reflection of what had happened to the ideals of the early Renaissance which had originally inspired him. The 1590's had begun—in spite of their professed admiration for his genius—to turn away from Spenser. Satire, of a realistic and mordant variety, was taking the place of literary idealism, and, particularly in the writings of Donne and Marston, was turning in the opposite direction from the order implied by allegory. The cult of melancholy —which became increasingly fashionable in the period—encouraged nothing but analysis and anatomy. It was based on something more realistic—or what seemed more realistic—than the optimism of a Neo-Platonist; it had affinities with the practicality of Machiavelli and with the skepticism of Montaigne. It saw, as Marston wrote in his "Cynic Satire" (1599), that though the other orders of nature fulfill their proper functions, man alone has lost his specific virtue:

> And now no human creatures, once disray'd
> Of that fair gem.
> Beasts sense, plants growth, like being as a stone,
> But out alas, our Cognizance is gone.[46]

Yet all this emphasis on man's tendency toward evil made his position only the more dramatic. It had been a commonplace of traditional humanism that what differentiated man from the other orders was that he could choose: he had free will. The angels were not called upon to choose; they were *above* choice because they directly understood universal truth through intellect. The animals were *below* choice because they failed to understand universal truth, being limited to sense. But the glory of man, who was half intellect and half sense, was that he could, through free will, decide to which level he belonged. According to Pico della Mirandola God had said to Adam—and to all other men as well—"Thou shalt have the power to degenerate into the lowest forms of life, the animal; thou shalt have the power, out of thy soul's judgment, to be reborn into the higher forms of life which are divine." [47] To Pico and the other earlier humanists, man belonged with the

---

[46] *Scourge of Villainy*, Satire vii.

[47] *Oratio de Hominis Dignitate*, trans. Elizabeth L. Forbes, *Journal of the History of Ideas*, III (1942), 348. See also G.-B. Gelli, *Circe*, bk. x.

angels. But to Montaigne, and the satiric, melancholy, realistic writers of the 1590's, he belonged with the beasts. The reawakened emphasis on man's bestiality, on his disruption, through wrong choice, of God's order in the world, in nature and in the state, was all the more tragic because of the potentialities it at once revealed and destroyed. The earlier Renaissance had emphasized the revelation of those potentialities by comparing man with the angels; the later Renaissance emphasized their destruction by comparing man with the animals. The result, at the end of the sixteenth century, was what Robert Frost, in our own day, has described in another connection:

> As long on earth
> As our comparisons were stoutly upward
> With gods and angels, we were men at least,
> But little lower than the gods and angels.
> But once comparisons were yielded downward,
> Once we began to see our images
> Reflected in the mud and even dust,
> 'Twas disillusion upon disillusion.
> We were lost piecemeal to the animals,
> Like people thrown out to delay the wolves.[48]

In Shakespeare's time many people felt in the same fashion. For though the old orderly scheme, which the new astronomy and the ideas of Montaigne and Machiavelli were shaking to its foundations, may have given a false view of reality, at least it represented a pattern to which thought and imagination could refer. To destroy it was to shake human confidence and to emphasize man's weakness and emptiness. "Doth any man doubt," asks Bacon in his essay on Truth, "that if there were taken out of men's minds vain opinions, flattering hopes, false valuations, imaginations as one would, and the like, but it would leave the minds of a number of men poor shrunken things, full of melancholy and indisposition, and unpleasing to themselves?" To

[48] "The White-tailed Hornet."

Bacon's question only an affirmative answer was possible. The age was ripe for tragedy.

For as we reflect upon the conflict which I have described as the essential element in Shakespeare's intellectual and emotional background, it appears that nothing could have been more propitious for the writing of great tragic drama. In the periods when great tragedy has been written, two things seem to have been necessary: first, a conventional pattern of belief and behavior, and second, an acute consciousness of how that conventional pattern can be violated. The convention may be a social one, and the violation a social violation: the result is the drama of Ibsen. Or the convention may be the law of the gods, and the violation, like that of Prometheus or Orestes, may be a religious violation: the result is the drama of Aeschylus. In Shakespeare's day the convention included everything—it was the whole inherited picture of man in the system of the universe, of Nature and of the state; it was religious, moral and social; it was a vast inclusive pattern of order. The violation of this order, as I have tried to show, was being felt everywhere at the end of the sixteenth century, and it was a violation which when it occurred in any one part, was felt throughout the whole structure. It was because Shakespeare, as he developed his art, was able to see individual experience in relation to the all-inclusive conflict produced by this violation, that his great tragedies have such wide reverberations and give us so profound a picture of the nature of man.

CHAPTER III

THE DRAMATIC CONVENTION AND SHAKE-SPEARE'S EARLY USE OF IT

I

What I have been saying so far has concerned the first of the three aims which this book is trying to achieve: an understanding of Shakespeare's intellectual background. We must now turn to the second of those aims: an understanding of Shakespeare's craft, namely, the development in the sixteenth century and in Shakespeare's own early plays, of the particular dramatic technique which enabled him to use, at the height of his powers, the deep conflict about man's nature which was given him by his age. Having described what was taken for granted when people thought of man's nature, we must now describe what was taken for granted when people thought of a play. And since, by Shakespeare's time, the drama had long roots in the past and was the product of a long tradition, we must begin by emphasizing certain features of that tradition and by trying to explain their significance for our understanding of Shakespeare.[1]

The medieval drama, as everyone knows, had grown up inside the church, and though an occasional morose preacher complained that it did more harm than good, it was usually approved by the authorities. And naturally so. For its chief subject matter was just that which it was the main business of the church to expound. In the fifteenth century, when we may

[1] For a much fuller treatment of this subject than I am able to give here, see Willard Farnham, *The Medieval Heritage of Elizabethan Tragedy*, Berkeley, Calif., 1936.

say that medieval drama was at its height, that drama did what every other serious form of literature did at the same time: it interpreted the two books, the book of the Scriptures and the book of Nature, which God had given to man. The cycle plays interpreted the book of the Scriptures, the morality plays interpreted the book of Nature. One gave, in a series of dramatizations of the Bible, an account of human history according to the revelation of God's word; the other abstracted from human nature various vices and virtues, personified them, and portrayed their battle for man's soul. Both described human history and human nature in relation to the pattern of the familiar tradition, and both made the drama a vehicle for the most important truths that could be told about man's place in the scheme of things.

The cycle plays had a magnificent theme, the greatest, it seems on the surface, that drama could desire. They showed the creation of man, the various, very human, episodes of the Old Testament—humorous, pathetic, and realistic—and their climax was the presentation, with all the convincing detail they could imagine, of the long story of Christ's death. It was the greatest episode in the history of the human race; all the other scenes led up to it, and those which followed, ending with the Last Judgment, were merely an epilogue which rounded the story out.

But in spite of the grandeur of its theme, the dramatization of the first of God's books never amounted to very much. Divided into thirty or forty scenes, presented on a series of carts instead of a single stage, and taking three days to perform, it was effective in individual episodes rather than in any unity of conception or organization. Neither dramatic technique nor, for that matter, the English language, was, in the fifteenth century, in a condition to be ready for a great dramatist. Furthermore the hero of the story was too perfect to be the hero of tragedy; dogma forbade that he should have a tragic flaw, and though his death could be so realistically presented that it might arouse a great deal of pity, it could not arouse terror, since Jesus was not a man like other men. In addition the meaning of the story was taken too much for granted; it was the same meaning and the same story that everyone had heard ever since he could remember; though individual scenes could be treated in new and lively ways, the main outline had to be orthodox, and there was no possibility for a creative imagination to shape the material afresh. The Biblical drama found no Aeschylus to exalt it into splendor.

But though it remained vulgar and crude, we must not underestimate its importance in Shakespeare's background. It was dying out in Shakespeare's day (the last performance of a full cycle was at Coventry in 1580), but it had created a tradition which affected both technique and subject matter. Its narrative method of telling a story was inherited by the chronicle play, and its use of the most important of all stories had accustomed generations of spectators to assume that drama would have a serious meaning underneath its surface entertainment.

Of much greater significance is the second main type of medieval drama, the morality play. It was a characteristic medieval invention; allegorical and didactic, it became an excellent medium for portraying the various elements which compose man's nature. It made the description of the second of Nature's books native to the drama; it was a *direct* expression—as Shakespeare's plays were later to be an indirect expression—of the familiar ideas which everyone took for granted. For these reasons it is important briefly to examine the moralities, for though most of them make heavy reading, they are extremely interesting for our purpose.

The history of the morality play and its descendants, as far as its serious side is concerned—I am not thinking, at the moment, of comedy—may be divided into four stages, which follow one another in roughly chronological order, though there is naturally a good deal of overlapping. The oldest type is the simplest, and all the seven English moralities which have survived from the fifteenth century conform to it. The hero is a personification of humanity in general; he is called Everyman, or Humanum Genus, or Anima, or Mankind, and the dramatic action, broadly speaking, consists in his corruption by personified vices and his ultimate salvation by personified virtues. The best of these plays, *Everyman,* is a simple and moving account of man's progress toward death, and does not use to any appreciable extent—nor do most of the others—the more elaborate ideas about man's nature which we have been describing. But that these ideas could be used for dramatic purposes is clearly shown by the play called *Wisdom,* or *Mind, Will, and Understanding,* which dates from the last half of the fifteenth century.[2] This play begins with the entrance of Wisdom, who is Christ, and of Anima the soul, dressed as a maid, who kneels to Wisdom telling him how much she loves him, and asking him how she can know God. "By knowing yourself," he replies, "you may have feeling of what God is in your sensible soul." So Anima asks what a soul is, and is told that a soul is the image of God but that it has been disfigured by Adam's sin and can only be purified by the Seven Sacraments which spring from the Death of Christ. He further explains that the soul is divided into two parts: one is sensuality and is served by what he calls the "five outward wits"; the other part is called reason, and is the image of God. Thus, he says,

> a soul is both foul and fair:
> Foul as a beast, by experience of sin,
>   Fair as an angel, of heaven the heir,
> By knowledge of God, by his reason within.[3]

[2] Throughout this chapter I follow the dating of plays as given by Alfred Harbage, *Annals of English Drama,* Philadelphia, 1940.

[3] *The Macro Plays* (London, 1907), ll. 157 ff. In l. 158 I translate "felynge" by "experience."

To make this clear, five virgins, representing the five senses, now enter, singing "I am black but comely, O daughters of Jerusalem"—for such is the body compared to the soul. Continuing his lesson, Wisdom goes on to explain that the second part of the soul has three powers, Mind, Will, and Understanding, which are an image of the Trinity. No sooner has he mentioned them than they spring smartly to attention:

> *Mind:* All three, here, lo, before your face!
>   Mind.
> *Will:* Will.
> *Understanding:* And Understanding, we three.

Wisdom calls on each to declare his significance and his specific property, which they all proceed to do. Mind says she is God's image, but is very humble about how she has failed to live up to her responsibilities. Will says that it is also the likeness and figure of God, that it must be well disposed, that before its judgments are acted on, the "library of reason" must be opened, and that everyone should struggle to keep will clean. Understanding explains that it is through him that knowledge of God is possible, and that whereas the angels desire direct knowledge of God, and the saints enjoy him assiduously, his creatures know him through his wonderful works.

After this explanation, Wisdom tells Anima that it is through Mind that she can know God the Father, through Understanding that she can know God the Son, and through Will that she can know God the Holy Ghost. And the first scene ends as Wisdom warns Anima that if she has three powers, she also has three enemies, The World, The Flesh and The Devil, and that she must keep her Five Wits from their clutches, lest the lower part of reason have domination over the higher.

But this good advice is not heeded. Immediately after Wisdom goes out, Lucifer enters with a roar, and he is so successful in tempting Mind, Will, and Understanding that he can boast of making Reason deaf and dumb. Mind, under Lucifer's direction, gives all his attention to extravagant dress, Understanding goes in for trickery and every kind of falseness, while Will enthusiastically devotes himself to fornication. They continue in this fashion for some time, and it is no wonder that when Anima appears (having apparently changed sex since the beginning of the play) he should "appear in the most horrible fashion, fouler than a fiend." Wisdom upbraids Anima with having in his soul as many devils as he has committed deadly sins, and, to confirm his point, from under the "horrible mantle of the Soul," there run out "six small boys in the likeness of Devils, and so return again." But the Soul is now repentant; Mind, Will, and Understanding are horribly ashamed of themselves; the Soul, awakened by contrition, is abandoned by the devils, and after listening to a long lecture by Wisdom, he finally returns to the church and hence to God.

Such is the way in which the earliest moralities use the traditional picture of man's nature to teach Christian doctrine, and the pattern represented by this play is typical of the whole morality convention; it extends to the interlude and passes into the tradition of Elizabethan drama. First we have an account of the optimistic picture of what man ought to be, we are then shown how man is led astray by the lower part of his nature, and finally we have a reconciliation between man and the ruler of the universe. It will be worth our while to keep this threefold division in mind when we consider Shakespearean tragedy.

In the second stage of its development, as it shades off into the interlude (we cannot easily draw the line between them), the morality undergoes a kind of gradual secularization, and though the aim of the plays is still didactic, it is not so intimately concerned with the salvation of the soul according to Church teaching. A very interesting example of this type of play is the one called *Nature,* written by Henry Medwall in about 1495. Man is again the hero, but his chief counsellor is Nature instead of Christ—a more humanistic substitution. The plot is simple: Nature gives Man at the outset the instruction necessary to live the good life, and gives him Reason, by whose guidance that instruction may be followed. Man has also two attendants, Innocence, his nurse, and Sensuality, an inevitable but dangerous companion whose activities must be vigilantly restricted by Reason. But—as usual—Man is quite unable to live up to what is expected of him, and as soon as Nature leaves him to himself, he is seduced by Sensuality so that he revolts against Reason and spends his life in the company of the seven deadly sins. Only when old age wakes him up to his folly does he make peace with Reason, industriously cultivate the seven cardinal virtues, and dedicate his life to God.

This brief outline can give no indication of how fully Medwall, for his dramatic material, uses the conventional views of man's place in the world. At the beginning of the play Nature describes herself as God's minister and deputy: she calls Man the chief of God's creatures, and Man himself tells how he partakes of every order of being, since he is the creature for whom the rest of the world was made. He has understanding and he has will—"in this point," he says, "I am half angelic,"

Unto thy heavenly spirits almost equal,—

and, such is the implication, it is his knowledge of his position in the scheme of things that should enable him to follow the counsel of Reason. All the familiar ideas are expounded, and the structure of the play repeats the tripartite pattern illustrated by *Wisdom*. For after Man's ideal position is described, we are shown how he violates it by becoming "as a brute beast that lacketh reason," and how, before he dies, he is reconciled to God.

The same pattern is used in a slightly later, and even more humanistic play, *The Nature of the Four Elements* (1517), by

John Rastell, the brother-in-law of Sir Thomas More.[4] Humanity is the hero, and, as in Medwall's play, he is instructed by Nature (called "Natura Naturate"). Rastell's Nature is even more explicit than Medwall's in impressing upon Humanity the necessity of knowing the whole world, beginning with the four elements, so that by knowing his own important place in it, he can rise to the ultimate felicity of knowing God. In fact the play is the most explicit of all the moralities and interludes in dramatizing the necessity of knowing the second of God's books; as the messenger says at the beginning of the play:

> How dare men presume to be called clerks
> Disputing of high creatures celestial
> As things invisible and God's high works
> And know not these visible things inferial;
> So they would know high things and know nothing at all
> Of the earth whereon they daily be.

And so, after Nature (here apparently a man) has instructed Humanity about his (Nature's) function as God's minister, he gives Humanity, who is accompanied by Studious Desire, a "figure" or map so that by studying it he can know the world he lives on and hence know himself.

There are other interludes which use a similar theme, such as the well-known *Wit and Science,*—but by the time *Wit and Science* was written (1539), the interlude was beginning to shake off its didactic character: both the allegory and the didacticism are only a shell for a yolk of very realistic farce. In plays like this we are already beginning to pass into the third stage of the morality tradition, where, from the strictly morality point of view, the tail is wagging the dog, and the scenes from real life are dramatically more important than the allegory to which they are supposedly secondary.

---

[4] The manuscript is incomplete, so that we do not possess the end of the play—the reconciliation scene. But there can be no doubt that it existed.

But the second stage of the development included other plays than those like *Nature* and *The Four Elements;* not only was the traditional psychology, the second of Nature's domains, used as dramatic material, the third domain, that of man in society, soon became dramatized too, and throughout the sixteenth century there are several plays which treat the problems of government, both universal and local. Sir David Lyndsay's *Satire of the Three Estates* (1540) has for its hero a character named Rex Humanitas, who is a representative of humanity in general and of kingship; he is an interesting example of how the two domains could be combined into one. And the play itself is about both subjects; the first part is a morality of the familiar tripartite kind; the second part is devoted to an attack on the various evils, religious and political, with which Scotland was at that time infested. The interlude called *Respublica* (1553) describes how the heroine of that name is despoiled by four vices, Avarice, Insolence, Oppression, and Adulation, so that the character called People, who is dependent on her, is in distress. She is finally reassured by Nemesis that all will be well, and the four vices who have used her for their own selfish purposes are exposed and discomfited.

This play, however, is almost the last which has in it merely abstract characters; by 1550 the various types were becoming confused, and the morality tradition was entering its third phase. Here Biblical, Classical, and historical figures begin to mingle with the abstractions, and the distinctions between the old dramatic types melt away. No one has ever satisfactorily made up his mind, for example, whether Bale's *King John* (1536?) is a chronicle play, a tragedy, or a morality, and there is no reason why anybody *should* make up his mind, since it is a mixture of all three. King John is both a historical figure and the personification of a good ruler; any abstract figure surrounding him may suddenly assume a concrete personality—Sedition, for example, turns into Stephen Langton; the action proceeds in a manner which is partly chronological and partly that of a morality; the king dies, as in a tragedy, but the play ends happily with a victory of the virtues over the vices. In fact, though it moves as sluggishly as a jellyfish swimming in glue, and is so dull that to read it to the end requires a cast-iron determination, *King John* is, theoretically, a very interesting example of how the particular and the general, the historical and the universal, were being brought together in the same dramatic structure. They are not fused, as they were later so superbly to be; but they are lying there side by side, and it needed only the creative force of genius to make their dead cells spring into unified life.

There are several other plays which contain the same mixture. *The Life and Repentance of Mary Magdalen* (1558) includes, besides its concrete Biblical heroine, the characters of Pride, Carnal Concupiscence, and their abstract companions; *King Darius* (1565) tells a story taken from the Bible, and surrounds it with virtues and vices; *Horestes* (1567) dramatizes (if that is the right word) the killing of Clytemnestra, and includes such characters, though they play relatively minor roles, as Nature and Revenge. *Cambyses* (1561) has everything—everything, that is, except dramatic or literary value—a classical story, a vice, and a set of morality abstractions such as Murder and Small Hability. It was only a slight step to the fourth and final stage of the morality tradition, where, as in *Gorboduc* (1561), the abstractions, taking on a new form, are relegated to a series of dumb-shows between the acts, and the moral of the play—for the moral is still very important—is shown in the action itself. The moral is stated by the wise counsellor Philander near the beginning of the play. What he says, he tells us, is intended to show

> by certain rules
> Which Kind [Nature] hath graft within the mind of man,
> That Nature hath her order and her course,

'Which being broken doth corrupt the state
Of minds and things, even in the best of all.

It is this order which Gorboduc violates by resigning his kingship and dividing his kingdom between his two sons, so that,
like King Lear, he is, as Philander says,

above them only in the name
Of father not in kingly state also.

By doing this he causes universal disaster, for the brothers fight
against each other, the king and queen are killed, and at the
end of the play the whole country is in the bloody chaos of civil
war.

It can be seen at once that for our purposes *Gorboduc* is of
the greatest interest. What the authors apparently set out to do
was to write a play that would warn Queen Elizabeth, three
years after her accession, of the necessity for a strong central
government, and in doing so they used at least three conventions which were given them by their age: the convention of
Senecan tragedy, the convention of the morality play, and the
conventional view that the order of the state was the order of
Nature. Without the morality tradition it is doubtful if the play
would have contained the balanced opposition of good and evil
counsellors which produces very much the same effect as the
opposition of virtues and vices in the moralities.[5] And what these
characters say is a repetition of the views with which we are
already so familiar. One of the counsellors, in fact, whose name
is Eubulus, could just as well be called Natura Naturate, for
he is as consistently the expounder of Nature's laws as, in the
earlier morality, is Nature himself. Nature, as Sir Thomas Elyot
had said in *The Governor*, and as Shakespeare was to repeat
in *Troilus and Cressida*, is revealed through order, and a violation of that order ends in universal catastrophe.

[5] See Farnham, *op. cit.*, p. 353.

Thus when tragedy first appeared on the English stage—for *Gorboduc* is the first English play that can properly be called a tragedy—it used both the habit of generalization and the subject matter of generalization which were native to the sixteenth century. The individual human being was seen in relation to a universal truth, and if the authors of the play failed to create an individual human being in whom we can believe (the characters in *Gorboduc* are as wooden as the blank verse in which they speak) at least they outlined the terms in which such human beings could later be conceived. The tradition of the morality, however greatly it might be changed, was firmly embedded in Elizabethan drama.

Yet the morality tradition is not the only tradition in *Gorboduc*; it can also be regarded as a chronicle play. Just as the characters in the moralities eventually took on proper names and became individuals instead of abstractions, so the dramatizations of narrative abandoned the Bible and included all kinds of secular subjects. But it is important to observe that when they did so, they continued to think of the individual situation invariably in relation to some universal power. For example one of the most popular types of narrative was the kind of story which described the downfall of a great man through the caprice of Fortune; various collections of such stories had been popular in the Middle Ages, and a fresh collection, which was to be continually added to for more than twenty years, had been published in 1559 under the title of *A Mirror for Magistrates*. The plots of no fewer than thirty Elizabethan plays are taken from this work, and when the dramatists studied those plots in their source they invariably found them employed to illustrate a general truth: that there is no use in being proud or ambitious, since Fortune's wheel is never still, and that if one day you are seated on a throne, on the next you may be grovelling in misery. There is some of this kind of moralizing in *Gorboduc,* and there is much of it in many other plays. The

THE DRAMATIC CONVENTION 63

moral may be trite, and the repetitions of it extremely tiresome, but it is there just the same, another kind of universality against which individual action can be placed and judged.[6]

In fact there was no form of serious entertainment in the sixteenth century which did not in some way or other see individual experience in relation to a general truth. When Queen Elizabeth passed through the City of London on the day before her coronation in 1558, she was presented with a pageant showing the throne of Government surrounded by men dressed as the political virtues who were subduing men dressed as the political vices; [7] just as the imitation of action in *Gorboduc* had its dumbshows, so the real action of Queen Elizabeth had its dumbshows; indeed those on the stage were an obvious imitation of those in real life. On another occasion, in 1581, at the reception of the French Ambassadors, there was a pageant which actually illustrated that identification of the cosmological hierarchy and the political hierarchy which was, as we know, so characteristically Elizabethan. The gallery in which the Queen sat, "the Castle or Fortress of Perfect Beauty," was first compared to the sun, and finally, for the purposes of the pageant, it turned into the sun itself.[8] Another pageant took place under a round vault, on which was painted the sun, and under the sun the sea and earth; the whole allegorical display had a cosmological background.[9] In fact the continued use of allegory in these pageants —which of course everybody wanted to see—is another illustration of how naturally the Elizabethans continued to think of human experience in general terms. The expression of the familiar ideas was not confined to the study or to books; it was taken for granted by all classes of people as one of the natural

---

[6] See Farnham, *op. cit.*, and Howard Baker, *Induction to Tragedy*, Baron Rouge, Louisiana, 1940.

[7] John Nichols, *Progresses . . . of Queen Elizabeth*, London, 1823, I, 44.

[8] *Ibid.*, II, 320 ff.

[9] *Ibid.*, II, 374.

ways of providing serious entertainment. And every conceivable kind of serious entertainment in the sixteenth century—pageants, chronicle plays, and tragedies—reflected the traditional association, however awkwardly it might be expressed, of the particular with the universal.

But the 'sixties and 'seventies and early 'eighties of the sixteenth century went by without the appearance of any dramatist great enough to take advantage of the admirable opportunities which the development of the drama offered him. Sir Philip Sidney, writing in about 1581, could look with well-justified gloom at the debased condition of the English theater; it had produced nothing since *Gorboduc* for which it was possible to find a word of praise. Yet if he had lived for ten years more he would have been forced to speak differently. For at the end of the 'eighties a dramatist of genius at last appeared on the scene, a dramatist whose mighty line exalted the tradition of the Biblical play and the chronicle play into the resounding splendor of *Tamburlaine* and enriched the tradition of the morality play and the serious interlude by describing the desperate ambition of Doctor Faustus. Since his work is an essential part of Shakespeare's background, we must, before we finally turn to Shakespeare himself, examine, however briefly, the remarkable achievement of Christopher Marlowe.

2

As far as the surface action is concerned, *Tamburlaine* is a crude, violent and bloody spectacle; a chronicle play describing the rise to power and the eventual death of an unscrupulous despot. But this is only the surface, for Marlowe conceives the character of Tamburlaine, especially in the first part of the play, as a typical Renaissance hero, who can glorify and ennoble his actions by thinking of them in general terms. Marlowe had a characteristic Renaissance mind, and no one made better dramatic use of the conventional view of man's excellence and potentialities than he. Many Renaissance writers, as we know, urged their readers to understand man's nature by contemplating the heavens; Marlowe's thought moved naturally among the stars, and when he was looking for a comparison or a simile, nothing came more readily to his soaring mind than a reference to the planets or the spheres.[10] It is this, among other things, which gives grandeur and magnificence to the very texture of his style, and it is his use of the traditional views of man's nature which gives grandeur and magnificence to his conception of Tamburlaine. In a famous passage which is often cited both as the key to the play and as the most characteristic expression of Marlowe's thought, Tamburlaine explains his ambitions, and he does so by weaving into a single concept the three interrelated domains of Nature—the domain of created beings, of the stars, and of the state—which, as we know, were the basis of Elizabethan thinking. Tamburlaine speaks as follows:

> Nature, that fram'd us of four elements
> Warring within our breasts for regiment,
> Doth teach us all to have aspiring minds:
> Our souls, whose faculties can comprehend
> The wondrous architecture of the world,
> And measure every wandering planet's course,
> Still climbing after knowledge infinite,
> And always moving as the restless spheres,
> Wills us to wear ourselves and never rest,
> Until we reach the ripest fruit of all,
> That perfect bliss and sole felicity,
> The sweet fruition of an earthly crown.

Most critics have despised the end of this speech as "Scythian bathos," and to modern ears it does seem an anticlimax. But to

---

[10] Caroline Spurgeon, *Shakespeare's Imagery*, Cambridge, 1936, p. 13: "This imaginative preoccupation with the dazzling heights and vast spaces of the universe is, together with a magnificent surging upward thrust and aspiration, the dominating note of Marlowe's mind. . . . No matter what he is describing, the pictures he draws tend to partake of this celestial and magnificent quality."

an Elizabethan mind it would have come as a natural conclusion to what precedes it. Nature's three domains were so closely related that to think of one was to think of the others, and the man whose ambitious mind could comprehend the wondrous architecture of the world would naturally want to fulfil his ambition by becoming a king.

> Is it not brave to be a king, Techelles?
> Is it not passing brave to be a king,
> And ride in triumph through Persepolis?

But in *Doctor Faustus* Marlowe goes more deeply, and in this finest of all morality plays ("How greatly is it all planned," said Goethe) [11] he probes profoundly into the nature of man. At the beginning of the play we see Faustus discarding every branch of normal human learning: logic, medicine, law and theology are briefly examined and tossed aside in favor of necromancy, which Faustus calls "heavenly." Actually, of course, it is quite the reverse, for the trouble with necromancy is that it carries the study of the second of Nature's books too far. A necromancer is a man who has acquired knowledge of Nature's laws not so that he can know himself and hence know God, but so that he can impiously control and manipulate Nature's laws for his own benefit. This is what the Bad Angel implies when he leads Faustus on:

> Go forward, Faustus, in that famous art
> Wherein all Nature's treasure is contain'd:
> Be thou on earth as Jove is in the sky,
> Lord and commander of these elements.

Faustus, in other words, is to have intellectual control of the world, as Tamburlaine had material control, and in order to enjoy this power for twenty-four years he sells his soul to

---

[11] Henry Crabb Robinson, *Diary*, London, 1869, II, 434, August 13, 1829: "I mentioned Marlowe's Faust. He (Goethe) burst out into an exclamation of praise. 'How greatly is it all planned!' He had thought of translating it."

Mephistophilis. Like the men of the early Renaissance, though in an illegitimate way, he wants to transcend human nature. He is, of course, doomed to failure.

It is interesting to see how the morality tradition is developed and expanded as Marlowe describes Faustus' career. He begins as a kind of *tabula rasa,* like the older personifications of Humanity; the progress of the action is a battle between good and evil for his soul, he sees the seven deadly sins, and his death—like the death of Everyman—ends the play by teaching a moral lesson. But Marlowe, great writer as he is, gives us much more than this. His hero is no abstract figure, but a concrete human being, and we have the moral conflict presented not merely externally, by the good and bad angels, but internally through the conflict in Faustus' soul. What is particularly interesting for our purpose is that this conflict is described in terms of the traditional view of man.

> *Faustus:* When I behold the heavens, then I repent,
> And curse thee, wicked Mephistophilis,
> Because thou hast depriv'd me of those joys.
> *Meph.:* 'Twas thine own seeking, Faustus, thank thyself.
> But think'st thou heaven is such a glorious thing?
> I tell thee, Faustus, it is not half so fair
> As thou, or any man that breathes on earth.
> *Faustus:* How prov'st thou that?
> *Meph.:* 'Twas made for man; then he's more excellent.
> *Faustus:* If heaven was made for man, 'twas made for me:
> I will renounce this magic and repent.

Again, the first lesson Faustus receives from Mephistophilis is a lesson in astronomy and astrology:

> As are the elements, such are the heavens,
> Even from the moon unto the imperial orb,
> Mutually folded in each others' spheres,

and he goes on to outline the details, telling Faustus that there are nine spheres, each with a "dominion or intelligentsia," and describing their motion. But when Faustus asks him who made the world, he will not answer, since no devil can name God; the final point of astronomical knowledge cannot be reached by learning that is divorced from religion. Nevertheless a knowledge of astronomy is about the only thing of any intellectual value that Faustus gets from his bargain. He took a journey through the universe in a chariot drawn by dragons to view

> the clouds, the planets, and the stars,
> The tropic zones, and quarters of the sky,
> From the bright circle of the horned moon,
> E'en to the height of *Primum Mobile*.

His dragons soared so high into the air,

> That looking down, the earth appear'd to me
> No bigger than my hand in quantity.

But apart from this, all he seems to be able to do with his supernatural power is to play tricks on the Pope, summon up the ghosts of the illustrious dead and get grapes out of season for a duchess. Whether or not the irony of this was intended by Marlowe, it is striking to a modern reader.

In Faustus' superb last speech, he again speaks of the stars: "Stand still, you ever-moving spheres of heaven," he cries, thinking of all possible means of escape from his terrible fate. He wishes that he could be changed

> Unto some brutish beast. All beasts are happy,
> For when they die,
> Their souls are soon dissolved in elements.

But this cannot be, and Faustus is carried off to hell, leaving the chorus to point the moral and urge the audience

> to wonder at unlawful things,
> Whose deepness doth entice such forward wits
> To practise more than heavenly power permits.

Such is one way in which the sixteenth-century views of man's place in the universe could be made an essential part of drama, and the tradition of the morality be awakened to a new and magnificent life. The individual hero, no longer a mere abstraction, is seen against the background of the cosmos, and the dramatic conflict, no longer a mere battle of virtues and vices, takes place inside a man's soul. By seizing upon and then transcending both the technique and the subject matter which his age gave him, Marlowe not only created his own splendid achievement; he laid the foundation for the greater achievement of Shakespeare.

3

We do not know just when Shakespeare left Stratford for London, but it was probably at the very end of the 'eighties, just as the plays of Marlowe were taking the town by storm. He could have come at no more fortunate moment. The theatrical business was rapidly expanding; new theaters, of a design never surpassed, or even equalled, before or after, had just been built; there were eager audiences and highly-trained actors, and there was, as we have seen, a dramatic tradition which enabled the playwright to enlarge the scope of his action by seeing it in relation to universal truths and to the chief current of thought in the time. From now on it will be our business to understand how Shakespeare made use of the great chance that his age offered him, and for the exalted employment of which Marlowe had set such a brilliant and challenging example.

Shakespeare, however, was a very different man from Marlowe, and we find in his first plays a much less direct use of the traditional views of man than in *Tamburlaine* and *Doctor Faustus*. Shakespeare was more interested in human beings in action than he was in astronomy, and though he might describe how

> The poet's eye in a fine frenzy rolling,
> Doth glance from heaven to earth, from earth to heaven—

a typical sixteenth-century description of the poet's activity [12]—
for the most part he is concerned with the entanglements of
lovers or the struggle for a throne. And yet, without the double
background of popular belief and of dramatic convention, the
earliest plays of Shakespeare, like the later ones, would be very
different from what they are.

Shakespeare began his dramatic career with two plays on the
subject of kingship—the second and third parts of *Henry VI,*
and almost immediately followed them by *Richard III;* in fact
the three plays should be considered as a trilogy, since there is
no real break between them.[13] They are directly in the dramatic
tradition we have so far been attempting to trace; the tradition
of the chronicle play with a serious theme. On the surface they
consist of the presentation of strong vigorous action and energetic personal conflict in a strong and energetic style, and as
we read them we are likely to be so caught by the speed of the
action that we forget how firmly it is conceived in relation to the
sixteenth-century view of kingship and the state. Yet when we
think of the trilogy as a whole, as Shakespeare thought of it,
we see an illustration of the disaster that comes to a kingdom
when order is violated through the weakness of its king, and
when government is destroyed by the machinations of those
who cause civil war by wanting to take the king's place. Clifford
in *3 Henry VI* (ii, 6, 11) sums up the theme with a comparison,
in typical Elizabethan fashion, between the sun and kingship:

> O Phoebus! hadst thou never given consent
> That Phaeton should check thy fiery steeds,
> Thy burning car never had scorch'd the earth;

[12] The pedantic Gabriel Harvey, Spenser's friend, when listing the qualities he
most admires in Chaucer and Lydgate, puts their knowledge of astronomy first.
"It is not sufficient for poets," he says, "to be superficial humanists: but they must
be exquisite artists, and curious universal scholars." *Gabriel Harvey's Marginalia,*
ed. G. C. Moore Smith, Stratford, 1913, pp. 160–161.

[13] I am assuming, with other Shakespeare scholars, that Shakespeare had very
little to do with the first part of *Henry VI.*

> And, Henry, hadst thou sway'd as kings should do,
> Giving no ground unto the house of York,
> They never then had sprung like summer flies.[14]

This is the central idea throughout; the action is a specific in-stance of how the weakness of Henry VI destroys the order of the state;

> Foul subornation is predominant,
> And equity exil'd your higness' land,
> (2 *Henry VI*, iii, 1, 145)

says the Duke of Gloucester, and it is not until the end of *Richard III* that the virtuous Richmond, as Henry VII, can look forward to a period when God will

> Enrich the time to come with smooth-fac'd peace,
> With smiling plenty, and fair prosperous days.

I do not mean to suggest, of course, that Shakespeare wrote this splendid trilogy as a political document, nor that, like the authors of *Gorboduc,* he was trying to teach a moral to Queen Elizabeth. He was naturally doing nothing of the kind. But in writing a successful play about English history he inevitably used the political views which his age gave him, and he in-evitably saw the various conflicts between individuals against a wider pattern of generalization. At one point, elaborating a hint from his source in Holinshed's chronicle, he even uses the technique of the morality play, and to emphasize the damage done by a weak king, he introduces a pair of personified abstrac-tions. When the civil war is at one of its climaxes (*3 Henry VI,* ii, 5), there enters a "Son that hath killed his Father," and a "Father that hath killed his Son," each carrying the body of his victim. They lament their wretched fates, and are joined by the king in an antiphonal keen over the miseries of war. It is

[14] This rather formal comparison of the two realms, the heavens and the state, is characteristic of Shakespeare's early way of writing; the two spheres are set side by side, as in a simile; later they would have been *fused,* as in a metaphor.

a rather stiff and artificial piece of dramatic writing, but it is a good example of how Shakespeare uses the conventions of his age to broaden the area of his subject.

Equally interesting is the way Shakespeare uses the traditional views to describe character. Though Henry VI is a poor sort of king he is a very good sort of man, and so we have him referring to himself as the deputy of God,[15] observing "how God in all his creatures works," [16] and expressing confidence in the prevalence of justice.[17] His views are as conventional as they are convincing in persuading us of the goodness of his character.

Even more striking is Shakespeare's characterization of an evil figure, the villain of the trilogy, Richard of Gloucester. For what distinguishes him is the fact that he is set apart from the rest of mankind, first by his malformed body, which is the outward sign of a malformed soul, and second by his thoroughgoing individualism. Order and society are nothing to him; he is the first of those Shakespearean villains who refuse to be a part of the order of nature and who refuse to see the interconnections between the various spheres of Nature's activity. He is, to use the old mistaken etymology of the word, ab-hominable; cut off from the rest of mankind.

> Then, since the heavens have shap'd my body so,
> Let hell make crook'd my mind to answer it.
> I have no brother, I am like no brother;
> And this word 'love,' which greybeards call divine,
> Be resident in men like one another
> And not in me: I am myself alone.
> (3 *Henry VI*, v, 6, 78)

"I am myself alone"; Iago and Edmund would have said the same.[18] And when at the end of *Richard III*, the two rivals

---

[15] 2 *Henry VI*, iii, 2, 285.

[16] *Ibid.*, ii, 1, 7.

[17] *Ibid.*, ii, 1, 201.

[18] In Kyd's *Spanish Tragedy*, the villain Lorenzo uses a similar Machiavellian

Richmond and Richard speak in soliloquy just before the final battle, the contrast between submission to order and extreme individualism is very clearly the contrast between good and evil. The flawless Richmond prays to God:

> O! thou, whose captain I account myself,
> Look on my forces with a gracious eye. . . .
> Make us thy ministers of chastisement,
> That we may praise thee in thy victory!

But Richard speaks in a different fashion:

> What! do I fear myself? There's none else by:
> Richard loves Richard; that is, I am I. . . .
> I shall despair. There is no creature loves me;
> And if I die, no soul will pity me.

Only when this cankered individual is extirpated, can the kingdom look forward to peace.

Such is the general plan of all Shakespeare's historical plays, as it was of the moralities, and as it is of the later tragedies— as it is, in fact, of all drama that has deep roots in the beliefs and conventions of its time. An existing order is violated, the consequent conflict and turmoil are portrayed, and order is restored by the destruction of the force or forces that originally violated it.

But Shakespeare, though the main outline of his historical plays may follow this conventional pattern, employs the pattern and the convention which it reflects chiefly to portray human beings. His greatness consists—and no historian of ideas should forget it for a moment—in his ability to create characters in whom we can believe, and it is only in so far as we are helped toward an understanding of how he does this, that a study of the conventions of his time is really useful.

---

phrase: "I'll trust myself, myself shall be my friend" (iii, 2, 119), and Marlowe's Barabas (misquoting Terence) says of himself, "Ego mihimet sum semper proximus" (*Jew of Malta*, i, 1, 184). See C. V. Boyer, *The Villain as Hero in Elizabethan Tragedy*, London, 1914, p. 41.

In his next presentation of kingship, in *Richard II* (1595–1596) it is very useful indeed. For the main fact about Richard's character is that he has become so intoxicated with the conventional, glorified view of the function of the king that he is quite unable to live up to his duties. As a king he thinks himself sacrosanct and inviolable (as Shakespeare well knew, Richard had been a king since he was ten years old, and hence the concept of kingship was ingrained in him), but as a man of action he proves himself a complete failure. The traditional glorifications of his position have become the essence of his being, and he lives in an unreal world in which he thinks of those glorifications as the only reality. The convention, the word, the illusion, are to him more important than external action. Shakespeare is careful to emphasize this again and again, but nowhere does he show it more clearly than when he puts into Richard's mouth an elaborate exposition of the familiar parallel between the cosmos and the state, the sun and the king:

> Discomfortable cousin! know'st thou not
> That when the searching eye of heaven is hid
> Behind the globe, and lights the lower world,
> Then thieves and robbers range abroad unseen,
> In murders and in outrage bloody here;
> But when, from under this terrestrial ball
> He fires the proud tops of the eastern pines
> And darts his light through every guilty hole,
> Then murders, treasons, and detested sins,
> The cloak of night being pluck'd from off their backs,
> Stand bare and naked, trembling at themselves?
> So when this thief, this traitor, Bolingbroke,
> Who all this while hath revell'd in the night
> Whilst we were wandering in the antipodes,
> Shall see us rising in our throne, the east,
> His treasons will sit blushing in his face,
> Not able to endure the sight of day,
> But self-affrighted tremble at his sin.
> Not all the water in the rude rough sea

Can wash the balm from an anointed king;
The breath of worldly men cannot depose
The deputy elected by the Lord.[19]

(iii, 2, 36)

Other characters in the play speak of Richard in the same way
—as if to re-inforce his own view of himself. To the Cardinal,
Richard is

the figure of God's majesty,
His captain, steward, deputy elect,

(iv, 1, 125)

and Harry Percy, when Richard humiliatingly enters on the
walls of Flint Castle, calls attention to him through use of the
same imagery that Richard himself employed:

See, see, King Richard doth himself appear,
As doth the blushing discontented sun
From out the fiery portal of the east,
When he perceives the envious clouds are bent
To dim his glory and to stain the track
Of his bright passage to the occident.

(iii, 3, 62)

To which the Duke of York replies:

Yet looks he like a king: behold, his eye,
As bright as is the eagle's, lightens forth
Controlling majesty: alack, alack, for woe,
That any harm should stain so fair a show! [20]

[19] It is worth while to remind ourselves how thoroughly the character of Richard
in this scene, as throughout, is Shakespeare's creation. Holinshed, Shakespeare's only
source as far as we know, has little to say about Richard's character, and it is
Shakespeare alone who so admirably uses the conventional views of kingship to
show what sort of person Richard is.

[20] Toward the end, in the deposition scene, Richard plays in highly characteristic
fashion with the image—in a different way. Confronted with the fact that Bolingbroke is now the real king, he transfers the familiar metaphor to him:

O! that I were a mockery king of snow,
Standing before the sun of Bolingbroke.

(iv, 1, 260)

But that is just Richard's difficulty; he is "so fair a show," and nothing more. To him that appearance is the reality, and tragedy is the inevitable result. We shall have much to say later about Shakespeare's use, in describing character, of the difference between appearance and reality; in his account of Richard we have one of the earliest illustrations of how he can use for dramatic purposes the views of man given him by his age. Here he limits himself to using the traditional views of kingship, and he is concerned with showing how a king who has accepted those views discovers, with a kind of sentimental desperation, that human suffering is the reality underneath:

> throw away respect,
> Tradition, form, and ceremonious duty,
> For you have but mistook me all this while:
> I live with bread like you, feel want,
> Taste grief, need friends: subjected thus,
> How can you say to me I am a king?
>   (iii, 2, 172)

But even this is not quite real; Richard gives himself away, as Shakespeare meant him to, by his punning on the word "subjected"; he means that he is under a burden, and also that he is a subject, instead of a king, and it is this double meaning, this verbal ambiguity, that chiefly moves him. As always with him the words control the thought; he is the opposite of Hamlet, whose thought controls the words. And the images that Richard uses are those which sixteenth-century convention supplied: the parallel between the sun and kingship, the parallel between the rule of the king on earth and the rule of God in heaven. To the last, he is an inveterate seeker of correspondences, and when he is alone in prison just before his death, he is still hunting for parallels, trying in vain to turn his prison into a macrocosm:

> I have been studying how I may compare
> This prison where I live unto the world:
> And for because the world is populous,

And here is not a creature but myself,
I cannot do it.

4

In his second great trilogy, the two parts of *Henry IV* and
Henry V, there is, as everyone knows, an enormous expansion
both of Shakespeare's extraordinary capacity for creating character, and of his ability to weave different threads of plot into
the texture of a single dramatic unity. And here again he owes
much to dramatic convention and to the traditional views of
kingship. Some scholars have even gone so far as to see, especially in the second part of *Henry IV*, a direct use of the
technique of the morality play, with Falstaff "as the lineal
descendant" of Gluttony, Lechery, Sloth, Avarice and Pride—
five of the seven deadly sins rolled into one "reverend Vice,"
one "grey Iniquity." According to this view, the second part of
the trilogy "depicts the conflict between Sir John and the Chief
Justice, after the manner of the Moralities, for the soul of
Prince Hal." [21]

This is certainly a possible way of thinking about the matter,
though I doubt if Shakespeare himself had quite so formal a
scheme in mind. One imagines him as being more interested in
character than in imitating directly a dramatic form which he
must have known was out of date, and even if he did have the
morality technique in mind as he wrote, he went beyond it in
his actual performance. And yet the conventional scheme of the
older serious drama is clearly present—the scheme which was a
blending of the Biblical play and the morality into the serious
chronicle play. A kingdom is in the chaos of civil war, and is only
restored to order by the right kind of king. Henry V is, of

[21] Robert A. Law, "Structural Unity in the Two Parts of *Henry the Fourth*,"
Studies in Philology, XXIV (1927), 242. See also, for similar views, A. Quiller-
Couch, *Shakespeare's Workmanship*, London, 1918, pp. 115 ff., and J. W. Spargo,
"An Interpretation of Falstaff," *University of Washington Studies*, IX (1922),
119 ff.

course, a much more important figure in this trilogy than Richmond is in the earlier one; he is present from the first as a major
character who, in typical royal fashion, the first time he speaks
seriously, compares himself to the sun:

> I know you all, and will awhile uphold
> The unyok'd humour of your idleness:
> Yet herein will I imitate the sun,
> Who doth permit the base contagious clouds
> To smother up his beauty from the world,
> That when he please again to be himself,
> Being wanted, he may be more wonder'd at.
>
> (Part 1, i, 2, 217)

In this speech Shakespeare wants to reassure his audience about
Hal's true character; he is not the wastrel he seems to be, and
it is perhaps not far-fetched to see, in his use of the familiar
analogy, a means of re-inforcing that assurance: if Hal thinks
along those lines, the audience will say, he must surely be a re-
liable prince.

There are other places in the first two plays where the role
of kingship is re-inforced by comparisons with the cosmos and
with the human body. Henry IV urges the rebellious Worcester
to

> move in that obedient orb again
> Where you did give a fair and natural light,
> And be no more an exhal'd meteor,
> A prodigy of fear and a portent
> Of broached mischief to the unborn times,
>
> (Part 1, v, 1, 17)

and on another occasion he says to Warwick,

> Then you perceive the body of our kingdom,
> How foul it is; what rank diseases grow,
> And with what danger, near the heart of it.
>
> (Part 2, iii, 1, 38)

The familiar interweaving of the three inter-related domains
of the cosmos, the state and the individual, proves, as usual, a

rich source of allusion and metaphor. Falstaff uses it in another way, in his famous defense of sherry: sherry, he says, "illumineth the face, which, as a beacon, gives warning to all the rest of the little kingdom, man, to arm; and then the vital commoners and inland petty spirits muster me all to their captain, the heart, who, great and puffed up with this retinue, doth any deed of courage; and this valour comes of sherris." (Part 2, iv, 3, 116.)

It is in *Henry V*, the third part of the trilogy, that we find the fullest description of what government and kingship should be. Hal has reformed—

> Consideration like an angel came,
> And whipp'd the offending Adam out of him,
> Leaving his body as a paradise,
> To envelop and contain celestial spirits.
> Never was such a sudden scholar made;
>
> (i, 1, 28)

and though to modern readers his behavior as Henry V by no means makes him a perfect individual, there can be no doubt that Shakespeare intended him to embody all that a king should be;

> a Christian king;
> Unto whose grace our passion is as subject
> As are our wretches fetter'd in our prisons.
> (i, 1, 241)

To set off this ideal monarch, Shakespeare uses a dramatic device which he was later frequently to employ. He puts into the mouth of one of his characters an account of the ideal situation which the action of the play is to illustrate; or—in the later plays—to violate. In this case, at the beginning of the play, both Exeter and the Archbishop of Canterbury describe the ideal of government; government, says Exeter,

> though high and low and lower,
> Put into parts, doth keep in one consent,

Congreeing in a full and natural close,
Like music.

(i, 2, 180)

The Archbishop, in a famous speech, develops the idea:

Therefore doth heaven divide
The state of man in divers functions,
Setting endeavour in continual motion;
To which is fixed, as an aim or butt,
Obedience: for so work the honey-bees,
Creatures that by a rule in nature teach
The act of order to a peopled kingdom.

And he expounds at length the comparison—familiar to everyone in Shakespeare's day, but never before so eloquently expressed—between a beehive and a commonwealth.[22]

They have a king and officers of sorts;
Where some, like magistrates, correct at home,
Others, like merchants, venture trade abroad,
Others, like soldiers, armed in their stings,
Make boot upon the summer's velvet buds;
Which pillage they with merry march bring home
To the tent-royal of their emperor:
Who, busied in his majesty, surveys
The singing masons building roofs of gold,
The civil citizens kneading up the honey,
The poor mechanic porters crowding in
Their heavy burdens at his narrow gate,
The sad-ey'd justice, with his surly hum,
Delivering o'er to executors pale
The lazy yawning drone.

[22] Shakespeare may have derived his description from Lyly's *Euphues*, where the
comparison is fully developed (*Works*, ed. Bond, II, 44 ff.), but it can also be
found in Vergil's fourth Georgic, in Pliny, *Natural History*, xi, ch. 4–22, in Sir
Thomas Elyot, *The Governor*, I, ii (who refers to Vergil, Pliny, and Columella,
bk. ix). A great many sixteenth-century treatises on government have some kind
of reference to it.

The effect of this description, given very near the beginning of the play, is obvious. This is the ideal way in which things are going to be run under the ideal king: everything will be orderly, everything, in the Archbishop's words, will "end in one purpose"—in the unity of government.

This picture of the ideal commonwealth is paralleled by a picture of the ideal individual, also given fairly early in the play (ii, 2, 126). It is not presented so directly, but for that very reason it makes a strong impression on our minds. The Lord Scroop is found guilty of plotting against the king, and the king arraigns him by listing the virtues he thought Scroop possessed, but which in reality were only a show. They give a very clear summary of what the king considers the right principles of conduct, and they give a picture of what sort of man the king is, for, being an ideal figure, he must himself embody the virtues he admires. The king speaks to Scroop:

> O! how hast thou with jealousy infected
> The sweetness of affiance. Show men dutiful?
> Why, so didst thou: seem they grave and learned? . . .
> Why, so didst thou: seem they religious?
> Why, so didst thou: or are they spare in diet,
> Free from gross passion or of mirth or anger,
> Constant in spirit, not swerving with the blood,
> Garnish'd and deck'd in modest complement,
> Not working with the eye without the ear,
> And but in purged judgment trusting neither? . . .
>   I will weep for thee;
> For this revolt of thine, methinks, is like
> Another fall of man.

This is the ideal aristocrat, dutiful, learned, religious, temperate, constant, controlling passion with reason, and ruling sense with judgment. It represents the same ideal which Shakespeare was to expound in other plays written about this time (1599). It is the ideal which Antony no doubt has in mind when he describes Brutus at the end of *Julius Caesar*:

> His life was gentle, and the elements
> So mix'd in him that Nature might stand up
> And say to all the world, "This was a man!"

It is the ideal which Hamlet has in mind when he describes Horatio:

> bless'd are those
> Whose blood and judgment are so well commingled
> That they are not a pipe for fortune's finger
> To sound what stop she please. Give me that man
> That is not passion's slave, and I will wear him
> In my heart's core, ay, in my heart of heart,
> As I do thee.
>
> (iii, 2, 73)

It is the ideal of the whole Hellenistic tradition of the nature of man, whose specific function, reason, should govern the passions which spring from the senses he shares with the animals, those beings below him in Nature's hierarchy to whose level he tends only too easily to fall.

In the character of Henry V we have a reflection of another aspect of human nature which seems, throughout the 1590's, to have concerned Shakespeare: the question of whether the pomp and ceremony which surround a king make him really distinguishable from other men. As we have seen, Richard II, in his strained and sentimental way, refers to the matter—

> I live with bread like you, feel want,
> Taste grief, need friends: subjected thus,
> How can you say to me I am a king?—

Henry V, in a more manly and realistic fashion, is troubled by the same question. Before the battle of Agincourt, when he is going about the camp in disguise, he says to the soldiers with whom he is conversing:

For, though I speak it to you, I think the king is but a man, as I am: the violet smells to him as it doth to me; all his senses have but human conditions: his ceremonies laid by, in his nakedness he appears but a man,

(iv, 1, 106)

and when he is left alone, his great speech on ceremony which follows is devoted to the same thought—that the pomp which Hamlet was later to call "absurd" is only a "proud dream."

> O ceremony! show me but thy worth:
> What is thy soul of adoration?
> Art thou aught else but place, degree, and form,
> Creating awe and fear in other men?

Ceremony is the only thing that distinguishes a king from other human beings, and it can do nothing to bring him health or happiness:

> 'Tis not the balm, the sceptre and the ball,
> The sword, the mace, the crown imperial,
> The intertissued robe of gold and pearl,
> The farced title running 'fore the king,
> The throne he sits on, nor the tide of pomp
> That beats upon the high shore of this world,
> No, not all these, thrice-gorgeous ceremony,
> Not all these, laid in bed majestical,
> Can sleep so soundly as the wretched slave,
> Who with a body fill'd and vacant mind
> Gets him to rest.

The idea is not a new one, but Shakespeare seems continually to dwell on it; Henry IV had spoken at length on the uneasy rest given to those who wear a crown, and as early as the third part of *Henry VI* (ii, 5) Shakespeare puts into his king's mouth a comparison between the simple life of the peasant and the cares of kingship. Henry VI, however, is a special case; it is the hot-bed of treason and violence which surrounds him rather than the general situation of being a king that makes him regret his position, and the chief view of kingship we get from the early trilogy is that it is a highly desirable state of existence. Richard

of Gloucester, for example, is as enthusiastic about kingship as
Marlowe's Tamburlaine:

> And, father, do but think
> How sweet a thing it is to wear a crown,
> Within whose circuit is Elysium,
> And all that poets feign of bliss and joy.
> (Part 3, i, 2, 28)

But Shakespeare's later heroes are not so naif, and Henry V's
awareness of the hollowness of the ceremony which surrounds
him is one of the main reasons why we think of him as a ma-
ture human being.

In fact Shakespeare's treatment of kingship, and his repeated
emphasis on the human reality underneath the outer cover of
ceremony, is only one aspect of his attitude, in the 'nineties, to
human nature in general. His most attractive and appealing
characters despise anything that is pretentious, as Mercutio despises the pretentiousness of Tybalt's Italian duelling terms, as
the Bastard, in *King John,* despises the boasting of the Duke of
Austria, and as Hotspur despises, among other things, the
supernatural pretensions of Glendower and the artificiality of
poetry. All these characters break through some kind of pre-
tense in order to discover, or assert, a common-sense point of
view that comes back to ordinary human reality. Romeo, when
we first see him, lives in a dream; his feelings, such as they are,
for Rosaline, make him go indoors when the sun begins to shine
and live in an artificial night; but when real love strikes him he
is another person, and at the end of the play he is forged, like a
sword through fire. In *The Merchant of Venice,* the Prince of
Morocco is fooled by the pretentiousness of the gold casket, and
the Prince of Aragon is fooled by the silver casket, each mis-
taking the appearance for the reality. Only Bassanio, whose wisdom consists in knowing that appearance is merely

The seeming truth which cunning times put on
To entrap the wisest,

(iii, 2, 100)

has the sense to choose the casket of lead where Portia's picture lies. This particular use of the difference between appearance and truth was given to Shakespeare, of course, by the old story, just as his common sense about humanity gave him his feeling for the genuine in human behavior as against the artificial and unreal; the plays of the 'nineties do not yet employ to the full that combination of Shakespeare's own wise observation of particular instances with the traditional picture of man's nature and the conflict suggested by it which was implicit in the time and which gives the wide grandeur of universality to the later tragedies. That was yet to come. In the best plays of the 'nineties—the three-dimensional plays as we may call them (in contradistinction to the great tragedies, which have, as it were, a fourth dimension)—the traditional views of human nature have a more local significance; they are used for the particular occasion; they bear on the particular action downwards; they do not exalt upwards the action and the characters. Admirably used as they are —in the plays about kingship for example,—they are used to *define* character, not to expand it into the kind of portrayal that defies definition, that is beyond definition. The characters in the plays of the 'nineties may be described, to use the terms of sixteenth-century psychology, by the discourse of reason, but in the sequence of tragedies which begins with *Hamlet*, we need (and I use this word in its sixteenth-century sense also) not merely reason, but a more exalted, a more intuitive and angelic faculty—the faculty which we may say that Shakespeare himself used in creating them—the faculty of understanding.

I do not mean to suggest, of course, that our knowledge of the plays of the 1590's is not immensely helped by an awareness of the traditional views of man. What Shakespeare could do, in dramatic terms, with the traditional view of kingship, in relation to both theme and character, we have just seen. And if we read such a play as *Love's Labour's Lost* in the light of the sixteenth-century views of man's nature, we can achieve a much clearer picture than we would have otherwise of Shakespeare's purpose and accomplishment. The date of the play is in some dispute, but the best opinion is now agreed on 1594 or 1595, and it seems clear that Shakespeare wrote it for a special audience, a more highbrow audience than that which frequented the popular theaters. The main plot (for which no source is known) concerns ideals of education and what happens to them when life breaks through; four young men, led by the king of Navarre, are to retire from the world for three years to study, but they are at once confronted by four young women with whom they fall in love, and the consequence is that their whole pretentious scheme collapses. The opening speech by the king sums up what the young men are trying to do—there is no speech in Shakespeare more characteristic of the optimism of the early Renaissance. They are to pursue fame in conquering their affections and their passions by the use of reason employed during three years' study in an academy:

> Let fame, that all hunt after in their lives,
> Live register'd upon our brazen tombs,
> And then grace us in the disgrace of death;
> When, spite of cormorant devouring Time,
> The endeavour of this present breath may buy
> That honour which shall bate his scythe's keen edge,
> And make us heirs of all eternity.
> Therefore, brave conquerors,—for so you are,
> That war against your own affections
> And the huge army of the world's desires,—
> Our late edict shall strongly stand in force:
> Navarre shall be the wonder of the world;
> Our court shall be a little academe,
> Still and contemplative in living art.

I do not believe it has been noted by previous students of Shakespeare that just before this play was written (if we follow Sir Edmund Chambers in dating it as of 1595), there appeared, in 1594, the third edition of the English translation of La Primaudaye's *French Academy*, that compendium of Renaissance knowledge and morality from which I have quoted in earlier chapters,[28] and which, of course, Shakespeare might have read as early as 1586, the date of the first English edition. La Primaudaye dedicates the work to Henry III of France, and begins his dedication by quoting Plato to the effect that "Commonwealths begin then to be happy, when kings exercise Philosophy, and Philosophers reign." The work itself opens with an account of how four young men of Anjou, after their study has been interrupted by the wars, take it up again, re-forming, under the direction of a wise philosopher, their Academy; and the body of the book consists of discourses by one of them after another, in which they show their fathers how much they have learned about the true nature of man.

It is tempting to suppose that Shakespeare derived his philosophic king of Navarre, who is one of four young men planning to study in an academy, from La Primaudaye. Possibly he did; the work was widely popular and he may very likely have known it. But whether he did or not, we may be sure that what the king of Navarre had planned to study would have been very similar to the traditional subject-matter expounded by the four young men from Anjou.

Our chief concern, however, is with what Shakespeare does with his idea, wherever it came from, and what he does is to show that the whole scheme is absurd, and that the "angel knowl-

[28] The full title of the first volume in the 1618 edition is: *The French Academy, wherein is discoursed the institution of manners, and whatsoever else concerneth the good and happy life of all estates and callings, by precepts of doctrine, and examples of the lives of ancient Sages and famous men.* The translator, in his preface, calls it a "treatise of moral philosophy," which it is.

edge," as Berowne calls it, which the king is pursuing, is not something that can be studied by itself, for it is intimately bound up with the rest of man's nature:

> For every man with his affects is born,
> Not by might master'd, but by special grace.[24]
>
> (i, 1, 150)

Berowne is much the most important character in the play, and he is a relative of Mercutio, of the Bastard, of Hotspur, in that he knocks down pretensions and always comes back to human reality. When all the lovers are revealed, he is delighted that nature has so asserted herself:

> Sweet lords, sweet lovers, O! let us embrace.
> As true we are as flesh and blood can be:
> The sea will ebb and flow, heaven show his face;

[24] Something similar to this view, and something which perhaps reflects Shakespeare's—the ex-schoolmaster's(?)—own view of education, occurs earlier, in the first act of *The Taming of the Shrew*. Lucentio says he has come to Padua to study, and, he says,

> Virtue and that part of philosophy
> Will I apply that treats of happiness
> By virtue specially to be achiev'd.

But his servant Tranio is not so high-flown; he wants to have learning related to life:

> *Mi perdonate*, gentle master mine,
> I am in all affected as yourself,
> Glad that you thus continue your resolve
> To suck the sweets of sweet philosophy.
> Only, good master, while we do admire
> This virtue and this moral discipline,
> Let's be no stoics nor no stocks, I pray;
> Or so devote to Aristotle's checks
> As Ovid be an outcast quite abjur'd.
> Balk logic with acquaintance that you have,
> And practice rhetoric in your common talk;
> Music and poesy use to quicken you;
> The mathematics and the metaphysics,
> Fall to them as you find your stomach serves you;
> No profit grows where is no pleasure ta'en;
> In brief, sir, study what you most affect.

Young blood doth not obey an old decree:
We cannot cross the cause why we were born;
Therefore, of all hands must we be forsworn.

(iv, 3, 215)

And shortly afterwards, in his famous speech in praise of love, he expands, with wonderful energy and eloquence, the idea that love develops the *whole* man, and re-inforces every part of him. The speech is greatly dependent on the traditional views of psychology, and Berowne, like so many other sixteenth-century characters, carries his thought from one sphere to another, from man up to the gods:

Other slow arts entirely keep the brain,
And therefore, finding barren practisers,
Scarce show a harvest of their heavy toil;
But love, first learned in a lady's eyes,
Lives not alone immured in the brain,
But, with the motion of all elements,
Courses as swift as thought in every power,
And gives to every power a double power,
Above their functions and their offices.
It adds a precious seeing to the eye;
A lover's eyes will gaze an eagle blind;
A lover's ear will hear the lowest sound,
When the suspicious head of theft is stopp'd:
Love's feeling is more soft and sensible
Than are the tender horns of cockled snails:
Love's tongue proves dainty Bacchus gross in taste.
For valour, is not love a Hercules,
Still climbing trees in the Hesperides?
Subtle as Sphinx; as sweet and musical
As bright Apollo's lute, strung with his hair;
And when Love speaks, the voice of all the gods
Makes heaven drowsy with the harmony.

(iv, 3, 324)

At the end of the play Berowne undergoes a change; even he is not close enough to reality. In the first place he changes his style of speaking—there are to be no more verbal extravagances and exaggerated conceits for him:

> Taffeta phrases, silken terms precise,
>   Three-pil'd hyperboles, spruce affectation,
> Figures pedantical; these summer flies
>   Have blown me full of maggot ostentation:
> I do forswear them; and I here protest,
>   By this white glove,—how white the hand, God knows,—
> Henceforth my wooing mind shall be express'd
>   In russet yeas and honest kersey noes.
>
> (v, 2, 407)

And in the second place he is condemned by his lady, Rosaline, to spend a year telling jokes in a hospital before she will marry him; he must visit the speechless sick, and converse with groaning wretches; he must know what suffering is as well as love. The play closes on an unexpected note of seriousness: the hospital we hear about at the end is a very different place from the "academe" we hear about at the beginning. That early Renaissance concept cannot stand up under the pressure of the facts. And just as the theme of the play dissipates illusion for reality, so does the language—not only as far as Berowne is concerned. It is surely no accident that the most verbally artificial and metrically elaborate of all Shakespeare's plays should end with the most rustic, simple and countrified of all his songs.

If in this play Shakespeare uses the traditional view of man's nature in relation to the moral sphere, in *Romeo and Juliet* he does something similar with the traditional view of the relation between man and the heavens, stretching far beyond what was given him by his source (the poem by Arthur Brooke called *Romeus and Juliet*) that conception of human action as dominated by a universal power which was so necessary a part of the Elizabethan dramatic heritage. Brooke's poem is merely an adjunct of the *Mirror for Magistrates,* and, as such, it is, in intention, an illustration of how Fortune brings people of high position to destruction. Fortune, that artificial abstraction, turns up on nearly every page of Brooke, and Brooke's insistence on Fortune's implacable insecurity, like a monotonous drum drowning out the singing violins in an orchestra, destroys the human reality of his protagonists.

Shakespeare, however, while recognizing the dramatic value of an exterior force which apparently determines the fate of his hero and heroine, hardly mentions Fortune at all. He identifies the exterior force with something much more immediate to the beliefs of his sixteenth-century audience, and instead of describing the fate of Romeo and Juliet as caused by a musty literary abstraction, he describes it as caused by the stars, agents of human destiny that his audience could really believe in. Romeo and Juliet are a pair of "star-cross'd lovers," Romeo, as he is about to meet Juliet, misgives "Some consequence yet hanging in the stars"; the Friar tells the Capulets that "The heavens do lour upon you for some ill"; Romeo, when he hears of Juliet's supposed death, and the forged sword of his character is clear at last, cries out with desperate authority, with a defiance only fully comprehensible to a believer in astrology: "Is it even so? Then I defy you, stars!"—the stars whose inauspicious yoke he at last shakes from his world-wearied flesh.

But the tragedy of Romeo and Juliet, unlike the later tragedies, is an external tragedy, and no matter how splendidly Shakespeare may see it in relation to the conventional belief in the influence of the stars on mankind, he does not make that belief, or the explosion of that belief, as he was to do later, a part of his analysis of character. Romeo and Juliet, unlike Hamlet and Othello, are "whole-souled," and though a knowledge of sixteenth-century views of man may help us to see how Shakespeare thought of their tragedy, they themselves are not aware of how their actions and what happens to them violate the accepted beliefs. Romeo's tragedy is caused by the stars above him, and he has to be told by an external commentator what is wrong with his passions. Friar Laurence is a chorus to the emotions of Romeo, just as—for the hierarchy of the state is important too—the Prince of Verona is a chorus to the feud. The Prince has to keep order in the state, to see that his authority is not destroyed by the quarrel between the Montagues and the Capulets, which ranges through all the orders of Veronese society, from servants to lords (as Shakespeare is careful to point out in the opening scene of the play), and the Friar, an embodiment of equal authority, has to keep order in Romeo's soul. The Prince, the symbol of secular government, can control the squabble only by shouting, "What ho! you men, you beasts," and the Friar, in trying to control Romeo's passion, uses the same familiar distinction between men and animals in an attempt to calm Romeo's personal turbulence:

> Art thou a man? thy form cries out thou art:
> Thy tears are womanish; thy wild acts denote
> The unreasonable fury of a beast.
>
> (iii, 3, 108)

But though the Prince and the Friar, the representatives of the political and psychological hierarchies, may comment and deplore, what they say does not, in any fundamental way, either determine the course of the action or increase an understanding of the protagonists. They are outside. In the later tragedies the views they expound, the conventions which they embody externally, are put by Shakespeare *inside* the consciousness of his heroes and heroines, and the split between appearance and reality, between man as tradition said he should be and what experience proved he was, is no longer an external matter, about which princes and priests may comment with a chorus-like equanimity; it is something which can tear a soul apart in pieces, as it tears the souls of Hamlet and of Lear.

CHAPTER IV

HAMLET AND *TROILUS AND CRESSIDA*

I

At the beginning of the seventeenth century, Shakespeare had behind him ten years of successful play-writing. He had proved himself a master of comedy, of the chronicle play, of a certain kind of tragedy, and he had proved himself a master of plot-construction, of character and blank verse. He had brilliantly developed the dramatic conventions given him by his time and he had admirably used the traditional sixteenth-century beliefs about man's nature as a mine for metaphor, as a means of describing character, and as a means of defining values by which character and action could be understood.

Toward the end of this period, as many students of Shakespeare have pointed out, there are indications of increasing seriousness, an anticipatory clouding over of Shakespeare's view of the human situation. His half-satiric, half-sympathetic portrayal of the melancholy Jaques in *As You Like It*, a tone of something alien to comedy in *Twelfth Night,* the seriousness which he gives to the character of Brutus in *Julius Caesar*, all appear to foreshadow the presentation of evil which is the basis of the later tragedies. [1] In *Hamlet* evil appears full-fledged, and we

---

[1] Brutus, incidentally, makes excellent metaphorical use of the familiar parallel between the body and the state in his famous lines:

> Between the acting of a dreadful thing
> And the first motion, all the interim is
> Like a phantasma, or a hideous dream:
> The genius and the mortal instruments
> Are then in council; and the state of man,
> Like to a little kingdom, suffers then
> The nature of an insurrection.

(ii, 1, 63)

have a very different kind of tragedy from anything that Shakespeare had previously written. For with *Hamlet* we feel as if Shakespeare had had a new vision of what a play could contain, and in this play, as in the other tragedies that follow it, the characters and events become larger than the characters of the 1590's; they make more reverberations in our minds; they take on a symbolic and universal meaning.

To describe how this is accomplished is one of the central problems in Shakespearean criticism: I suggest that we can understand it best by realizing that in *Hamlet* Shakespeare for the first time used to the full the conflict between the two views of man's nature which was so deeply felt in his age. On one side was the picture of man as he should be—it was bright, orderly and optimistic. On the other was the picture of man as he is—it was full of darkness and chaos. Shakespeare puts an awareness of this contrast into the character of Hamlet, and his having done so is one of the main reasons for *Hamlet's* greatness. Previously Shakespeare had used the traditional beliefs *descriptively* as part of the background—the sun is compared to the king, the human body is compared to the state—and there is no question as to whether the beliefs are true. But in *Hamlet* they are not in the background, they are an essential part of the hero's consciousness, and his discovery that they are not true, his awareness of the conflict between what theory taught and what experience proves, wrecks him. Shakespeare had used the difference between appearance and reality as a dramatic device many times before, but never like this, and never in such close relation to the thought and feeling of his time.

For Hamlet, before his mother's second marriage, had been, as Shakespeare is careful to point out, the ideal Renaissance nobleman; according to Ophelia, he had a "noble mind," "the courtier's, soldier's, scholar's, eye, tongue, sword." He was

> The expectancy and rose of the fair state,
> The glass of fashion and the mould of form;

he had, to use Bradley's somewhat romantic expression, "an unbounded delight and faith in everything good and beautiful." He was conceived by Shakespeare, in other words, as a young man who had been trained to believe, and by temperament was inclined to believe, in the traditional optimistic view of the nature of man. But the discovery of his mother's lust and the fact that the kingdom is in the hands of a man he considers unworthy—these shatter his belief into ruins, and the world, the state and the individual are to him suddenly corrupt. There is no better illustration than *Hamlet* of the fact that in Shakespeare's day the three spheres were so closely related that to destroy one was to destroy the others as well. Nor is there any better illustration of the sixteenth-century dramatic convention which invariably placed individual action against the background of a universal truth. In *Hamlet* the two traditions, the tradition of belief and the tradition of dramatic practice, are magnificently fused in the creation of the most absorbing character the stage has ever known.

There are two related aspects of Hamlet's thought which Shakespeare deliberately emphasizes in first presenting him to the audience. Hamlet is preoccupied with the difference between appearance and reality, and he extends his feelings about his particular situation to cover his feelings about the world as a whole.

> *King:* But now, my cousin Hamlet, and my son,—
> *Hamlet:* (*Aside.*) A little more than kin, and less than kind.
> *King:* How is it that the clouds still hang on you?
> *Hamlet:* Not so, my lord; I am too much i' the sun.

Again, when the queen asks him why the death of his father seems so particular with him, he answers,

> Seems, madam! Nay, it is; I know not 'seems,'

and he discourses, roused for the first time, on the contrast between the outer trappings of grief, and the feeling within
"which passeth show."

So much he can say in public, but when he is left alone, we
see that his whole view of life is turned upside down. It is
characteristic of Shakespeare's conception of Hamlet's universalizing mind that he should make Hamlet think first of the
general rottenness; to him *all* the uses of the world are weary,
stale, flat and unprofitable; things rank and gross in nature
possess it completely. From this he passes to the king, the head
of the state, bitterly comparing his god-like father to his satyr-
like uncle, and he finally dwells at length on individual per-
version, the lustfulness of his mother, who has violated natural
law by the brevity of her grief and the haste of her marriage.

> O God! a beast, that wants discourse of reason,
> Would have mourned longer.

Hamlet's thought, like that of so many men of the time, involves the world, the state and the individual, and one reason
this first soliloquy is so broken, its rhythms so panting, is that
it reflects Hamlet's disillusionment about all three spheres
at once.

Hamlet's generalizing mind is everywhere emphasized;
his thought invariably leaps out to embrace the world as a
whole, he talks of infinite space, his rhetoric includes the stars.
It is characteristic of him that when he approaches Laertes
after Laertes has jumped into Ophelia's grave, he should ask
who it is who

> Conjures the wandering stars, and makes them stand
> Like wonder-wounded hearers,

when, as a matter of fact, Laertes had not mentioned the stars
at all. It is as if Hamlet were attributing to Laertes a thought
that would be natural to him, but not to Laertes. Again, the
first thing that Hamlet exclaims after the ghost has given his

message is "O all you host of heaven!"; and in his mother's closet, when he upbraids her with her marriage, he describes it not merely as violating human contracts, but as affecting the world as a whole:

> heaven's face doth glow,
> Yea this solidity and compound mass,
> With tristful visage, as against the doom,
> Is thought-sick at the act.

But the occasion on which Hamlet speaks at greatest length of the heavens is, of course, when he describes his state of mind to Rosencrantz and Guildenstern in the second act. The situation is a critical one for Hamlet. He knows that his former fellow-students are spies of the king, and he obviously cannot tell them the real cause of his distemper. What explanation can he give them? He gives them just the kind of explanation that would be most clearly understood by young intellectuals, particularly young intellectuals who were familiar with his own generalizing type of mind and who might be expected to have shared his previous acceptance of the optimistic view of the world. All three young men had been taught that the surest way to comprehend man's place in the universe and to realize the magnificence of God's creation, was to contemplate the glory of the superior heavens which surrounded the earth, those heavens of which Spenser had so glowingly written in his "Hymn of Heavenly Beauty," and which Thomas Digges, in his *Perfect Description of the Celestial Orbs* (1576) described more scientifically, but with equal enthusiasm.[2] La

---

[2] Digges wrote of the motionless heaven of fixed stars according to the Copernican system, and in his case, as in others, the acceptance of Copernicus did not mean that the universe was not beautiful. "This orb of stars," he says, "fixed infinitely up extendeth himself in altitude spherically and therefore immoveable, the palace of felicity garnished with perpetually shining glorious lights innumerable, far excelling our sun in quantity and quality, the very court of celestial angels, devoid of grief and replenished with perfect endless joy, the habitacle for the elect."

Primaudaye and countless other Renaissance writers had written in the same way, and had inevitably turned, as Hamlet turns, from the contemplation of the stars to the contemplation of man, for whom all this splendor had been made. But Hamlet reverses the application, and the clearest way he can explain his melancholy to his fellow-students is to tell them that he sees in the heavens, as well as in the world around him, the reality of evil underneath the appearance of good. Nothing could be more plausible, for everyone knew that such were the opinions of the man afflicted with melancholy. For example in 1599, just before Shakespeare wrote *Hamlet,* there appeared an English translation of a French medical work called *Of the Diseases of Melancholy* by a certain Dr. Du Laurens. Like the other sixteenth-century writers on melancholy, Du Laurens describes a state of mind very similar to Hamlet's. He begins with the usual exaltation of man: "Coming to extol man unto the highest degree and step of his glory, behold him I pray thee the best furnished and most perfect of all other living creatures, having . . . in his soul the image of God, and in his body the model of the whole world." [3] But the melancholy man is a very different object, he is "the most caitiff and miserable creature that is in the world, spoiled of all his graces, deprived of judgment, reason and counsel, enemy of men and of the Sun, straying and wandering in solitary places; to be brief, so altered and changed, as that he is

---

See Francis R. Johnson, *Astronomical Thought in Renaissance England,* Baltimore, 1937, p. 166. Digges' tract is published in *The Huntington Library Bulletin,* No. 5, April, 1934, by F. R. Johnson and S. V. Larkey. Perhaps Shakespeare knew of his description; Digges was a kind of sixteenth century Eddington or Jeans, his book went through six editions before 1600, Shakespeare could have found these words merely by looking at the title page where they are inscribed in a diagram, and Hamlet's description of the heavens sounds more like the motionless outer sphere of Copernicus than the revolving heavens of Ptolemy.

[3] *A Discourse of the Preservation of the Sight,* etc., trans. Richard Surphlet, *Shakespeare Association Facsimiles,* No. 15, London, 1938, p. 80.

no more a man, as not retaining anything more than the very name." [4]

Hamlet, of course, enlarges this concept, as he enlarges everything, but the conventional views of man, both general and specialized, gave him an excellent groundwork to build on, and both his two interlocutors and the audience would have understood Hamlet's magnificent generalizations more richly than we do, since they had been trained in the same beliefs as his own:

I have of late,—but wherefore I know not,—lost all my mirth, forgone all custom of exercises; and indeed it goes so heavily with my dis-

[4] Many other symptoms of the melancholy man, as Du Laurens (among other specialists) describes him, are shared by Hamlet: the melancholy man has "dreadful dreams" (p. 82); he is "witty" and "excels others" (p. 86); "sadness doth never forsake him, suspicion doth secretly gall him, sighings, watchings, fearful dreams, silence, solitariness . . . and the abhorring of the sun, are as it were unseparable accidents of this miserable passion" (p. 89). Melancholy men "conceive of death as a terrible thing, and notwithstanding (which is strange) they often times desire it, yea so eagerly, as that they will not let to destroy themselves" (p. 92). Hamlet says (ii, 2, 635):

> The spirit that I have seen
> May be the devil: and the devil hath power
> To assume a pleasing shape; yea and perhaps
> Out of my weakness and my melancholy—
> As he is very potent with such spirits—
> Abuses me to damn me.

Du Laurens tells us that the imaginations of melancholic persons are troubled in three ways; "by nature, that is to say, by the constitution of the body; by the mind, that is to say, by some violent passion, whereunto they had given themselves; and by the intercourse or meddling of evil angels, which cause them often-times to foretell and forge very strange things in their imaginations" (p. 100). I am indebted to Dr. John Floyd for calling my attention to Du Laurens' treatise. Parallels between *Hamlet* and another contemporary medical work, Timothy Bright's *A Treatise of Melancholy* (1586), have been pointed out by Miss Mary Isobelle Sullivan, "Hamlet and Dr. Timothy Bright," *P.M.L.A.*, XLI (1926), 667–79. Miss Sullivan thinks that Hamlet's character was moulded directly from Bright's description. But, apparently unaware of Du Laurens or the other contemporary descriptions of melancholy, she over-states her case: we cannot say that Shakespeare relied on any one text; he merely used the ideas which were part of the common knowledge of his time.

position that this goodly frame, the earth, seems to me a sterile promontory; this most excellent canopy, the air, look you, this brave o'erhanging firmament, this majestical roof fretted with golden fire, why, it appears no other thing to me but a foul and pestilent congregation of vapours.

And from this consideration of the macrocosm he passes at once to the microcosm; the sequence of thought was, in his time, almost automatic; and again he uses the familiar vocabulary of his age, describing the natural hierarchy in the technical language he could count on his school-fellows to understand:

> What a piece of work is a man; how noble in reason, how infinite in faculties; in form and moving, how express and admirable in action; how like an angel in apprehension; how like a god! the beauty of the world; the paragon of animals. And yet to me, what is this quintessence of dust? Man delights not me.[5]

This use of generalization, which is one of the most important and attractive sides of Hamlet's character, is also a further example of how Shakespeare weaves into the texture of his play a standard of value or a point of view so that the particular action can stand out more clearly. It is a device which the dramatic tradition gave him, and which he had used many times before, notably in *Henry V,* but it had never before been made so important a part of character. A further example can be seen in what Hamlet has to say about reason, the specific virtue of a human being (which Montaigne had so ingeniously labored to minimize). Horatio speaks (i, 4, 73) of the "sovereignty of reason," as does Ophelia, but Hamlet himself, as is appropriate in a play where the conflict is so deeply psychological, is the one who describes the traditional view most fully (iv, 4, 33):

[5] My punctuation is based on that of the second quarto and of J. Dover Wilson, which alone makes sense in terms of Elizabethan psychology. The whole speech should be compared with the quotation from La Primaudaye, above, pp. 3–4.

> What is a man,
> If his chief good and market of his time
> Be but to sleep and feed? a beast, no more.
> Sure he that made us with such large discourse,
> Looking before and after, gave us not
> That capability and god-like reason
> To fust in us unus'd.

It is worth observing in what terms Shakespeare speaks of reason in important passages throughout the play. Reason, the specific function of man in the order of Nature, is twice referred to as "noble," an adjective, like "sovereign" (also applied to reason), that has connotations in the political order, and, in the passage I have just quoted, it is described as "god-like," an adjective that, to an Elizabethan, would have cosmological connotations as well. It may not be fantastic to see in this adjectival microcosm an image of the macrocosm we have been trying to define.

At all events, the standard which Hamlet's soliloquy describes is not only the standard which his own lack of action so agonizingly seems to violate, it is also the standard which was violated by Gertrude in mourning so briefly for her first husband, and in unnaturally yielding to her lust, so that her reason, in Hamlet's words, has become a pander to her will (her fleshly desire), thus disgustingly reversing the natural order. Hamlet's own standards are high. "Give me that man," he says to Horatio

> That is not passion's slave, and I will wear him
> In my heart's core, ay, in my heart of heart,
> As I do thee.

And it is because he has this high standard that he is so torn apart by discovering that the traditional order in which reason should be in control of passion is only an appearance, and that the reality of his mother's action proves human beings to be only beasts, their specific function gone.

2

Shakespeare uses the traditional views of kingship in the same way that he uses cosmology and psychology. Throughout *Hamlet* there is an emphasis on the importance of the king as the center of the state. Rosencrantz and Guildenstern describe the accepted ideal most fully (iii, 3, 8):

> *Guildenstern:* Most holy and religious fear it is
> To keep those many many bodies safe
> That live and feed upon your majesty.
> *Rosencrantz:* The single and peculiar life is bound
> With all the strength and armour of the mind
> To keep itself from noyance; but much more
> That spirit upon whose weal depend and rest
> The lives of many. The cease of majesty
> Dies not alone, but, like a gulf doth draw
> What's near it with it; it is a massy wheel,
> Fix'd on the summit of the highest mount,
> To whose huge spokes ten thousand lesser things
> Are mortis'd and adjoin'd; which, when it falls,
> Each small annexment, petty consequence,
> Attends the boisterous ruin. Never alone
> Did the king sigh, but with a general groan.

Hamlet himself is described by Laertes at the beginning in the same terms in which Rosencrantz describes Claudius. Laertes tells Ophelia that Hamlet

> may not, as unvalu'd persons do
> Carve for himself, for on his choice depends
> The safety and the health of the whole state;
> And therefore must his choice be circumscrib'd
> Unto the voice and yielding of that body
> Whereof he is the head.
>
> (i, 3, 19)

Once more we have the kingdom compared to the human frame, and once more we have an illustration of how careful

Shakespeare is, from the very beginning of the play, to emphasize the political side of the action. Much state business is transacted before the king, in the second scene of the first act, finally turns to the particular problem of Hamlet's melancholy; Shakespeare deliberately puts Hamlet's situation in a political environment. This not only increases the scope of the play, it also emphasizes the dramatic conflict. For from whatever side we regard the action there is something politically wrong. From Claudius' point of view it is bad for the state to have a disaffected heir, particularly since he is so much loved by the multitude. From Hamlet's point of view it is abominable to have an unworthy and lustful king. And the appearance of the ghost emphasizes in more general terms our sense of uneasiness about the condition of the state. It bodes, says Horatio, "some strange eruption to our state," Hamlet dwells on the fact that the ghost is armed, and the armor implies that the ghost has more than a private purpose in showing himself. No wonder Marcellus says that there is something rotten in the *state* of Denmark. He, and the king, and the ghost, reinforce Hamlet's feelings about the situation, and the speeches of Rosencrantz and Laertes on kingship apply not only to an immediate necessity but also to the importance of kingship itself, and hence they emphasize the enormity of Claudius' previous action in murdering his kingly brother. Again it is worth remembering the strength of Hamlet's feeling about his uncle's unworthiness as a king—a feeling that shocks, as Hamlet means it to do, the conventional Guildenstern (iv, 2, 30):

> *Hamlet:* The king is a thing—
> *Guildenstern:* A thing, my lord!

Hamlet's description of the king is much stronger elsewhere: he is the "bloat king"—a "king of shreds and patches"—and

Hamlet's tendency to generalization surrounds the notion of kingship as it surrounds all his thoughts:

> Imperious Caesar, dead and turned to clay,
> Might stop a hole to keep the wind away.

A king may go a progress through the guts of a beggar; the illusion of kingly power is not the reality; nothing is but thinking makes it so. What is true of the king, of the queen, is true of the whole "drossy age," where the orders of society have broken down, and "the age is grown so picked, that the toe of the peasant comes so near the heel of the courtier that he galls his kibe." "To be honest, as this world goes, is to be one man picked out of ten thousand." "I am very proud, revengeful, ambitious; with more offenses at my back than I have thought to put them in, imagination to give them shape, or time to act them in. What should such fellows as I do crawling between heaven and earth? We are arrant knaves all." The discovery of individual evil, and the inevitable generalizations, once granted Shakespeare's conception of Hamlet's character, that follow upon it, almost crack his comprehension: cruelty to the innocent Ophelia, again expressed in generalization, is one of the consequences.

In fact the way Hamlet treats Ophelia, like the way he treats love in general, is a further striking example of Shakespeare's handling of the contrast between appearance and truth. For here too there is an ideal in the background against which the present reality seems coarse and vile. The relation between Hamlet's mother and father had been perfect; he was as fine a husband as he had been a king, his

> love was of that dignity
> That it went hand in hand even with that vow
> (He) made to her in marriage;
>
> (i, 5, 48)

he was, says Hamlet,

> so loving to my mother
> That he might not beteem the winds of heaven
> Visit her face too roughly.
>
> (i, 2, 140)

But this ideal, an ideal as deeply embedded in the sixteenth-century mind as the ideal of kingship and of human reason, is violated by Gertrude's marriage to Claudius, which he calls "incestuous," as according to the law of Nature, it actually was.[6] Hamlet throughout the play can think of the relations between the sexes only in the coarsest terms; he tortures both Ophelia and himself by doing so, attributing to her in his usual generalizing way the faults of her sex as a whole which his mother's behavior had revealed. And the innocent Ophelia herself, in delirium, sings songs at which her maidenly sanity would have blushed.

This sense of the reality of evil—in the cosmos, in the state, and in man—this enlargement of dramatic dimension by significant generalization, this dramatic use of one of the essential conflicts of the age, is what helps to make *Hamlet* so large an organism, and to give it, as the expression of a universal situation, so profound a meaning. Hamlet's disillusionment is a partial expression of a general predicament; the emotions he gives voice to were shared in his own time and have been shared ever since by many people less miraculously articulate than himself. His discovery of the difference between appearance and reality, which produced in his mind an effect so disillusioning that it paralysed the sources of deliberate action, was a symptom that the Renaissance in general had brought with it a new set of problems, had opened new psychological vistas, which the earlier views of man had not so completely

[6] See J. Dover Wilson's edition of *Hamlet*, Cambridge (England), 1936, p. 152. Miss Victoria Schrager has suggested to me that Shakespeare's audience would remember that Henry VIII's marriage to Catherine of Aragon was proved illegal because it violated the law of Nature: it was incestuous because he had married, like Claudius, his brother's wife.

explored. As we look back on the period, it appears that the contrast between outward seeming and inner truth had begun, at the beginning of the seventeenth century, to seem the most easily available example of a more portentous awareness, which could by no other means be so readily described. It is one of the keys to an understanding of Shakespearean tragedy, to that stretching into hitherto inarticulate reaches of experience, which is one of the chief emotional legacies of the Renaissance.[7]

3

But we can find, if we return to the play itself, more in Shakespeare's conception of Hamlet's character than an embodiment, however profound, of the difference between appearance and reality. Shakespeare had made several earlier experiments with the development of character; in portraying Romeo and Prince Hal, among others, he had shown his ability to make a hero change as the result of the play's action. But just as *Hamlet* illustrates both a more expanded and a more fused control of dramatic convention and traditional belief than the earlier plays, so it shows a greater mastery of how to describe the growth, inside dramatic limits, of a hero. This can be clearly seen if we examine, in order, Hamlet's great soliloquies. When we first see Hamlet alone, he is emotionally in pieces, and the chaos of his thought and feeling is reflected in the grammatical chaos of his utterances; before he can finish a sentence some new agonizing disruptive thought explodes to distract his mind.[8] The order of the world, of the state, and

[7] The difference between appearance and reality is continually referred to throughout the play by other people besides Hamlet himself; Polonius, the ghost, the king, all mention it in one way or another; the frequency with which images of painting, of covering up hidden diseases, are used is another illustration of its prevalence; and it is the central idea of Hamlet's meditations in the graveyard.

[8] J. Dover Wilson quite rightly uses the very light punctuation of Q2 to illustrate Shakespeare's apparent intention in this matter.

of the individual are all in pieces, and the chaotic grammar reflects the universal chaos of his thought. The same is true of his second great soliloquy, the one beginning,

> O, what a rogue and peasant slave am I!

in which he bursts into violent self-deprecation as he thinks of the difference between stage-playing and real action. But even in this speech, at the end, he pulls himself together and orders his thought to plan the testing of the king. Planned action takes the place, as it had not before, of emotional desperation.

In the soliloquy that follows (as far as the audience is concerned, about three minutes later), the "To be or not to be" soliloquy, we see a Hamlet who is able to generalize on a new level. No longer is there a grammatical torrent, and no longer is Hamlet thinking about existence as opposed to non-existence only in relation to himself; he has grown, psychologically and philosophically, so that he can think of the problem more universally. In the first soliloquy it was *"This* too too solid flesh"—Hamlet's own—about which he was concerned. Now, as the play reaches its center, it is no longer "I," but "we"—all humanity—that he reflects upon: "When *we* have shuffled off this mortal coil" . . .

> And makes *us* rather bear those ills *we* have
> Than fly to others that *we* know not of.
> Thus conscience doth make cowards of *us all.* . . .

Even the soliloquy in the fourth act—"How all occasions do inform against me"—when Hamlet compares his behavior to that of Fortinbras, combining, as usual personal and general reflection—even this agonized soliloquy has much more order, both logically and grammatically, than the first two violent outbursts. In fact there can be little doubt that Shakespeare thought of Hamlet as growing much older, emotionally, intellectually and even physically, during the course of the play, than the literal time covered by the action could possibly justify.[9] At the beginning Hamlet is fresh from the university; he is about twenty. In the graveyard scene he is unmistakably described as thirty. Shakespeare was in the habit of using concrete numerical details to make a particular scene vivid, regardless of previous data, and this is an obvious example of how his view of his hero had changed, perhaps unconsciously, at the end of the play. Throughout the fifth act, Hamlet is a very different man from the distracted undergraduate he was at the beginning. At the beginning there was a horrible split between his view of the world as it should be and the world as it is. At the end he is reconciled; and his reconciliation has both matured and ennobled him. He sees himself no longer in relation to a lustful mother and a vicious king; the immediate is replaced by the universal:

> and that should learn us
> There's a divinity that shapes our ends
> Rough-hew them how we will.[10]

He is no longer *in* the tumult, but above it; he is no longer "passion's slave," but a man who sees himself as a part of the order of things, even though his final view of that order, exhausted, resigned, and in a way exalted, is very different from the youthful rosy picture his Renaissance theoretical education had given him.

[9] It has long been noticed that there are "two series of times" in *Hamlet*, as in many Elizabethan plays, "the one suggestive and illusory, the other visible and explicitly stated." See Furness, *Variorum Hamlet*, Philadelphia, 1877, I, pp. xv–xvii. "At the close," says Furness, "as though to smooth away any discrepancy between his mind and his years, or between the execution of his task and his years, a chance allusion by the Grave-digger is thrown out, which, if we are quick enough to catch, we can apply to Hamlet's age, and we have before us Hamlet in his full maturity."

[10] See Hardin Craig, "Hamlet's Book," *Huntington Library Bulletin*, Nov., 1934, for an interesting analogy between Hamlet's ideas and those expressed by Cardan, in his widely read *Comfort*. In this article Professor Craig, as elsewhere, gives a most illuminating picture of the relation between Shakespeare and the intellectual life of his time. See especially *The Enchanted Glass*, New York, 1936.

If it be now, 'tis not to come; if it be not to come, it will be now; if it be not now, yet it will come: the readiness is all.

The thought may be a neo-stoic Renaissance commonplace, but Hamlet's expression of it, through his incomparable control of rhythm, enlarges our feeling about Hamlet's character. To be resigned, as Hamlet is resigned, is to be made, by experience instead of by theory, once more aware of the world's order. The last time we know Hamlet emotionally, he has transcended his own situation; he is no longer a victim of it. That is why we feel so moved, so in a way glorified, by the inevitability of his death. We have seen the purgation of a soul, and when Fortinbras enters at the end to be the king that Hamlet might have been, we know in another way and on another level—a more practical level that brings us back to the world in which we live—that we have also seen, with the accomplishment of Hamlet's revenge, the purgation of a state.

4

We must not forget, in thinking of Shakespeare's portrayal of the nature of man, that he was also a practical playwright, and that in two or three weeks he could toss off, at about the same time that he wrote *Hamlet,* a farce like *The Merry Wives of Windsor,* perhaps at the request of his sovereign. But the *Merry Wives* is a feeble performance; Falstaff in love is a perfunctory character, a victim, not a master, of strategy, verbal or otherwise, and it is clear that Shakespeare was interested in other reaches of awareness. For almost immediately after he had written *Hamlet,* he began further to explore the human mind. Once more he used an old story, and once more he developed it, employing the views of human nature given him by his age, to probe with a new profundity and a sharper intellectual and emotional examination, into what happens when a preconceived picture of life is blasted by experience.

Troilus and Cressida is a puzzling play, both in execution and intention, and the uncertainty of the Folio editors as to where to place it (at the last minute they squeezed it between the Histories and the Tragedies) has been reflected ever since in the comments of the critics.[11] If we are to have a clear view of it, we must first remember three things; that it was in all probability written for a special audience of law students, that it was very probably influenced by the contemporary fashion for dramatic satire, and that Shakespeare was dealing with a story more familiar to his audience than, say, the story of Hamlet, and that he was therefore less free to change the outline of its events. This last fact is particularly important when we think of the end of the play. The old story, as Chaucer and many other writers had told it, was unsatisfactory for tragedy because its conclusion was so indefinite: Cressida keeps on living as Diomed's mistress, and Troilus keeps on fighting the Greeks until he is eventually killed by Achilles in an irrelevant way that has nothing to do with his previous actions. Shakespeare was too close to his audience to be able to change—as Dryden later was able to change—this undramatic trailing-off of the sequence of events, and it is this trailing-off which more than anything else has made the play seem unsatisfactory. Death was the essence of tragedy to an Elizabethan audience, but to follow the old story of Troilus and Cressida meant to keep them alive at the end. Yet if, as modern critics have pointed out, "Shakespeare's picture of the Troy story is an experiment in the middle ground between comedy and tragedy,"[12] the traditional ending could be very useful. If we ex-

[11] In discussing the play I am indebted to W. W. Lawrence, *Shakespeare's Problem Comedies*, New York, 1931, to O. J. Campbell, *Comicall Satyre and Shakespeare's Troilus and Cressida*, San Marino, California, 1938, and to my own article (with which I no longer entirely agree), "A Commentary on Shakespeare's *Troilus and Cressida*," *Studies in English Literature*, Tokyo, XVI (1936), 1 ff. See also J. E. Phillips, Jr., *The State in Shakespeare's Greek and Roman Plays*, New York, 1940.

[12] O. J. Campbell, *op. cit.*, p. 187.

amine the play more closely we shall discover that, governed by these facts which I have mentioned, Shakespeare was in all probability experimenting with a new kind of dramatic form.

There are two main themes in the play: the theme of war and the theme of love. The first is represented by Hector, the second by Troilus, and the climax of the action is that both these heroes are destroyed. At the end Hector removes his armor, and Achilles, not even single-handed, but accompanied by a gang of Myrmidons, attacks him in the most cowardly fashion and he is killed without a chance for self-defense. Cressida, the object of Troilus' passionate devotion, after swearing to him that she will be forever true, betrays him the very first night after their separation. The result is that we have, in the case of Troilus, a worse kind of tragedy than death, the tragedy of continued existence after everything that matters has been destroyed. There is nothing here of that inevitability which ennobles the end of *Hamlet*.

The two dastardly climaxes of the action, the murder of Hector and the betrayal of Troilus, are all the more shocking because of the way Shakespeare planned the play. For in *Troilus and Cressida,* almost more elaborately than anywhere else, Shakespeare sets up a standard of conduct which the main action of the play violates. In the first act, when the Greeks are discussing among themselves why it is that their siege is unsuccessful, Ulysses delivers that long and magnificent speech on order with which we are already familiar,[13] and which is the finest expression in Shakespeare's work of the traditional view of the state and of Nature. The "specialty of rule"—the special art of government—says Ulysses, has been neglected in the Greek camp, and that specialty, namely the maintenance of order and degree, must be enforced if the state, and also the heavens, the elements, society and the individual, are to fulfill their proper functions. The argument is one that must have

[13] See pp. 21–22 above.

been recognized at once by the law-students before whom the play was probably first performed. But what we see on the stage is a complete violation of the whole traditional belief. Instead of order we have anarchy, instead of degree there is violent personal rivalry. Both Ajax and Achilles stand out as petulant and proud individualists, and Ulysses, who acts throughout as the voice of common sense and practical wisdom, learns that there is nothing he can do which will enforce the standards of order and perseverance which he so eloquently describes. The action of the war ends in chaos; the fifth act, apart from the scene describing Cressida's betrayal, is a series of brutal combats ending with a curse.

The Trojans, though they may seem to be nobler than the Greeks as far as their action in war is concerned, are equally ineffective. Like the Greeks they too have a debate (act ii, scene 2) among themselves, in which a proper standard of action is set up, and then dismissed for a less rational course. The point at issue is whether or not they shall return Helen to Menelaus; Hector thinks they should, Troilus passionately argues that they should not, since honor demands that they keep what they have taken. Paris, naturally enough, supports him, but Hector rebukes both of them for the superficiality of their views—they cannot determine between right and wrong because their arguments come from "the hot passion of distemper'd blood." The right lies on the opposite side, and, Hector says:

> Nature craves
> All dues be render'd to their owners: now,
> What nearer debt in all humanity
> Than wife is to the husband? if this law
> Of nature be corrupted through affection,
> And that great minds, of partial indulgence
> To their benumbed wills, resist the same,
> There is a law in each well-order'd nation
> To curb those raging appetites that are
> Most disobedient and refractory.

> If Helen then be wife to Sparta's king,
> As it is known she is, these moral laws
> Of nature, and of nations, speak aloud
> To have her back return'd: thus to persist
> In doing wrong extenuates not wrong,
> But makes it much more heavy. Hector's opinion
> Is this, in way of truth—

This is the traditional view, and all rational opinion would support it; to do otherwise is to go against Nature. But what happens? Hector immediately switches to the opposite, irrational side, and supports the argument of passion:

> Hector's opinion
> Is this, in way of truth; yet, ne'ertheless,
> My spritely brethren, I propend to you
> In resolution to keep Helen still;
> For 'tis a cause that hath no mean dependence
> Upon our joint and several dignities.

It would be hard to find a more lame and impotent conclusion than this, and though we may say that Shakespeare was forced by the familiar story to end the argument in such a fashion (for the Trojans did keep Helen, as everyone knew), nevertheless he need not have introduced the argument in the first place. Having done so, and having made Hector reach a conclusion which only too clearly implies that the Trojans are staking their lives on a cause which violates the law of reason, of Nature and of nations, he gives us only the feeblest kind of confidence in the validity of their enterprise and in the success of its outcome. In another fashion, but just as clearly, the Trojans, like the Greeks, are doomed to disintegration.

But Shakespeare does not rely merely on the violation of the conventional standards to give his picture of disruption, he uses another feature of the old story, the character of Thersites, to act as a reviling and denigrating chorus to the whole action. In many previous versions of the story, dramatic and otherwise,

Thersites had been described as a railer, and in making him rail, Shakespeare was only giving the members of his audience what they expected. But they can never before have heard such effectively corrosive railing as this. Thersites' entrance is carefully prepared for by several mentions of his name, and when he first appears with Ajax, at the beginning of the second act, his violence makes everything he thinks of either bestial or diseased. "Agamemnon," he begins—and we must remember that as the leader of the Greek state Agamemnon should be, in Ulysses' words of the previous scene, like the hive "to whom the foragers shall all repair"—"Agamemnon," says Thersites, "how if he had boils? full, all over, generally? And those boils did run? Say so, did not the general run then? were not that a botchy core?"

There are plenty of disease images in *Hamlet*,[14] in fact more than in any other play, but Thersites speaks with a destructive venom that is peculiar to himself. "A botchy [an ulcerous] core" does not promise a healthy fruit, nor does a king who is running with boils promise a healthy state. And as Thersites and Ajax curse one another while Ajax beats Thersites with his fists, image after image is piled up of corruption and bestiality: in fifty lines they call each other *dog, bitch-wolf's son, horse, toadstool, porpentine, whoreson cur, ass,* and *camel;* they speak of diseases like the murrain, the scab, and the scurvy—all is degradation and corruption. This is the tone of Thersites throughout: he can see only "Lechery, lechery; still, wars and lechery: nothing else holds fashion."

For he is not merely a commentator on the warriors, he is a

[14] See Caroline Spurgeon, *Shakespeare's Imagery*, New York, 1936, p. 316. But in discussing *Hamlet* Miss Spurgeon fails to point out the interesting fact that the great majority, about 85 per cent., of these images of disease appear after the middle of the third act; in other words Shakespeare uses images from the decay of the body of man with increasing frequency as his plot shows the decay, under Claudius as king, of the body of the state.

commentator on the lovers too, and he adds his harsh, grating emphasis to the peculiar bitterness which is so deeply a part of Troilus' emotion. Troilus is a very different kind of lover from Romeo—the difference shows even in the texture of his speech. When Romeo addresses Juliet, his images are the conventional images of romantic love (ii, 2, 10):

> It is my lady; O! it is my love:
> O! that she knew she were.
> She speaks, yet she says nothing: what of that?
> Her eye discourses; I will answer it.
> I am too bold, 'tis not to me she speaks:
> Two of the fairest stars in all the heaven,
> Having some business, do intreat her eyes
> To twinkle in their spheres till they return.
> What if her eyes were there, they in her head?
> The brightness of her cheek would shame those stars
> As daylight doth a lamp; her eyes in heaven
> Would through the airy region stream so bright
> That birds would sing and think it were not night.

But when Troilus speaks of his love for Cressida (i, 1, 51), we have no such exalted language. Romeo's images are full of lightness, brightness—*stars, daylight, lamp, heaven, airy region,* birds singing. They are images that lead us upward. But the images of Troilus lead us down; they are violent and harsh. As Troilus speaks of love he uses such words as *drown'd, deep, indrench'd, mad, ulcer, ink, ploughman's hand, gash, knife.* When we listen carefully the effect is very striking:

> O Pandarus! I tell thee, Pandarus,—
> When I do tell thee, there my hopes lie drown'd,
> Reply not in how many fathoms deep
> They lie indrench'd. I tell thee I am mad
> In Cressid's love: thou answer'st, she is fair;
> Pour'st in the open ulcer of my heart
> Her eyes, her hair, her cheek, her gait, her voice;
> Handlest in thy discourse, O! that her hand,

> In whose comparison all whites are ink,
> Writing their own reproach; to whose soft seizure
> The cygnet's down is harsh, and spirit of sense
> Hard as the palm of ploughman: this thou tell'st me,
> As true thou tell'st me, when I say I love her;
> But, saying thus, instead of oil and balm,
> Thou lay'st in every gash that love hath given me
> The knife that made it.
>
> (i, 1, 50)

In Troilus' love for Cressida there is a strong element of sensuality, though his love is not, as some critics [15] would have it, sensuality and nothing else. He thinks a great deal of the physical fruition of his passion:

> I am giddy, expectation whirls me round.
> The imaginary relish is so sweet
> That it enchants my sense.
>
> (iii, 2, 17)

But he has also exalted the worthless Cressida into an ideal, and we know, from the debate about Helen, that he is a worshipper of honor. He tells us himself, somewhat priggishly perhaps, that he is

> as true as truth's simplicity,
> And simpler than the infancy of truth.
>
> (iii, 2, 176)

And Ulysses, whose words are always meant to be trusted, speaks very highly of him indeed:

> The youngest son of Priam, a true knight:
> Not yet mature, yet matchless; firm of word,
> Speaking in deeds and deedless in his tongue;

---

[15] For example O. J. Campbell, *op. cit.*, pp. 210 ff. Mr. Campbell reduces the stature of Troilus' character to that of Cressida; they are "two virtuosi in sensuality." Mr. Campbell has to adopt this view in order to fit the play into the type of "Comicall Satyre" which he has invented. As a result his otherwise excellent discussion minimizes and distorts the great speeches of Troilus.

Not soon provok'd, nor being provok'd soon calm'd: [16]
His heart and hand both open and both free;
For what he has he gives, what thinks he shows;
Yet gives he not till judgment guide his bounty,
Nor dignifies an impure thought with breath. . . .
Thus says Aeneas; one that knows the youth
Even to his inches, and with private soul
Did in great Ilion thus translate him to me.

(iv, 5, 96)

This is obviously someone to respect, and it is an error in criticism not to see at least as much idealism as sensuality in Shakespeare's conception of Troilus' character. Therefore when he discovers Cressida's betrayal, her surrender to Diomed on the very first night after her separation from him, the evil reality under her apparently true protestations of eternal fidelity nearly breaks him apart. The scene in which this happens is an admirable example of the dramatic experimentation which is one of the chief characteristics of the play (v, 2). We have just had Thersites' speech about Diomed—

They say he keeps a Trojan drab,[17] and uses the traitor Calchas' tent. I'll after. Nothing but lechery! all incontinent varlets—

[16] This line is similar to two other famous speeches in Shakespeare. Polonius says to Laertes (*Hamlet* i, 3, 63):

Beware
Of entrance to a quarrel, but, being in
Bear't that th' opposed may beware of thee.
And Othello describes himself (v, 2, 344) as
One not easily jealous, but, being wrought,
Perplexed in the extreme.

[17] One of the striking differences between Chaucer's version of the story and Shakespeare's is that in Shakespeare everyone seems to know all about Cressida's affairs, whereas in Chaucer they are kept secret. The medieval convention of privacy and honor has disappeared, and as a result the sordidness of Cressida's character is emphasized, as anything is emphasized the more it is talked about. In the same way Achilles' love affair with Polixena is well known, to Achilles' surprise. "Ha! known!" he exclaims, when Ulysses refers to it (iii, 3, 195), and Ulysses answers him in a speech which is characteristic of his view of the state—and characteristic of the Renaissance view as well:

when the scene opens in front of Calchas' tent. From the purely technical point of view I know nothing like this scene in previous Elizabethan drama. We see the situation from no fewer than four angles—it should be imagined on the Elizabethan stage for its full effect to be conveyed. At the back on the inner stage, are Cressida and Diomed, the main focus of attention; on one side of the front stage are Troilus and Ulysses; Thersites is on the other. Cressida and Diomed talk, she strokes his cheek, and their talk and action are interpreted for us by Troilus—emotional, agonized, incredulous—by Ulysses, rationally trying to control Troilus, and by Thersites, to whom all is lechery. Passion, reason and cynicism form the discordant chorus to action; they are three emotional mirrors which reflect the demonstration of the evil reality, Cressida's whorishness, under what had seemed so fair an appearance.

After she has left the stage, mildly and unconvincingly self-reproachful, we see the full effect of her behavior on Troilus. Throughout the play we have felt a sense of strain, of pressure, in the complex of his emotion toward Cressida—"This is the monstruosity in love, lady, that the will is infinite, and the execution confined; that the desire is boundless, and the act a slave to limit (iii, 2, 84)." There is not much in common between Hamlet and Troilus, but they do share one characteristic: they are aware, in what is perhaps a peculiarly masculine way, of the inexplicable, the almost incomprehensible gap between what the mind can think and desire, and what the body can perform. And

---

> Is that a wonder?
> The providence that's in a watchful state
> Knows almost every grain of Plutus' gold,
> Finds bottom in the uncomprehensive deeps,
> Keeps place with thought, and almost, like the gods,
> Does thoughts unveil in their dumb cradles.
> There is a mystery—with whom relation
> Durst never meddle—in the soul of state,
> Which hath an operation more divine
> Than breath or pen can give expressure to.

when Cressida's faithlessness is revealed to him this peculiar tension in Troilus' mind produces an outburst of what can only be called metaphysical anguish.

> Never did young man fancy
> With so eternal and so fix'd a soul—

But his devotion is now a chaos.

For like every Elizabethan he feels that with the destruction of one element in his universe, the whole structure is in pieces. Because the appearance and what he believes to be the reality do not fit, the very concept of unity itself, on which the whole Elizabethan vision of the world was based, lacks order and rule. What he has just seen makes reason and its opposite, the loss of reason, seem the same thing; and something which cannot be separated, his view of Cressida combined with Cressida as she really is, is at the same time split in two and an indivisible unity. The thought is almost more than he can bear, and the difficulty he faces almost strains comprehension. Professor Campbell, writing of this speech, says that "Troilus, in attempting to preserve his characteristic self-deceit in the face of contradictory objective fact, forces his logical machine to perform feats of prestidigitation that make it creak ridiculously." [18] I cannot believe the speech should be interpreted in this fashion. On the contrary, its rhythm beats with emotional torture, and the intellectual effort, as in metaphysical poetry elsewhere, only increases and stiffens the tension.

> This she? no, this is Diomed's Cressida.
> If beauty have a soul, this is not she;
> If soul guide vows, if vows be sanctimony,
> If sanctimony be the gods' delight,
> If there be rule in unity itself,
> This is not she. O madness of discourse,
> That cause sets up with and against itself;
> Bi-fold authority! where reason can revolt

[18] *Op. cit.*, p. 216.

> Without perdition, and loss assume all reason
> Without revolt: this is, and is not, Cressid.
> Within my soul there doth conduce a fight
> Of this strange nature that a thing inseparate
> Divides more wider than the sky and earth;
> And yet the spacious breadth of this division
> Admits no orifice for a point as subtle
> As Ariachne's broken woof to enter.
> Instance, O instance! strong as Pluto's gates;
> Cressid is mine, tied with the bonds of heaven:
> Instance, O instance! strong as heaven itself;
> The bonds of heaven are slipp'd, dissolv'd, and loos'd;
> And with another knot, five-finger-tied,
> The fractions of her faith, orts of her love,
> The fragments, scraps, the bits, and greasy reliques
> Of her o'er-eaten faith, are bound to Diomed.

After this he can do nothing but rage against the Greeks, and take his fruitless part in the general turmoil of fighting and betrayal with which the play concludes.

From the beginning his passion had been under a cloud, for the only way he could communicate with Cressida was through Pandar, and Shakespeare describes Pandar as a very coarse, worldly character, who speaks a vulgar prose, and who surrounds the love story, as Thersites in a different way surrounds the war story, with his sordid, chorus-like comments on the physical aspects of love. In fact Pandar, groaning with the pox, speaks the last lines of the play—an address to those people in the audience who are, like himself, "traders in the flesh."

When Troilus discovers that the object of his passionate, strained love is no better than her uncle, no wonder his reason almost cracks, and the coarse images of food [19] with which his speech ends are an indirect reflection of what he now knows to

[19] Miss Spurgeon (*op. cit.*, pp. 320 ff.) points out that there are 42 images of food, cooking, etc., in *Troilus;* twice as many as in any other play: a reflection, she rightly suggests, of the coarseness embedded in the whole action.

be Cressida's true nature. Thersites' comment is justified: "Lechery, lechery; still, wars and lechery; nothing else holds fashion."

5

Troilus and Cressida, though it follows *Hamlet* chronologically, is obviously not an improvement on it as a play. But it is not the ambiguous failure it has often been thought to be. Indeed, so far as our subject is concerned, it marks an extension of awareness in Shakespeare's presentation of man's nature. Whatever name we give it, whether we call it a tragedy, or a history, a comedy or a "comicall satyre," it describes in a new way the difference between man as he ought to be and man as he is. He ought to be part of an ordered state in an ordered universe; he ought to act according to reason and not according to passion. But these ideals are expounded only to be refuted by example after example: Achilles is a proud and selfish individualist who, when he is finally roused, acts like a bully; Cressida is a whore; and the nobility of Troilus, shining through his own sensuality and the murky lustfulness of his environment, is disillusioned and betrayed. The conflict between the two views of man which was implicit in Shakespeare's age is presented in concrete terms through the medium of the old story, and without that conflict the story could not have taken such a vivid, if bitter and disillusioned, form. *Troilus* is the kind of experiment which was necessary before *King Lear* could be written.

CHAPTER V

OTHELLO AND *KING LEAR*

I

After *Troilus and Cressida*, if the chronology of modern scholarship is correct, Shakespeare chose two stories which were poor material for dramatization; they appeared as *All's Well that Ends Well*, in 1602–03, and *Measure for Measure* in 1604. About the first there is nothing revealing to be said; with the exception of one or two characters and an occasional scene, it is a dispiriting and tasteless performance. *Measure for Measure,* though it also is unsatisfactory, is more interesting, for, like *Troilus and Cressida,* it seems to express the darkening view of man's nature, the consciousness of difference between outward show and inner truth, the growing awareness of the possibilities of interior chaos, which at this time were apparently characteristic of Shakespeare's imagination.

The difference between appearance and reality is clearly illustrated in this play by the character of Angelo. The Duke of Vienna gives him the government of the city, because Angelo seems to be an ideal human being, and his external behavior is apparently the reflection of his inner, admirable and socially-minded nature. But such is not the case. The whole city of Vienna is corrupt with lust (some of the best dramatic scenes in the play describe life in a bawdy house), and Angelo proves to be no exception to the general situation; the moment he sees Isabella he wants to possess her, and all his virtue is thrown to the winds:

> I have begun:
> And now I give my sensual race the rein,

he tells her; and he proposes an infamous bargain: he will free her brother (who is condemned to death for lust), if she will satisfy his lust for her. The resulting situation is strained and forced, and though Shakespeare gets some admirable poetry out of it, he does little to make any of the characters convincing.

It is wrong to say, however, as many critics have said, that the play should have ended tragically, for it is impossible to see how a credible tragedy could have been made out of the circumstances of the plot; nevertheless there is no doubt that the "happy ending," if so it can be called, is awkwardly manoeuvred. For the last act is a patched-up affair, and we see the old duke, like a *deus ex machina* turned into a needle, busily and boringly sewing up the characters and the pieces of the story into a kind of crazy-quilt that is meant to cover, but does not, the failure of the play.

The tone of this play may be more clearly understood if we think of it for a moment in contrast to *Love's Labour's Lost*. In *Love's Labour's Lost* the intellectual ideal of the King of Navarre is broken down by romantic love. But the ideal apparently embodied in Angelo is broken down by lust. Such is the difference between the early comedies and the comedies which are a part of Shakespeare's tragic period. In *Measure for Measure* we are shown that the baser elements in human nature are the important ones—lust, not reason, motivates mankind. Perhaps it may not be too fanciful to see, in the fifth act of the play, with its elaborate glossing over of the facts, a last attempt on Shakespeare's part to show, in spite of everything, that the existence of lust in human nature does not necessarily imply, as it did in *Hamlet* and *Troilus*, the destruction of everything valuable. If this is so, Shakespeare's honesty, his vision of evil (combined, it may be, with his anxiety to satisfy a popular demand for tragedy) soon broke through, and after *Measure for Measure* he used the contemporary vision of the evil reality in man's nature, which he seems so fully to have shared, to the limit of his powers. Between 1605 and 1608 he wrote *Othello, King Lear, Macbeth, Antony and Cleopatra, Coriolanus* and drafted *Timon of Athens*. He was, for the time being, a confirmed writer of tragedy, and it is our present business to discover how variously and how profoundly, in the light of what we know, and in the light of what *he* knew, he presented to his audiences his tragic picture of man.

2

In making a tragedy out of Giraldi Cinthio's story about an anonymous Moor (it had not even been translated into English), Shakespeare was entirely unhampered, or unassisted, by any previous dramatic treatment of the subject. He could assume—as he could not when he wrote about Troy—that the audience knew nothing of the plot; hence he was free to do with it as he pleased. What he did was to make it, almost more than any of his other plays, a tragedy of character. It is solely because Othello is the kind of man he is that a man like Iago can destroy him. Consequently, since *Othello* is a personal tragedy, we do not find in it, as we do in *Hamlet* and *Troilus*, much use of the political or cosmological hierarchies. It is more a close and intensive study of man himself, and of the terrible contrast between the good and evil, the nobility and the bestiality, of which he is composed.

Yet the state and the outside world of nature are by no means absent from the play; in fact they surround the personal situation like a kind of double shell, and only when we have pierced through them, do we arrive at the heart of the action, the conversion of man into a beast. In the first act Othello's position in the state is of almost equal importance with his position as Desdemona's husband, and the trust reposed in him by the Venetian Senators naturally enlarges our view of him. He is, as are all Shakespeare's characters, placed against the background of a given society.

External nature also plays its role, and the storm at Cyprus not only destroys the Turkish fleet, thus clearing up the public situation, and allowing us to concentrate on Iago and Othello, it also gives us a foretaste—a chaos in the macrocosm—of what is to happen within Othello's soul. We are not meant, of course, to apply it directly, but there can be no doubt that the vivid description of the tempest in external nature given by Montano and the two gentlemen is similar to the internal tempest shortly to be revealed to us:

> For do but stand upon the foaming shore,
> The chidden billow seems to pelt the clouds;
> The wind-shak'd surge, with high and monstrous mane,
> Seems to cast water on the burning bear
> And quench the guards of the ever-fixed pole:
> I never did like molestation view
> Of the enchafed flood.
>
> (ii, 1, 11)

The emphasis on the storm is clearly a deliberate invention by Shakespeare, for Cinthio's story says nothing about it; on the contrary Cinthio tells us that Othello and Desdemona arrived safely at Cyprus "with a perfectly tranquil sea—*con somma tranquillità del Mare*—" [1] exactly the reverse of the situation in Shakespeare. Nor has Cinthio anything to say about a Turkish fleet; in his version the only reason why Othello leaves Venice is that the Signoria "made a change in the troops whom they

---

[1] Furness Variorum edition, p. 378. It is tempting to guess that some technician in Shakespeare's theater, about 1604 or so, invented a new device for making off-stage noises, and that Shakespeare wrote storm-scenes so that it could be used. The richness of psychological and metaphysical overtones, in drama as in all art, is likely to be suggested by practical necessities, the physical conditions that shape the form, and these often can be, and should be (ask any playwright), the orig-inating cause for the most striking dramatic effects. One of Shakespeare's most won-derful creations, the part of the Fool in *Lear*, was perhaps invented—as various scholars have supposed—because the well-known comic actor in Shakespeare's company, Robert Armin, needed a good role after the miserable one given him in *Othello*.

used to maintain in Cyprus, and they appointed the Moor commander of the soldiers whom they dispatched thither." Shakespeare adds both the danger in the political world and the danger in the physical world as important preliminaries to the disaster in the psychological world, and that world is enlarged and intensified as a result.[2]

Nor are the heavens left out of the background to the psychological chaos. Just after Othello has killed Desdemona he exclaims:

> O heavy hour:
> Methinks it should be now a huge eclipse
> Of sun and moon, and that the affrighted globe
> Should yawn at alteration,

and he explains the murder to Emilia by saying:

> It is the very error of the moon;
> She comes more near the earth than she was wont,
> And makes men mad.

Yet these images, as Mr. Wilson Knight very justly observes, are "something against which the dramatic movement may be silhouetted, but with which it cannot be merged. This poetic use of heavenly bodies serves to elevate the theme, to raise issues infinite and unknowable. Those bodies are not, however, implicit symbols of man's spirit, as in *Lear:* they remain distinct, isolated phenomena, sublimely decorative to the play." [3] The play itself is primarily concerned with the effect of one human being on another.

3

In presenting the character of Othello to his audience, Shakespeare emphasizes very strongly his grandeur, self-control and

---

[2] For an illuminating account of how the storm scene and Othello's arrival at Cyprus may be produced on a modern stage, see G. Wilson Knight, *Principles of Shakespearean Production*, London, 1936, pp. 134 ff. Mr. Knight's comments on Othello in his *Wheel of Fire*, Oxford, 1930, are also suggestive.

[3] *The Wheel of Fire*, p. 109.

nobility. Almost as soon as we see him, he tells us, though his
modesty has kept it previously a secret, that he is of kingly
blood:

> 'Tis yet to know,
> Which when I know that boasting is an honour
> I shall promulgate, I fetch my life and being
> From men of royal siege, and my demerits
> May speak unbonneted to as proud a fortune
> As this that I have reach'd.
>
> (i, 2, 19)

He is "our noble and valiant general" (ii, 2, 1); Iago (and we
can here take Iago at his word) describes him as being of "a
free and open nature" (i, 3, 405), "of a constant, loving, noble
nature" (ii, 1, 301). Before his frightful transformation he is,
in Lodovico's words,

> the noble Moor whom our full senate
> Call all-in-all sufficient . . . the noble nature
> Whom passion could not shake.
>
> (iv, 1, 275)

His love for Desdemona is in keeping with such a character;
entirely unlike the love of Troilus for Cressida, it has no sensuality in it; when he asks to be allowed to take Desdemona to
Cyprus with him, he explicitly describes—in the terms of Elizabethan psychology—the exalted quality of his devotion:

> I therefore beg it not
> To please the palate of my appetite,
> Nor to comply with heat,—the young affects
> In me defunct,—and proper satisfaction,
> But to be free and bounteous to her mind;
> And heaven defend your good souls that you think
> I will your serious and great business scant
> For she is with me. No, when light-wing'd toys
> Of feather'd Cupid seel with wanton dulness
> My speculative and offic'd instruments,
> That my disports corrupt and taint my business,

> Let housewives make a skillet of my helm,
> And all indign and base adversities
> Make head against my estimation!
>
> (i, 3, 263)

Like Horatio, Othello appears to all the world as a man who is not passion's slave; his higher faculties, his "speculative and offic'd instruments" are apparently in complete control.

This control, and the nobility that goes with it, are reflected in the rhythm of his speech; in his lines there is an assured grandeur, an exalted authority, as he rises without effort to any emergency:

> Keep up your bright swords, for the dew will rust them. . . .
>
> Most potent, grave, and reverend signiors,
> My very noble and approv'd good masters. . . .

No one else in Shakespeare speaks like that, just as no one else speaks like Hamlet or like Lear.

> This only is the witchcraft I have used:
> Here comes the lady; let her witness it.

And yet there *is* a kind of witchcraft, or rather magic, about Othello. His remote origin, and the glimpses we have of his career—the "antres vast and deserts idle,"

> The Anthropophagi, and men whose heads
> Do grow beneath their shoulders—
>
> (i, 3, 140)

the magical handkerchief given by an Egyptian charmer to his mother—these things, which are part of his romantic past, add strangeness and mystery to his grandeur and self-possession. In his own eyes they have great importance. There is something remarkable to Othello himself about his own history, and when he refers to anything connected with it, he is at his grandest. Hence it is superbly characteristic of him that, when he recovers his lost control at the end, and he requests the Venetians to describe him as he is, he should recall, as the climax to his speech, an episode from his own past, an episode which showed his devotion to the state of Venice:

> And say besides, that in Aleppo once,
> Where a malignant and a turban'd Turk
> Beat a Venetian and traduc'd the state,
> I took by the throat the circumcised dog,
> And smote him thus.

4

All this, this noble and remarkable career which has taken so long and has ranged so far, Othello has given over to Desdemona. She is the place, he says,

> where I have garner'd up my heart,
> Where either I must live or bear no life,
>   (iv, 2, 56)

and it is no wonder that when he thinks her unworthy, his whole being, that splendidly proportioned and controlled work of art, should be broken. "Excellent wretch!" he says to Desdemona,

> Perdition catch my soul
> But I do love thee! and when I love thee not
> Chaos is come again.

And chaos—the disordered state of the elements before the world was created—does come again; in the microcosm of Othello's own world. Hamlet sees himself and his situation in relation to the universe, and his generalizations are generalizations about the world as a whole; Othello's generalizations, his expansion of his immediate situation into a wider realm of implication, are concerned with his view of himself. His is not a philosopher's mind—it is the mind of a man of action; but his generalization is none the less grand:

> O! now, for ever
> Farewell the tranquil mind; farewell content!

Farewell the plumed troop and the big wars
That make ambition virtue! O, farewell!
Farewell the neighing steed, and the shrill trump,
The spirit-stirring drum, the ear-piercing fife,
The royal banner, and all quality,
Pride, pomp, and circumstance of glorious war!
And, O you mortal engines, whose rude throats
The immortal Jove's dread clamours counterfeit,
Farewell! Othello's occupation's gone!

(iii, 3, 348)

It is this magnificent human being who is turned by Iago into chaos, into a beast. The passion which he apparently has under such superb control masters him; he is possessed by a monster; and there is nothing to distinguish him from an animal as he cries "O! blood, blood, blood!" In him, under the devilish machinations of Iago, the psychological hierarchy horribly breaks down, and we find an appalling reality under the noble appearance. Gertrude's lust had made the idealistic Hamlet see the whole world as an unweeded garden, but he could find some relief in universal speculation through his unequalled command of words; Othello, the man of action, who is his own world, and has given that world to Desdemona, when he finds lustfulness, as he thinks, in *her*, can for the time being only grovel on the floor. His period of actual bestiality, to be sure, does not last long, and though he strikes Desdemona in public, and with hideous irony treats her as an inhabitant of a brothel, when he actually comes to kill her, he does it from the noblest motives. That is what is so terrible. For in the pursuit of his misguided aim he uses all those resources of grandeur and nobility which are part of his character, and he sees himself, victim of appearance that he is, as the instrument of universal justice.

It is the cause, it is the cause, my soul;
Let me not name it to you, you chaste stars!
It is the cause.

5

Iago exists in other dimensions. If we look at him from the formalistic point of view, keeping the moralities and the interludes in mind, we can see him as the equivalent of the Vice, who manipulates all the action, until he is exposed at the end. From another point of view we can think of him as the typical Machiavellian, all intrigue, egoism and *virtú*, who enjoys evil, like Marlowe's Barabas, for its own sake. Or we can think of him as a neo-Senecan villain-hero, out to justify himself against a set of circumstances that have combined to oppress him. Literary historians have seen him in all three aspects, separately or combined, and if we enjoy being literary historians it may help us to understand him to think of him in these terms. But I doubt if Shakespeare thought of him in such a fashion, and it is perhaps wiser to discuss Iago in more direct relation to human nature.

In his earlier plays, the plays of the 1590's, Shakespeare, as we know, had made various experiments in portraying the bluff, honest man, the man who, like Mercutio, Berowne, the Bastard, and Hotspur, saw through all pretensions and stood up for the facts. It is apparently a favorite type with Shakespeare, and in the 'nineties he always presents it favorably. But as his awareness of evil expands, he sees that even this type of man may be only an appearance. For Iago is this type of man gone wrong. Shakespeare himself, in another play, gives an admirable description of one aspect of Iago's character. In *King Lear* Cornwall mistakenly describes Kent as follows:

> This is some fellow,
> Who, having been prais'd for bluntness, doth affect
> A saucy roughness, and constrains the garb
> Quite from his nature: he cannot flatter, he,
> An honest mind and plain, he must speak truth. . . .
> These kind of knaves I know, which in this plainness
> Harbor more craft and more corrupter ends

> Than twenty silly-ducking observants,
> That stretch their duties nicely.
>
> (ii, 2, 101)

It is a poor description of Kent, as it is meant to be; but it is an admirable description of Iago.

The terrible thing about Iago, if we think of him (as Shakespeare thought of him) in terms of Elizabethan psychology, is that he is a thoroughly rational human being. As Bradley says, "not Socrates himself, not the ideal sage of the Stoics, was more lord of himself than Iago appears to be." [4] Othello's nobility, his apparent control of his passions, was directed, until Iago got hold of him, to good purposes; to the service of the state, to the right kind of love. But Iago is a man without passions; he is an embodiment of one layer of human activity which has no relation to any other layers; he is separated from ordinary human beings on both sides of his nature, the lower and the higher. He has no lust to link him with the animals, and he has no capacity for seeing himself in relation to the state or the universal order of things. He is an unscrupulous individualist.

> "Virtue! a fig! 'tis in ourselves that we are thus, or thus. Our bodies are our gardens, to the which our wills are gardeners; so that if we will plant nettles or sow lettuce, . . . either to have it sterile with idleness or manured with industry, why, the power and corrigible authority of this lies in our wills." [5]
>
> (i, 3, 322)

He knows all the right things, but he perverts the familiar doctrine to his own cynical ends:

[4] *Shakespearean Tragedy*, London, 1904, p. 218.

[5] Gardens, as microcosms of the world of human nature, occur very frequently in Shakespeare. The gardener in *Richard II* (iii, 4) delivers an elaborate, characteristically externalized, homily in the manner of the early plays, on the parallel between a garden and a commonwealth; Hamlet's first thought is of the world as an "unweeded garden"—in fact the image is everywhere, and if we follow Shakespeare's use of it, from the earliest plays to the latest (where flowers, not weeds, abound), we may find a kind of symbolic microcosm of the macrocosm—Shakespeare's changing view of man—which it is the aim of this book to describe.

"If the balance of our lives had not one scale of reason to poise another of sensuality, the blood and baseness of our natures would conduct us to most preposterous conclusions; but we have reason to cool our raging motions, our carnal stings, our unbitted lusts, whereof I take this that you call love to be a sect or scion."

The last phrase gives him away—"I take this that you call love"; it is obvious that he knows nothing about it. He is an emotional eunuch. That is why he talks so much about lust. Lust is something that as a man of the world he has always heard about, and so he attributes it to everybody, even himself, since he wants to be like other people. For example, he urges himself forward to his attack on Othello by forcing an artificial set of emotions, based on a sexual jealousy about which he really knows nothing:

> Now, I do love her too;
> Not out of absolute lust,—though peradventure
> I stand accountant for as great a sin,—
> But partly led to diet my revenge,
> For that I do suspect the lusty Moor
> Hath leap'd into my seat; the thought whereof
> Doth like a poisonous mineral gnaw my inwards.
>   (ii, 1, 303)

Coleridge's notorious phrase about Iago's soliloquies, that they represent the "motive-hunting of a motiveless malignity," is true in one sense, for although we do not have to think of Iago as an abstract personification of evil, he does, in the very reasons (none of them followed up) that he gives for his villainous actions, try to see himself in relation to ordinary human motives and behavior. He gives one explanation after another for his hatred of Othello, partly to make his behavior superficially plausible, and partly to assure himself that it is justified. But none of these reasons is convincing; they do not even sound convincing to Iago himself—"the thought whereof doth like a poisonous mineral gnaw my inwards": this is fairly stagey language; it has no real feeling in it, and we are not surprised never to hear of Iago's jealousy again. That venomous opportunist has merely conjured it up as one of his several attempts to make himself seem natural, and to make his villainy seem natural to the audience.

We can obtain further light on Iago's character if we think of him in relation to the difference between appearance and reality. In one of his earliest speeches, where he is revealing himself to Roderigo and the audience, he first describes himself as a thorough-going egoist:

> Others there are
> Who, trimm'd in forms and visages of duty,
> Keep yet their hearts attending on themselves,
> And, throwing but shows of service on their lords,
> Do well thrive by them, and when they have lin'd their coats
> Do themselves homage: these fellows have some soul;
> And such a one do I profess myself.
>
> (i, 1, 49)

This is in the familiar tradition of Elizabethan villainy, but Iago, developing it, goes on to tell us that the outward appearance he gives to the world bears no relation to the reality inside:

> Were I the Moor, I would not be Iago:
> In following him, I follow but myself;
> Heaven is my judge, not I for love and duty,
> But seeming so, for my peculiar end:
> For when my outward action doth demonstrate
> The native act and figure of my heart
> In compliment extern, 'tis not long after
> But I will wear my heart upon my sleeve
> For daws to peck at: I am not what I am.

In fact we may think of Iago as being compounded of three concepts of human nature—not merely literary concepts—that were at this time familiar to both Shakespeare and his age: the concept of the difference between outer show and inner fact, the concept of the evil man as an individualist, and, connected with this, the concept of the evil man as the *incomplete* man, the man who does not contain all the psychological levels that should make up a human being. Shakespeare's vision of evil probed very deep when he conceived Iago, for the frightening thing about Iago, as I have said, is that from one point of view he represents the Renaissance ideal of the man whose reason controls his passions, and yet he is wholly bad.

The concept of the difference between outer show and inner truth is not only important as a part of Iago's character; it permeates the whole play. The essence of Othello's tragedy is that he judges wrongly by appearances; he thinks that Iago is honest and that Desdemona is false, and he thinks that he is performing a just action in cruelly murdering his spotless wife. And when he finds out the true reality, that noble nature can only say of himself, "O fool, fool, fool!" No suicide was ever more dramatically inevitable than Othello's. He had given his world to Desdemona; she had apparently betrayed him; as a minister of justice he had killed her. But her lustfulness was only an appearance; the evil lay elsewhere—in the "demi-devil" Iago who seemed the soul of honesty. When Othello stabs himself at the end he is restoring for a final moment that lost self-respect which can only be reclaimed, since he has already killed his world in killing Desdemona, by killing himself.

6

Shakespeare uses the three inter-related hierarchies given him by the assumptions of his age to make *King Lear* the largest and the most profound of all his plays. Nowhere else does he so completely fuse the contemporary concepts of the world, the individual and the state into a single unity; correspondences and parallels between them, amalgamations of one concept with another, are everywhere; they embody the vision of life and they form the texture of the style. At the height of his career, with his dramatic craftsmanship developed to a remarkable pitch of virtuosity, daring and assurance, Shakespeare uses the old story of Lear to present his terrible picture of the microcosm and the macrocosm, the picture which shows how, under the good appearance, the evil in man's nature can bring chaos in a kingdom and a soul, and be reflected in the chaos of the external world.

As we think of the technique of this play, and it is with technique that we should begin, two words come at once to mind: re-inforcement and expansion. The sub-plot re-inforces the main plot; it is not, as in all the other plays where a sub-plot occurs, a contrast to it. Both Lear and Gloucester are the victims of filial ingratitude; the blinding of Gloucester is the physical equivalent to the madness of Lear; and both, as a result of their terrible experiences—though in very different degrees—achieve more wisdom at the end than they had at the beginning. The assumed madness of Edgar re-inforces the real madness of Lear, and the character Edgar assumes, that of a man who was once well off in the world, re-inforces, as he stands by Lear on the heath, the situation of the man who was once a king. The bareness of the heath itself—

> for many miles about
> There's scarce a bush—

re-inforces and reflects what the king discovers there, that "unaccommodated man is no more" than "a bare, forked animal." Just at the moment when Lear cries out "O fool! I shall go mad," there is (in the Folio) a stage direction, "*storm and tempest*"; even more obviously than in *Othello*, the storm in outer nature is meant to be a reflection of the storm in man. The Fool does more than *distract* the king; he calls attention, from another emotional angle, to Lear's situation, and hence emphasizes it:

Lear: Dost thou call me fool, boy?

Fool: All thy other titles thou hast given away; that thou wast born with.

(i, 4, 164)

In the same fashion, the mad speeches of Edgar on the heath have again and again a bearing on Lear's situation, and affect us like probings into an open wound.

The main action is also re-inforced in this play by more characters than in any other who act as a chorus. In *Othello* there is, if we except Lodovico at the end, no chorus type of character whatever; that is one reason why *Othello* is so tense, and its tragic agony so taut and constrained; there is no one to relieve our feelings by expressing them. But in *Lear*, in addition to such minor figures as Curan, two or three Gentlemen and Cornwall's servants, we have Kent, the Fool, Edgar and Albany—all of whom, in various ways, comment on the action and both re-inforce and expand its implications. Even Lear himself in his madness—and at this point Shakespeare uses to the fullest possible extent the resources of the Elizabethan stage convention of presenting mad scenes—even Lear himself acts as a chorus to his own situation, and in the fourth act, his madness giving him an extra personality, he comments with desperate irony on the general evil and injustice which for the moment are more universal than the particular evil and injustice that have driven him insane.

Every cruelty in the action is re-inforced. There is not one evil daughter, there are two; in the scene of the blinding of Gloucester, Regan invariably presses her husband's violence as far as possible by adding to it—it is she, for example, who, immediately after one of Gloucester's eyes is put out, eagerly urges Cornwall to put out the other. In what is, as far as tragic terror is concerned, the climactic scene of the play, the scene in which the blind Gloucester meets the crazed Lear, Lear *rubs in* (there are no other words for it) his mad, cruel mockery of Gloucester's blindness:

Glo.: Dost thou know me?

Lear: I remember thine eyes well enough. Dost thou squiny at me? No, do thy worst, blind Cupid; I'll not love. Read thou this challenge; mark but the penning of it.

Glo: Were all the letters suns, I could not see.

(iv, 6, 139)

No wonder that the feelings of the audience have to be relieved by Edgar's aside:

> I would not take this from report; it is,
> And my heart breaks at it.

And there is the final overwhelming re-inforcement of cruelty in the death of Cordelia; when all the villains are destroyed, and everything seems to be settled, Lear suddenly enters "with Cordelia dead in his arms."

"If my sensations could add anything to the general suffrage," said Dr. Johnson, "I might relate, that I was many years ago so shocked by Cordelia's death, that I know not whether I ever endured to read again the last scenes of the play till I undertook to revise them as an editor."

7

In Lear, says Mr. Wilson Knight, as others have also said, "a tremendous soul is, as it were, incongruously geared to a puerile intellect." [6] And the greatness of Lear's soul is as clearly indicated by his way of speaking and his use of images, as the smallness of his intellect is shown by his division of the kingdom and his testing of his daughters' love. He naturally and invariably sees himself both in relation to large natural forces and to the gods that control them. He swears "by the sacred radiance of the sun,"

> By all the operation of the orbs
> From whom we do exist and cease to be;

[6] *The Wheel of Fire*, Oxford, 1930, p. 177.

he calls on Nature—"hear, dear goddess, hear!"—to revenge him on Goneril; he invokes "all the starr'd vengeances of heaven;" he conjures the "taking airs," the "nimble lightnings," "the fen-suck'd fogs," and in the great storm speeches he urges all the destructive forces in Nature, the winds, the cataracts and hurricanes, the lightning and the thunder, to destroy—not merely his daughters—but everything:

> Strike flat the thick rotundity o' the world!
> Crack nature's moulds, all germens spill at once
> That make ingrateful man!
>
> (iii, 2, 7)

With characteristic violence Lear universalizes his own experience; it is no wonder that other characters in the play think of him in macrocosmic terms. Before he appears on the heath, a Gentleman tells us what to expect, that the king

> Bids the wind blow the earth into the sea,
> Or swell the curled waters 'bove the main,
> That things might change or cease,

and he tells us that Lear, the microcosm,

> Strives in his *little world of man* to out-scorn
> The to-and-fro conflicting wind and rain.
>
> (iii, 1, 5)

So Gloucester, in the fourth act, as he contemplates the destruction of Lear's sanity, at once associates Lear with the macrocosm:

> O ruin'd piece of nature! This *great world*
> Shall so wear out to naught.
>
> (iv, 6, 137)

At the close of the play, for the third time, Lear is seen as a reflection of the universe. When he enters with Cordelia's body, the sight so affects Kent and Edgar that they think of the Last Judgment; the overwhelming terror and pity of Lear's individual situation makes them imagine the end of the whole world.

> *Kent:* Is this the promis'd end?
> *Edgar:* Or image of that horror?

And Albany, looking on and sharing their emotions, asks that the entire order of Nature—such is the implication of his words —shall "fall and cease," thus echoing the desire for universal destruction which Lear himself had expressed at the height of the storm.

Miss Spurgeon's analysis of the imagery in this play brings out very clearly how closely interwoven are the world of Nature and the world of man. There is "an overtone," she says, "running through the crisis of the tragedy, the fury of the elements, described, be it remarked, wholly in terms of the human body. They are wild, fretful, unquiet . . . with these, the old king, with his heart-struck injuries, is contending, tearing his white hair

> Which the impetuous blasts, with eyeless rage,
> Catch in their fury." [7]
>
> (iii, 1, 8)

The destruction which Lear invokes the elements to accomplish in the macrocosm, "that things might change or cease," actually occurs, of course, in the microcosm of Lear himself. Even when he is sane, he is a man quite lacking in wisdom; nothing he does in the first act is good or sensible, and we can easily believe Regan when she says that her father "hath ever but slenderly known himself." *Nosce teipsum* was a piece of advice to which King Lear had never paid any attention. The division of the kingdom and the testing of his daughters are only the climax to a life composed of hasty imperious decisions, based on an unthinking acceptance of his own importance and of what was due to him as king and father—a life that has had this ac-

---

[7] *Shakespeare's Imagery*, New York, 1936, p. 342.

ceptance ingrained in it for many years. No wonder that when he gives up the reality of kingly power, he believes that he can still keep the appearance—

> Only we shall retain
> The name and all th' addition to a king;
> The sway, revenue, execution of the rest,
> Beloved sons, be yours.
>
> (i, 1, 137)

And no wonder that when the appearance of kingly authority —his retinue of a hundred knights—turns into a rabble of "epicurism and lust," and is taken from him, or that when the daughters whom he had expected to fulfill the natural law by honoring their father, fail him by turning out to be either, like Cordelia, too honest, or like her sisters, too cruel (Cordelia's appearance of cruelty covering the reality of love, and her sister's appearance of love covering the reality of cruelty) —no wonder that his reason should crack, and the false, insecure order he had lived by, should disrupt into such chaos and madness that the hierarchy of his being should disintegrate, and everything be turned loose.

That is what happens in *King Lear: everything* is turned loose. Lear's own passions, the fury of the elements, the lustful desires of Regan and Goneril, all are horribly released from order. The chaos is more widespread, less local, than in *Hamlet*, for Hamlet himself, in spite of what he may say about the general human situation, is always the prince of Denmark—"This is I; Hamlet the Dane." Lear's kingdom, on the other hand, is only irrelevantly Britain; it is any kingdom, or all kingdoms, as Lear, granted his circumstances, is any king, or all kings. And the chaos is more universal than in *Othello*, for *Othello* is a play of intensification, and the turmoil in Othello's mind breaks only an individual world, however splendidly it may be conceived. *King Lear* is orchestrated more broadly, and the instruments for which Shakespeare wrote his score are stretched to the limits of their tonal capacity. Re-inforcement through expansion, expansion through re-inforcement, in the worlds of nature, of the individual and of the state, each inseparably linked to the others so that when one falls, they all fall—such is Shakespeare's technique in *King Lear*. It is a technique that would have been impossible without the picture of man's nature and the conflict it included that was taken for granted in Shakespeare's intellectual and emotional background. Shakespeare's mastery of his craft, at the service of his own deep vision, enabled him to use that picture to create a huge portrayal of devastation that, more excruciatingly than any other, moves us to pity and terror for the protagonists and for ourselves.

8

King Lear may also be described as a study in relationships. It is concerned with the relations of children to their parents, with the relation of man to the state, and with the relation of the gods to man. Natural law, justice and religion are concepts which permeate the play, the validity of which the action seems to violate. Lear, like Gorboduc, violates natural law—and the law of nations as well—by dividing his kingdom, and his daughters violate natural law by their ingratitude, a vice which, like the bestial jealousy that overcomes Othello, is called "monstrous"—it is outside the order of Nature. The *unnaturalness* of Goneril and Regan is what Lear cannot bear, as Gloucester cannot understand the apparent unnaturalness of Edgar, and Lear's daughters are fittingly described in those animal images—tigers, wolves, vultures, serpents—which are, as Bradley observes, scattered everywhere through the play.[8]

[8] *Shakespearean Tragedy*, p. 266. Shakespeare uses the word "unnatural" 37 times in all his plays; one fifth of these uses is in *Lear*. It is also interesting to note, from a study of the Concordance, that the word "nature" is used a great deal more in the plays written between 1601 and 1608 than in any others—40% of the uses occur in 22% of the plays. It occurs most frequently in *Lear*: 40 times. In *Hamlet* the word appears 30 times.

The unnaturalness, the upsetting of order, which is illustrated
by the fact that Goneril and Regan, the children, are dominating Lear, the father, is re-inforced by one of the chief themes
which run through the apparently irrelevant speeches and songs
of the Fool. The fact is another illustration of how one character or *motif* re-inforces the others. For the Fool is continually referring to things that are upside-down or backside-
foremost, or out of the natural order, as things are in Lear's
erstwhile kingdom. He says to Lear that, when he divided his
realm, "thou borest thine ass on thy back o'er the dirt" (i, 4,
176); he sings of the cuckoo that bit off the head of its foster-
parent (i, 4, 238); he speaks of the cart drawing the horse
(i, 4, 246); his songs are often a comment on the main situation:

> The man that makes his toe
> What he his heart should make,
> Shall of a corn cry woe,
> And turn his sleep to wake.
>
> (iii, 2, 31)

Such a false sense of values as this is obviously a reflection of
Lear's action toward his daughters; Lear, like the man in the
song, had mistaken the non-essential for the essential.

Goneril and Regan not only violate natural law by their behavior to their father, they also violate their proper functions
as human beings by their lust for Edmund, a lust which ends in
murder and suicide, and which makes the description of them
as animals doubly appropriate. One violation leads to another.
As Albany says to Goneril:

> That nature, which contemns its origin,
> Cannot be border'd certain in itself;
> She that herself will sliver and disbranch
> From her material sap, perforce must wither
> And come to deadly use.
>
> (iv, 2, 32)

The lust of Regan and Goneril is the clearest indication of their degeneration; here, as in *Hamlet, Troilus* and *Othello*, lust is, to Shakespeare, apparently the chief element in humanity that drags men and women (particularly women) down to the level of animals in the natural hierarchy. Like everything else that is presented in *King Lear* lust is emphasized both by specific action and by universalizing comment; we see Regan and Goneril lusting for Edmund, and the universality of lust in the world is made peculiarly appalling because the eighty-year old Lear himself is the character who generalizes about it:

> When I do stare, see how the subject quakes.
> I pardon that man's life. What was thy cause?
> Adultery?
> Thou shalt not die: die for adultery! No:
> The wren goes to't, and the small gilded fly
> Does lecher in my sight.
> Let copulation thrive; for Gloucester's bastard son
> Was kinder to his father than my daughters
> Got 'tween the lawful sheets.
> To't luxury, pell-mell! for I lack soldiers.
>
> (iv, 6, 111)

Lust, to Lear, is the evil truth under the false appearance of virtue:

> Behold yond simpering dame,
> Whose face between her forks presageth snow;
> That minces virtue, and does shake the head
> To hear of pleasure's name;
> The fitchew nor the soiled horse goes to't
> With a more riotous appetite.
> Down from the waist they are Centaurs,
> Though women all above. . . .

And this destructive generalization about the world of the individual, which re-inforces and expands what we have seen exemplified in the lustful behavior of Goneril and Regan, is developed, in Lear's next long speech, to include the world of the state. There too, the appearance is false, order is broken, and what pretends to be justice is corruption:

Lear: See how yond justice rails upon yon simple thief. Hark, in thine ear: change places; and, handy-dandy, which is the justice, which is the thief? Thou hast seen a farmer's dog bark at a beggar?
Glo.: Ay, sir.
Lear: And the creature run from the cur? There thou mightst behold the great image of authority; a dog's obey'd in office.

In other words, animal nature prevails in government as in the individual. Lear, whose specifically human property, reason, has been destroyed in a storm of passion and who has unnaturally abandoned his kingly function as the administrator of justice, is the fittingly ironic commentator on a world of government that has also lost all distinction, that has no justice, that cannot authorize any discrimination between good and evil:

Thou rascal beadle, hold thy bloody hand!
Why dost thou lash that whore? Strip thine own back;
Thou hotly lust'st to use her in that kind
For which thou whipp'st her. The usurer hangs the cozener.
Through tatter'd clothes small vices do appear;
Robes and furr'd gowns hide all. Plate sin with gold,
And the strong lance of justice hurtless breaks;
Arm it in rags, a pigmy's straw doth pierce it.
None does offend, none, I say none . . .

Lear's mad generalizations are a kind of indirect comment on what has happened in his own kingdom when he selfishly and arrogantly gave up his proper office.

His act has had further ramifications. Almost as soon as he has broken political order by dividing Britain between Cornwall and Albany, we hear from Gloucester that because of disorder in the heavens, there is disorder and disaster in the realm of politics and of nature:

These late eclipses in the sun and moon portend no good to us: though the wisdom of nature can reason it thus and thus, yet nature finds itself scourged by the sequent effects. Love cools, friendship falls off, brothers divide: in cities, mutinies; in countries, discord; in palaces, treason; and the bond cracked between son and father.

(i, 2, 115)

And this generalization, which, incidentally, might be considered as a particular illustration of what Ulysses, in *Troilus and Cressida*, had said about how disorder can corrupt the world —this generalization is borne out by what we shortly hear of the civil war in the state. As in *Gorboduc*, division of authority leads to disruption and violence:

Curan: Have you heard of no likely wars toward, 'twixt the Dukes of Cornwall and Albany?
Edmund: Not a word.
Curan: You may do then, in time.

(ii, 1, 11)

Shakespeare has so many other things to show us that he cannot show us these wars in actual operation, but he refers to them three times, and that is enough. The political chaos is as obvious as the chaos in man and in the universe.

Man's relation to the gods, the forces that should order him supernaturally, is as much emphasized as his relation to the state that should order him politically and the self-control by reason that should order his own nature. In fact Shakespeare seems in this play deliberately to use the way a man thinks of the gods as an indication of character. All the characters with whom we are meant to sympathize—Lear, Gloucester, Edgar, Kent and Albany—continually appeal to the gods, and in their different ways think of human affairs as controlled by supernatural power. The bad characters, particularly Edmund (in this respect, as in others, he resembles Richard III and Iago), are incorrigible individualists and egoists.

Shakespeare emphasizes the distinction as early in the play as he can, in the conversation between Gloucester and Edmund in the second scene of the first act. Gloucester sees everything as conditioned by the heavens, and all the right thinking people in Shakespeare's audience would have agreed with him. But when he leaves the stage, Edmund illustrates the villainy of his own nature, his cynical disregard of correspondences and inter-relations, by taking the opposite point of view from that of his father:

> This is the excellent foppery of the world, that, when we are sick in fortune,—often the surfeit of our own behavior,—we make guilty of our disasters the sun, the moon, and the stars; as if we were villains by necessity, fools by heavenly compulsion, knaves, thieves, and treachers by spherical predominance, drunkards, liars, and adulterers by an enforced obedience of planetary influence; and all that we are evil in, by a divine thrusting on: an admirable evasion of whoremaster man, to lay his goatish disposition to the charge of a star!
>
> (i, 2, 132)

Later in the play Kent, an invariably "good" character, directly contradicts this attitude: "It is the stars," he says, "the stars above us, govern our conditions." The contrast is clear throughout.

It is natural, of course, for a bastard, who is an outcast from the law of nations (as Edmund himself says) to think of humanity only in relation to the vices of which he is a product; the Nature whom Edmund invokes as his goddess is a more animal kind of goddess than the Nature later invoked by King Lear. But however natural it may be to Edmund, his view of man, like that of Iago—"Virtue! a fig! 'tis in ourselves that we are thus, or thus"—is, as far as the audience is concerned, a clear indication of villainy.

Yet though the sympathetic figures in the play, unlike Edmund, call frequently upon the gods, and see human affairs in relation to divine control, the gods are highly ambiguous figures, and their rule is not necessarily beneficent. As Dowden says, Shakespeare's *King Lear* differs from the old play which was its main source, in being deliberately placed in heathen times, "partly, we may surmise, that [Shakespeare] might be able to put the question boldly, 'what are the gods?' " [9] The gods are mentioned many times, in relation to circumstances that are invariably evil; but God, the God that would have meant something to Shakespeare's audience, is mentioned only once, when Lear is delusively looking forward to a blissful life with Cordelia.[10] Though Albany, who, as the action develops, eventually emerges as a good and responsible character, may exclaim, hearing of Cornwall's death:

> This shows you are above,
> You justicers, that these our nether crimes
> So speedily can venge—
>
> (iv, 2, 78)

nevertheless Gloucester's terrible observation, made when he is at the bottom of his fortunes, apparently expresses the final truth about the relation between man's fate and the forces that control it:

> As flies to wanton boys, are we to the gods;
> They kill us for their sport.

What is most characteristic of *King Lear* is, on one occasion, summed up by Albany. The animal imagery, the interweaving of relationships, the rapid shift of thought from man as an individual to man as a prince and from man to the heavens, the re-inforcement of the degeneracy in one hierarchy by the degeneracy in another, the doubt concerning divine control of man's affairs, the monstrous chaos and destruction into which man's unassisted nature will lead him—all these things which form the macrocosm of the play are woven in a typical fashion

[9] *Shakespeare, His Mind and Art*, New York, 1903, p. 240. I can merely repeat Bradley's praise of Dowden's observations on *King Lear*. But there is one point which I would dispute with Dowden: in my opinion he over-emphasizes the superstitious side of Gloucester's character. I do not believe that an Elizabethan audience would have thought of him in those terms.

[10] In *Hamlet* God is mentioned 19 times.

into the microcosm of a single speech. "What have you done?"
Albany asks Goneril,

> Tigers, not daughters, what have you perform'd?
> A father, and a gracious aged man,
> Whose reverence the head-lugg'd bear would lick,
> Most barbarous, most degenerate! have you madded.
> Could my good brother suffer you to do it?
> A man, a prince, by him so benefited!
> If that the heavens do not their visible spirits
> Send quickly down to tame these vile offences,
> It will come,
> Humanity must perforce prey on itself,
> Like monsters of the deep.
>
> (iv, 2, 40)

9

As we have seen, Shakespeare uses his consciousness of the
difference between appearance and reality in many places and
in many connections throughout the play; it is particularly
striking in relation to what happens to Lear himself. He begins
with all the assurance of long-established authority, his speeches
are nearly all imperatives, but one by one his pretensions are
stripped away. He gives away his power, his hundred knights
are cut to fifty, to twenty-five, to ten, to five—until Regan's
"What need one?" drives him to the verge of madness:

> O! reason not the need; our basest beggars
> Are in the poorest thing superfluous:
> Allow not nature more than nature needs,
> Man's life is cheap as beast's.
>
> (ii, 4, 267)

And on the bare heath life does become as "cheap as beast's."
For when he sees the disguised Edgar, as the storm still thun-
ders, Lear finds out what man is really like, and he starts to tear
off even the covering of his garments:

Is man no more than this? Consider him well. Thou owest the worm no silk, the beast no hide, the sheep no wool, the cat no perfume. Ha! here's three on's are sophisticated; thou art the thing itself; unaccommodated man is no more but such a poor, bare, forked animal as thou art. Off, off, you lendings! Come; unbutton here.

(iii, 4, 105)

This stripping off of layers of appearance to arrive at the bare truth is the final and tragic expression of that common Shakespearean theme which derides all affectation, as Berowne derides it, which questions the validity of ceremony, as Henry V questions it, and which tries to describe man as he really is. Lear's description is a terrible one, but even in this play, dark as it is, it is not the whole answer. The movement is not all downward, there is a counter-movement upward. Lear himself is not merely stripped, he is purged, and hence there is a possibility of redemption. The storm makes him think, for the first time in his eighty years, of what happens to "poor naked wretches" in "seasons such as these":

> O! I have ta'en
> Too little care of this. Take physic, pomp;
> Expose thyself to feel what wretches feel,
> That thou mayst shake the superflux to them,
> And show the heavens more just.
>
> (iii, 4, 32)

And thoughts of this kind make possible his later recovery into love.

But if we are to understand the full dramatic force of the scenes on the heath, we must imagine their effect in the theater, for in spite of Lamb's remarks, Shakespeare obviously thought of the play in practical dramatic terms; it is as wrong to think of *King Lear* apart from a stage as it is to think of Beethoven's *Ninth Symphony* apart from an orchestra. And these particular scenes should be imagined in relation to the opening of the play; the contrast of visual impression, the contrast in *tableau*, must be as concretely perceived by the eye as the contrasts of rhythm and word are heard by the ear. In the opening scene Lear is surrounded by his court: a page holds the gold crown on a velvet cushion, the King of France, the Duke of Burgundy and a crowd of brilliantly dressed courtiers all wait upon his imperious commands. But in the heath scenes his only companions are a fool and a madman. Kent and Gloucester may be looking out for him, but one is in disguise and the other is in disgrace; on the heath it is to the "bitter Fool" and the "loop'd and window'd raggedness" of Edgar that Lear must turn for companionship.

> There the king *is* but as the beggar.

We see him reduced to relying on the lowest dregs of human nature, his mind in pieces, trying to get to reality by stripping off his clothes.

Never before or since has there been such dramatic writing as this. In presenting man's nature as below any rational level, Shakespeare's control of poetic and dramatic counterpoint enables him as it were to transcend man's nature. Though Lear, Edgar and the Fool are human beings in whom we can believe, what Shakespeare makes them say is beyond normal human speech, and we are in a world where comedy and tragedy are the same. The real madness of Lear, the assumed madness of Edgar, the half-madness of the Fool all play against one another to make out of chaos an almost incredible harmony. These scenes suggest the technique of music as well as the technique of drama, the use of a dramatic orchestration so broad that it stretches our comprehension as no drama had stretched it before. It would have been impossible to foretell that the tradition of the morality play, and the tradition represented by *Gorboduc*, could ever be used and transcended as Shakespeare transcends it in *King Lear*.

10

Of course everything is not evil in *King Lear;* Kent, Edgar and, above all, Cordelia are, as good characters, very sharply set against the evil of Goneril, Regan and Edmund. And yet, be it noticed, in the world of *Lear,* goodness has to *hide.* Cordelia is banished, Kent has to disguise himself, Edgar not merely pretends to be mad, but unnecessarily conceals himself from his father in several other ways. And evil seems to conquer crushingly when Lear enters with Cordelia dead in his arms.

But if we look more closely at this last scene, we shall find that for Lear himself, evil does not conquer after all. For in spite of what he says—

> I know when one is dead, and when one lives;
> She's dead as earth—

Lear cannot believe that this is the reality. He asks for a looking-glass, he thinks that the feather he holds in his trembling hand is stirred by Cordelia's breath. Three times he alternates between believing that the reality is death and believing that the reality is life. The audience knows it is death, but Lear does not. For though, at the very end, he may say

> No, no, no life!
> Why should a dog, a horse, a rat, have life,
> And thou no breath at all? Thou'lt come no more,
> Never, never, never, never, never!

he suddenly cries out, before he dies,

> Do you see this? Look on her, look, her lips,
> Look there, look there!

In his own mind she lives; and it is the discovery that Cordelia is alive, that life is the reality under the appearance, that the reality is *good,*—it is this that breaks his heart at last. As Bradley says, "it seems almost beyond question that any actor is false to the text who does not attempt to express, in Lear's last accents and gestures and look, an unbearable *joy.*"

Chapter VI

MACBETH AND *ANTONY AND CLEOPATRA*

I

One of the most remarkable things about Shakespeare is that although he uses the same materials for the achievement of size and universality in his great tragedies, he creates in each a distinctive and particular world. In *Macbeth*, as in *King Lear*, the individual, the state, and external nature are seen as inter-related parts of a single whole, so that a disturbance in one disturbs the others as well—and yet the atmosphere and tone of the two plays are very different; we may say that *Lear* is a play that opens out, whereas *Macbeth* is a play that closes in. Lear's sufferings end in release, but Macbeth, in the course of his career, becomes trapped by his own crimes, until he sees himself, at the end, as a captured animal:

> They have tied me to a stake; I cannot fly,
> But bear-like I must fight the course.
> (v, 7, 1)

In *Macbeth* there is nothing like the purgation of King Lear. As the action of *King Lear* progresses the main character *loses* his bad qualities; in the course of *Macbeth*, the main character *develops* them. This is something new. Iago, for example, does not become increasingly evil as the play goes on; he is thoroughly and completely bad from the beginning. But Macbeth *grows* into evil; that is why those critics are right who describe the play as a more intense study of evil than any other. Unlike *King Lear* it portrays, not the whitening, but the blackening of a soul.

153

Macbeth is the shortest of the tragedies, and the speediest; at the very beginning we are enveloped in its distinctive atmosphere of darkness, of blood, of a general "hurly-burly" which includes thunder and lightning in the heavens and the turmoil of conflict in the state. All these are suggested by the dozen short lines spoken by the witches in the opening scene; they end with characteristic ambiguity:

> Fair is foul, and foul is fair;
> Hover through the fog and filthy air.

The lines that immediately follow are equally characteristic; Duncan addresses a bleeding Sergeant;

> What bloody man is that? He can report,
> As seemeth by his plight, of the revolt
> The newest state.

Blood, revolt, fog, fair interchanged with foul—such is the confused and murky atmosphere out of which Macbeth himself emerges, his first words echoing the words of the weird sisters to whom he is so closely linked:

> So foul and fair a day I have not seen.

In *Macbeth* the elements which compose the Elizabethan picture of man seem to be more closely fused than in any other tragedy. The confusion in the political world is not merely reflected in the world of Nature and the individual; it is—such is the power of the poetic imagination—*identified* with those worlds, even more intimately than it had been in *King Lear*.

This can be clearly seen if we examine the way in which Shakespeare handles the central event in the play, the murder of Duncan. In the first place, the murder occurs in a dark, dead, haunted period of time. As Macbeth himself says,

> Now o'er the one half-world
> Nature seems dead, and wicked dreams abuse
> The curtain'd sleep; witchcraft celebrates

Pale Hecate's offerings; and wither'd murder,
Alarum'd by his sentinel, the wolf,
Whose howl's his watch, thus with his stealthy pace,
With Tarquin's ravishing strides, toward his design
Moves like a ghost.

(ii, 1, 49)

Lennox describes this terrible night in terms of a confusion which extends to the earth itself:

The night has been unruly: where we lay,
Our chimneys were blown down; and, as they say,
Lamentings heard i' the air; strange screams of death,
And prophesying with accents terrible
Of dire combustion and confus'd events
New hatch'd to the woeful time. The obscure bird
Clamour'd the livelong night: some say the earth
Was feverous and did shake.

(ii, 3, 60)

It is to this same night that Ross and the old man refer as they describe the unnatural events that have taken place in the external world. "Unnatural deeds," as Lady Macbeth's doctor says later, "Do breed unnatural troubles."

Ross: Thou seest, the heavens, as troubled with man's act,
Threaten his bloody stage: by the clock 'tis day,
And yet dark night strangles the travelling lamp. . . .
Old Man: 'Tis unnatural,
Even like the deed that's done. On Tuesday last,
A falcon, towering in her pride of place,
Was by a mousing owl hawk'd at and kill'd.
Ross: And Duncan's horses,—a thing most strange and certain,—
Beauteous and swift, the minions of their race,
Turn'd wild in nature, broke their stalls, flung out,
Contending 'gainst obedience, as they would
Make war with mankind.
Old Man: 'Tis said they eat each other.
Ross: They did so; to the amazement of mine eyes,
That look'd upon't.

(ii, 4, 5)

Never before in any of Shakespeare's dramatic worlds had the breakdown in Nature's order gone so far as this. It is not only man who sinks below his natural level; in the disrupted chaos that is the universe of *Macbeth* even the animals are unnatural. They eat each other, and would make war with mankind, whom, according to all accepted belief, they were created to obey and serve.

Such is the consequence of man's disruption of the order of Nature, exemplified by Macbeth's murder of the virtuous Duncan, who is both his kinsman and his King. No wonder that Macduff exclaims, when he discovers the murder,

> Confusion now hath made his masterpiece!
> Most sacrilegious murder hath broke ope
> The Lord's anointed temple, and stole thence
> The life o' the building!
>
> (ii, 3, 72)

The confusion is centered, of course, on Macbeth himself; he is the individual whose pursuit of evil has made the world and the state a chaotic horror. It is thoroughly appropriate, in an atmosphere where fair is foul and foul is fair, that Lady Macbeth should use the traditional difference between man and animals to encourage her husband in an act that perverts the natural distinction between them. When Macbeth, his mind a turmoil of indecision, hesitates to commit the crime, he says:

> I dare do all that may become a man;
> Who dares do more is none,

Lady Macbeth answers him:

> What beast was't, then,
> That made you break this enterprise to me?
> When you durst do it then you were a man;
> And, to be more than what you were, you would
> Be so much more the man.
>
> (i, 7, 46)

To Lady Macbeth, who had denaturalized herself—"unsex me here"—Macbeth was a man only when he dared to perform the unnatural act of murder.

The murder is crucial in the development of Macbeth's character. At the beginning of the play he is, like the weather, both fair and foul—neither one nor the other, and with potentialities for either. The witches, the symbols both of external destiny and of his own character, send him toward evil, as does his wife. Brewing their disgusting potions from the filthiest parts of the vilest sort of animals, the witches represent a different degree, though not a different kind, of dramatic orchestration from that in the mad scenes of *King Lear*. They, too, are on a bare heath, like Edgar, Lear and the Fool, but they are completely depersonalized from humanity, being, in spite of their connection with human affairs, supernatural, or subnatural, or both; whereas Edgar, Lear and the Fool, no matter how mad they are or appear to be, are nevertheless human beings. The chorus of weird sisters represents a different kind of abstraction from the abstractions that are developed from the human mind.

From another point of view the weird sisters—sponsors and prophets of chaos and of order, of delusion and reality—may be regarded as a final dramatic realization of the Elizabethan dramatic convention which invariably tended to see individual human experience in relation to some power—God, the stars, or Fortune—larger than itself. An earlier, a more didactic and moralistic dramatist would have made only too obvious what abstraction they were supposed to personify. Shakespeare was wiser. We never know, as we see or read *Macbeth*, whether the weird sisters control Macbeth's fate, or whether their prophecies are a reflection of Macbeth's own character. The problem of predestination and free-will is presented, but is left unanswered. Or, to put it in more Shakespearean terms, the dictation of what seems to be external destiny and the impulses of individual character are seen as parts of the same vision, and, in a technical sense, as parts of the same dramatic whole.

2

One of the reasons why *Macbeth* is so dark a play is that the striking emphasis on the unnaturalness of both the chief and the subsidiary events is paralleled by a continually expressed uncertainty as to what is real. In his previous plays Shakespeare presents many aspects of the difference between appearance and fact, but never was the subject so ubiquitous as in the murky fog of *Macbeth*. Are the witches only a product of imagination, or have they a true existence? "I' the name of truth," says Banquo,

> Are ye fantastical, or that indeed
> Which outwardly ye show?
>
> (i, 3, 53)

Macbeth himself is troubled by a similar confusion in his mind:

> My thought, whose murder yet is but fantastical,
> Shakes so my single state of man that function
> Is smother'd in surmise, and nothing is
> But what is not.
>
> (i, 3, 139)

Illusion and reality change places with each other; Macbeth's imaginary dagger is as

> palpable
> As this which now I draw,

just as the hand of Lady Macbeth cannot be sweetened from its imaginary smell of blood by all the perfumes of Arabia. The "horrible shadow," the "unreal mockery," of Banquo's ghost is only a stool to Lady Macbeth. The prophecies of the witches about the man not of woman born and about Birnam wood coming to Dunsinane—both, incidentally, *unnatural* circumstances—turn out to be only an appearance, so that Macbeth cries out:

> And be these juggling fiends no more believ'd,
> That palter with us in a double sense;
> That keep the word of promise to our ear,
> And break it to our hope.
>
> (v, 6, 48)

At least twice in the play the difference between appearance and reality is made the basis for a very effective dramatic irony. In the first act, Duncan says of the revolted Cawdor:

> There's no art
> To find the mind's construction in the face;
> He was a gentleman on whom I built
> An absolute trust.
>
> (i, 4, 11)

And immediately after this comment on the falseness of appearance, Macbeth enters, apparently a loyal general, but with murder already in his heart. Again Duncan's famous description as he enters Macbeth's castle—

> This castle hath a pleasant seat; the air
> Nimbly and sweetly recommends itself
> Unto our gentle senses—
>
> (i, 6, 1)

which is taken up by Banquo—

> This guest of summer,
> The temple-haunting martlet, does approve
> By his lov'd masonry that the heaven's breath
> Smells wooingly here—

this description is clearly in ironic contrast to the true nature of Macbeth's habitation and what takes place there:

> The raven himself is hoarse
> That croaks the fatal entrance of Duncan
> Unto our battlements.
>
> (i, 5, 39)

Macbeth realizes that his situation demands that he and his wife must

> make our faces vizards to our hearts,
> Disguising what they are;
>
> (iii, 2, 34)

and in fact the progress of both Macbeth and Lady Macbeth throughout the play is an ironic and terrible comment on the difference between what seems and what is. Lady Macbeth believes that "a little water clears us of this deed"; she does not conceive that the deed has left an indelible stain that nothing can remove. Macbeth himself—and this is the final irony—discovers that his crimes lead to nothing, they turn to ashes in his mouth. The crown for which he had "filed" his mind is in reality, like everything else, sterile, empty and meaningless. He too, like Hamlet, comes to a conclusion about life, but his conclusion is not a neo-stoic acceptance of things, nor is it, like Othello's last speech, a momentary recapturing of a lost nobility. Macbeth's final generalization is something much more terrible—a fitting conclusion to a scene of disorder, confusion and disillusionment:

> Out, out, brief candle!
> Life's but a walking shadow, a poor player
> That struts and frets his hour upon the stage,
> And then is heard no more; it is a tale
> Told by an idiot, full of sound and fury,
> Signifying nothing.

3

Yet out of this "great perturbation of nature," to use the doctor's words, which is the tragedy of *Macbeth*, naturalness and order eventually emerge. As in *Lear*, there is an upward movement into order as well as a downward movement into chaos; the difference being that in *Lear* the upward movement occurs in the realm of the individual, while in *Macbeth* it occurs in the realm of the state. In the fourth act we have a reversal of the usual situation in the play and instead of the appearance being good and the reality evil, it is the other way around, for the appearance is evil while the reality is good. Malcolm, the prospective king of Scotland, describes himself at length as a mass of lechery and avarice, as the worst possible type of king, as much worse, even, than Macbeth. But in reality he is quite otherwise; he is as chaste as he is generous,

> would not betray
> The devil to his fellow,

and he delights "No less in truth than life."

This scene, to a modern reader, seems unsatisfactory; it is a kind of static set-piece, dramatically a decided let-down from the superb vivid stagecraft we have become accustomed to. It is usually omitted in modern productions. But to omit it is to blur what were apparently Shakespeare's plans, even though he found an unsatisfactory way of working them out. For he had made the difference between appearance and reality so integral a part of the texture of the whole play that at this point, where we have a promise of ultimate good, he wants to use it too, and Malcolm deliberately blackens his own character, "in whom I know," he says,

> All the particulars of vice so grafted,
> That, when they shall be open'd, black Macbeth
> Will seem as pure as snow, and the poor state
> Esteem him as a lamb, being compar'd
> With my confineless harms.
>
> (iv, 3, 51)

He speaks like this so that the reality of good which shines under the false appearance may offset and contradict the reality of evil which is Macbeth.

Parallel to this, and dramatically more successful, is what happens as Macbeth is finally defeated. For, again in terms of the difference between seeming and fact, what had appeared to be unnatural turns out to be natural after all. Everything about Macbeth is a violation of Nature—the witches, his murder of his king and kinsman, the portents in the external world, and finally, his apparent security against death. He can only be killed by a man not born of a woman, and when Birnam wood comes to Dunsinane. But Birnam wood *does* come to Dunsinane, carried by men, and Macbeth is killed by Macduff, who, though he was untimely ripped from his mother's womb, is obviously a human being. Macbeth, tragic victim of appearance that he is, moved throughout the play by unnatural forces and desires, fights desperately and in vain against the reality of natural and normal good. And he dies at the hands of normal human beings who will restore, in Malcolm's words, "by the grace of Grace" what Macbeth has unnaturally destroyed, and will perform what needful else, "in measure, time, and place," to re-establish the state that has been ruined by the "watchful tyranny"

Of this dead butcher and his fiend-like queen.

4

When we move from *Macbeth* to *Antony and Cleopatra* we are at once in a different atmosphere. The main action of *Macbeth* describes the hardening of a soul that is, as it were, vulcanized to insensitivity by evil; it takes place in a northern kingdom haunted by witches and overspread by the terrors of darkness. But *Antony and Cleopatra* opens in a southern empire of sunlight, of gold, of perfumes, of luxury and grandeur. It is, in Mr. Granville-Barker's words, "the most spacious of the plays. . . . It has a magnificence and a magic all its own, and Shakespeare's eyes swept no wider horizon." [1] In *Antony and Cleopatra* human passion does not, as in *Hamlet*, *Lear* and *Macbeth*, produce spiritual disaster; it puts an end to a career of

[1] *Prefaces to Shakespeare*, Second Series, London, 1930, p. 111.

Empire. The situation is exposed, not probed, and though there is much to move us, there is nothing to hurt us, as there is in *Othello* and in *Lear*.

The full significance of this for an understanding of Shakespeare's development is something we shall discuss later. At the moment our concern is to see how, by a fresh use of the three inter-related hierarchies of Nature, the world and the state, Shakespeare gave to this play the breadth and size which his vision of the subject demanded, and which was so much richer than anything he found in Plutarch.

The opening scene sets the tone at once. Antony's situation is described by Philo:

> Take but good note, and you shall see in him
> The triple pillar of the world transform'd
> Into a strumpet's fool.

Such is the view of public opinion. But as soon as Antony and Cleopatra speak we find that to them their love has a dimension as large as any political world it may seem to have destroyed.

> *Cleopatra:* I'll set a bourn how far to be belov'd.
> *Antony:*   Then must thou needs find out new heaven, new earth.

The size, to them, of their world of love, is deliberately set against the size of the political world which their love may reject.

> Let Rome in Tiber melt, and the wide arch
> Of the rang'd empire fall! Here is my space.
> Kingdoms are clay; our dungy earth alike
> Feeds beast as man; the nobleness of life
> Is to do thus; when such a mutual pair
> And such a twain can do't, in which I bind,
> On pain of punishment, the world to weet
> We stand up peerless.
>
> (i, 1, 33)

A little later Cleopatra gives their love the same immensity:

> Eternity was in our lips and eyes,
> Bliss in our brows bent; none our parts so poor
> But was a race of heaven; they are so still,
> Or thou, the greatest soldier of the world,
> Art turn'd the greatest liar.
>
> (i, 3, 35)

Antony himself is a figure of more than human proportions: "the greatest soldier of the world";

> Your Emperor
> Continues still a Jove,
>
> (iv, 6, 28)

says one of Caesar's warriors; to Eros, Antony's face is

> that noble countenance
> Wherein the worship of the whole world lies.
>
> (iv, 12, 85)

When he has stabbed himself, the guards comment:

> *Second Guard:*   The star is fallen.
> *First Guard:* And time is at his period.
>
> (iv, 12, 106)

And Antony himself, as he is dying, sees his life in large and noble terms:

> Wherein I liv'd, the greatest prince o' the world,
> The noblest.[2]

Caesar thinks of Antony in a similar fashion. When he hears of Antony's death, he says:

> The breaking of so great a thing should make
> A greater crack; the round world

[2] Plutarch: "considering that while he lived, he was the noblest and greatest prince of the world." It is interesting to notice how Shakespeare alters the order of the adjectives to get the emphasis he wants.

Should have shook lions into civil streets,
And citizens to their dens. The death of Antony
Is not a single doom; [3] in the name lay
A moiety of the world.

(v, 1, 14)

But it is Cleopatra who, in speaking of Antony, uses most majestically and most magically the concept of the microcosm and the macrocosm; to her he is not merely the "Lord of lords" (iv, 8, 16), not merely the crown of the earth and the garland of the war, he is the macrocosm itself. There is no hint of this in Plutarch; Shakespeare's magnificent poetry is developed from the images his own age gave him:

His face was as the heavens, and therein stuck
A sun and moon, which kept their course, and lighted
This little O, the earth. . . .
His legs bestrid the ocean; his rear'd arm
Crested the world; his voice was propertied
As all the tuned spheres, and that to friends;
But when he meant to quail and shake the orb,
He was as rattling thunder. For his bounty,
There was no winter in't, an Antony [4] 'twas
That grew the more by reaping; his delights
Were dolphin-like, they show'd his back above
The element they liv'd in; in his livery
Walk'd crowns and crownets, realms and islands were
As plates dropp'd from his pocket.

(v, 2, 79)

[3] Cf. Rosencrantz (*Hamlet*, iii, 3, 15):
The cease of majesty
Dies not alone, but like a gulf doth draw
What's near it, with it.

[4] "Antony" is the Folio reading here. Theobald emended it to "autumn," and every subsequent editor, with the exception of Furness, has (I believe) unquestioningly followed him. The test is to speak the line aloud. If it is properly spoken, it is quite clear that Shakespeare meant Cleopatra's thought to come suddenly back to Antony, so that by a particularly intense reversion, he appears to her more than ever a microcosm of bounty. If we see a sexual reference, which is by no means unlikely, all difficulties of meaning disappear.

In thinking of Antony, the individual man, her thought takes in the whole Ptolemaic universe, the world of Nature, and the world of the state; no wonder that she says that such a man "is past the size of dreaming" and that

>   to imagine
> An Antony were nature's piece 'gainst fancy,
> Condemning shadows quite.

5

Cleopatra uses the familiar concepts in a different fashion from that in which they are used in Shakespeare's earlier plays. In fact there are three ways in which they occur in Shakespeare's work; each is characteristic of a different stage in his development as a poet and playwright. In the plays of the 'nineties, as we have seen, the traditional beliefs appear as part of the background. In *Hamlet, Troilus and Cressida, Othello, Lear* and *Macbeth*, they are part of the consciousness of the protagonists, and the splitting of a soul is the splitting of a world. In *Antony and Cleopatra*, they are used in a third way, not merely as background, not as elements in a psychological chaos, but as part of the texture of the poetry, as a way of enlarging the magical aura that surrounds the characters. They do not intensify the situation, they expand it, but—contrary to the way Shakespeare uses them at the beginning of his career—they are not the frame of the picture, they are a part of the painting itself; they are part of its Titian-like richness. And in this play they are expanded to give a picture of *glory*, though it may be defeated glory, not as in *King Lear*, to give a picture of destruction.

The difference between the second and third style may be seen if we compare the characters of Othello and Antony in one important aspect. Both are great warriors, and when each is destroyed, the art of war itself, in typical Elizabethan fashion, is seen to be broken also. But when Othello says farewell to his profession—"Othello's occupation's gone"—he says it *himself;*

the general truth that grows from his particular situation is revealed by his own recognition of it through the collapse of his inner world. This is not true of Antony. It is Cleopatra, not he, who cries,

> O! wither'd is the garland of the war,
> The soldier's pole is fall'n; young boys and girls
> Are level now with men; the odds is gone,
> And there is nothing left remarkable
> Beneath the visiting moon.
>
> (iv, 13, 64)

Moving as Cleopatra's expression of it may be, this situation is not unnatural or monstrous; [5] it has no terror mixed with its grandeur, as has the passage in *Othello*. The difference is typical of a wider difference between two styles, between two kinds of thought, in Shakespeare's portrayal of human nature.

6

"A world-catastrophe!" exclaims Brandes, as he starts to describe *Antony and Cleopatra*. Shakespeare, he continues, "has no mind now to write of anything else. What is sounding in his ears, what is filling his thoughts, is the crash of a world falling to ruin." [6] A more sober examination tends to confirm Brandes' somewhat melodramatic description. As Miss Spurgeon has noted, the word "world" occurs 42 times in this play—a number which is double that to be found in any other,[7] and it occurs in every kind of association.

[5] It is interesting to note, for what it is worth, that in *Othello* the words *monster* or *monstrous* occur 12 times, but only 4 times in *Antony and Cleopatra*, and that when they do occur in the latter play, they have no bearing, as they do in *Othello*, upon the immediate situation of the main characters.

[6] *Shakespeare*, London, 1898, II, 142.

[7] *Shakespeare's Imagery*, New York, 1936, p. 352. "The group of images in *Antony and Cleopatra* which, on analysis, immediately attracts attention as peculiar to this play, consists of images of the world, the firmament, the ocean and vastness generally" (p. 350). Mr. G. Wilson Knight, in his *Shakspearian Tem-*

It is, among other things, part of Antony's salutation to Cleopatra—"O thou day o' the world!"—and from the beginning of the play to the end, Antony and Caesar are described in terms of the macrocosm they rule. To Octavia the prospect of a war between her husband and her brother would be "as if the world should cleave" (iii, 4, 31); Enobarbus, hearing of the dismissal of Lepidus from the triumvirate, comments on it in his own fashion:

> Then, world, thou hast a pair of chaps, no more;
> And throw between them all the food thou hast,
> They'll grind the one the other.
>
> (iii, 5, 14)

The impression of largeness given by the imagery is re-inforced by the way the action shifts from Egypt to Rome and back again, and by the way Shakespeare uses the place-names he found in Plutarch. Antony, says Caesar, has proclaimed his sons the kings of kings:

> Great Media, Parthia, and Armenia
> He gave to Alexander; to Ptolemy he assign'd
> Syria, Cilicia, and Phoenicia. . . .
>   He hath assembled
> Bocchus, the King of Libya; Archelaus,
> Of Cappadocia; Philadelphos, King
> Of Paphlagonia; the Thracian king, Adallas;
> King Malchus of Arabia; King of Pont;
> Herod of Jewry; Mithridates, King
> Of Comagene; Poleman and Amintas
> The Kings of Mede and Lycaonia
> With a more larger list of sceptres.
>
> (iii, 6, 13 ff., 68 ff.)

---

pest, Oxford, 1932, pp. 210 ff., points out that the play has many sea images, but that none of them is tempestuous; they are all peaceful—another contrast to *Othello*. "The tragedy, such as it is," he says, "is shown clearly as a human conflict played on a stage of gentle and peaceful nature; nature thus harmonizing with the love-theme, not the conflict."

This is the empire which, in Caesar's words, Antony has "given up to a whore"; "the noble ruin of her magic, Antony," loses all this for Cleopatra.

We must not forget, however, that large as this world is, it is a very different world from that of *Lear*. It may be immensely imposing, it may be rich, spacious and magnificent—but it is a world of the senses; it is physical. Lear's world is metaphysical; it is the world of the soul. Antony's world, for all its grandeur, is smaller, and when he loses it, though he may be passionately moved, there is no reason why, like Lear, he should go mad. What happens to Antony is, after all, in the nature of things; he has had his luck and his glory, and he knows what he is doing; battle as he may, his end is to be expected: Fortune (the word occurs more frequently here than in any other play) will bring about his downfall. In *Antony and Cleopatra* there is no awareness, on the part of any character, that what happens is unnatural; nothing is hideous or monstrous, like the real lust of Gertrude, the apparent lust of Desdemona, the cruelty of Goneril and Regan, or the criminality of Macbeth. The geographical reach of the Roman Empire may be vast, and Antony's warm gold share of it may fall into the dry manipulating hands of Caesar; the passion of Antony and Cleopatra may destroy them—but that, we feel, is how things happen. It is not unjust; it is how things are. Shakespeare's final vision of man, though still under a tragic guise, is already in sight.

7

Though the stretch of empire is both the background and an essential part of the action of *Antony and Cleopatra*, and though it conditions the expansive form of the dramatic structure which Shakespeare handles with such masterly ease, it is obviously only half the picture; Shakespeare devotes as much care to describing the characters and passion of Antony and Cleopatra themselves as he does to describing the huge environment in which that passion flames.

Here, too, he uses the familiar language of his time; from one point of view Antony loses everything because he fails to be a rational human being. After he has followed Cleopatra in fleeing from the naval battle, Cleopatra asks Enobarbus (a character—of Shakespeare's invention—who acts like a chorus in reflecting an ordinary human view of these great events):

> Is Antony or we, in fault for this?

And Enobarbus replies:

> Antony only, that would make his will
> Lord of his reason. What though you fled
> From that great face of war, whose several ranges
> Frighted each other, why should he follow?
> The itch of his affection should not then
> Have nick'd his captainship; at such a point,
> When half to half the world oppos'd, he being
> The mered question.
>
> (iii, 11, 2)

But this, of course, is only a comment—an outsider's opinion. We do not need to be *told* such things; at this stage of his career Shakespeare can do better than that; he can show us what such a woman as Cleopatra is like, so that, if she were ours instead of Antony's, we too might consider—in Dryden's phrase —"the world well lost" for her sake.

An analysis of Cleopatra's character is, unfortunately, beyond our present scope; what is important for our purpose is to see how, as Antony gives up everything for her, we see him gradually being stripped of the huge and glamorous world which surrounds him, as, in so different a fashion, Lear's world was stripped from *him*. The process is a long one, and Shakespeare manages it with admirable skill.

Until the middle of the third act (I use the word "act" for convenience; Shakespeare himself wrote without thinking of acts or scenes; to him the play unrolled like a continuous un-broken scroll)—until the middle of the third act Antony has apparently the best of both worlds, the world of passion and the world of empire. In the sixth scene of this act we learn from Caesar how magnificently he lives with Cleopatra, and how many kings he has at his command; the scene deliberately em-phasizes Antony's worldly magnificence just before it is, in his own word, to "discandy." From then on he loses one thing after another until there is nothing left but Antony himself and the private world of passion for which he had thrown the public world away. He first loses the naval battle—as Scarus says,

> The greater cantle of the world is lost
> With very ignorance; we have kiss'd away
> Kingdoms and provinces;
>
> (iii, 8, 16)

Canidius and his legions go over to Caesar, so that Antony has only his schoolmaster to send as an ambassador:

> An argument that he is pluck'd, when hither
> He sends so poor a pinion of his wing,
> Which had superfluous kings for messengers
> Not many moons gone by.
>
> (iii, 10, 3)

He challenges Caesar to single combat—a futile proceeding, as Enobarbus realizes:

> I see men's judgments are
> A parcel of their fortunes, and things outward
> Do draw the inward quality after them,
> To suffer all alike. That he should dream,
> Knowing all measures, the full Caesar will
> Answer his emptiness! Caesar, thou hast subdu'd
> His judgment too.
>
> (iii, 11, 31)

Antony looks on himself in a similar fashion:

But when we in our viciousness grow hard,—
O misery on't!—the wise gods seel our eyes;
In our own filth drop our clear judgments; make us
Adore our errors; laugh at's while we strut
To our confusion.

(iii, 11, 111)

One by one, everything abandons Antony; the

good stars, that were my former guides,
Have empty left their orbs, and shot their fires
Into the abysm of hell;

(iii, 11, 145)

Enobarbus also steals away:

and I see still,
A diminution in our captain's brain
Restores his heart. When valor preys on reason
It eats the sword it fights with. I will seek
Some way to leave him.

(iii, 11, 196)

Antony, by "one of those odd tricks which sorrow shoots out of the mind," bids a touching farewell to his servants before the last battle, and immediately afterwards we have that strange and haunting little scene, developed from Plutarch, in which the soldiers on guard hear the music of hautboys under the stage:

Fourth Soldier: Peace! what noise?
First Soldier: List, list!
Second Soldier: Hark!
First Soldier: Music i' the air.
Third Soldier: Under the earth.
Fourth Soldier: It signs well, does it not?
Third Soldier: No.
First Soldier: Peace, I say!
                    What should this mean?
Second Soldier: 'Tis the god Hercules, whom Anthony lov'd,
                    Now leaves him.

(iv, 3, 11)

The stars, his own judgment, his soldiers, Enobarbus and the god from whom his family are descended—all have left him, and we know that no matter how jocund Antony may seem after his last "gaudy-night" with Cleopatra, the outcome of the final battle can only be disastrous. Which it is, for there Cleopatra leaves him too.

> This grave charm,
> Whose eyes beck'd forth my wars, and call'd them home,
> Whose bosom was my crownet, my chief end,
> Like a right gipsy, hath, at fast and loose,
> Beguil'd me to the very heart of loss.
>
> (iv, 10, 38)

There is nothing left of his world.

Before he kills himself, he pauses—the pause gives a very effective release, for the moment, to the emotional tension—and once more draws an analogy between nature and himself. He speaks of clouds that appear to be dragonish, that take the forms of citadels, rocks,

> A forked mountain, or blue promontory
> With trees upon 't, that nod unto the world
> And mock our eyes with air. . . .
> That which is now a horse, even with a thought
> The rack dislimns, and makes it indistinct,
> As water is in water.
>
> (iv, 12, 5)

The appearance melts, as the grandeur of Antony has melted:

> My good knave, Eros, now thy captain is
> Even such a body: here I am Antony;
> Yet cannot hold this visible shape, my knave.

But the tragedy does not end here, and Antony's death is not a defeat but a kind of triumph. As Professor Case has pointed out,[8] both Othello and Antony imagine that they will meet the

---

[8] In his introduction to the Arden edition of *Antony and Cleopatra*, London, 1906, p. xv.

women they have loved in the next world; but with what different emotions! Othello says of Desdemona:

> When we shall meet at compt,
> This look of thine will hurl my soul from heaven,
> And fiends will snatch at it.
>
> (v, 2, 272)

Antony's vision is of another kind; he and Cleopatra are to be *together* in the next world, not separated by the gulf between heaven and hell. The contrast marks the contrast in tone between two kinds of tragedy.

> Where souls do couch on flowers, we'll hand in hand,
> And with our sprightly port make the ghosts gaze;
> Dido and her Æneas shall want troops,
> And all the haunt be ours.
>
> (iv, 12, 51)

And before his death Antony's grandeur is, by Cleopatra's image of him in cosmic terms, in a way restored. "O sun!" she cries,

> Burn the great sphere thou mov'st in; darkling stand
> The varying star o' the world. O Antony!
>
> (iv, 13, 9)

At the beginning of the play, when Cleopatra says, "I'll set a bourn how far to be belov'd," Antony had replied: "Then must thou needs find out new heaven, new earth." At the end, through the poetic glory of Cleopatra's re-creation of Antony, we feel that in a sense the new heaven and earth have been found.

8

Antony and Cleopatra, unlike the chief characters of the other great tragedies, are never disillusioned, for they have had no illusions to start with. Antony knows what he is doing when he chooses Egypt instead of Rome, and their deaths are, as I have said, part of the order of things. Yet in his presentation of Cleopatra at the end Shakespeare gives a further range to his action by referring, as he had done so often before, to the fact that under all the trappings of royalty, there are only human beings. To Cleopatra, when Antony dies, all distinction and difference have disappeared:

> Young boys and girls
> Are level now with men.
> (iv, 13, 65)

And she rebukes Iras for calling her Empress:

> No more, but e'en a woman, and commanded
> By such poor passion as the maid that milks
> And does the meanest chares.

So when she is dead, she is not, to Charmian, a queen, but "a *lass* unparallel'd." [9] This simplicity is re-inforced by the clown who brings the basket of figs with the asps. There has been no one remotely like this in the play before, and Shakespeare has him speak in flat prose to make him as simple a fellow as possible. He is at one end, the bottom end, of the human scale. But the moment he leaves, we are at the top once more. There is a sudden leap from the humblest peasant to the highest grandeur. As she is about to die, Cleopatra is still an empress:

> Give me my robe, put on my crown; I have
> Immortal longings in me.

And in another fashion, with the paradoxical reversal that is the essence of her charm, when she applies the asp to her breast, she both spurns and spans the same range—from the heavens to the most simple human act—that has been spanned

---

[9] J. Middleton Murry, *Shakespeare*, London, 1936, p. 357: " 'A *lass* unparallel'd.' Who dare risk it? Who but the man to whom these things were no risk at all? Every other great poet the world has known, I dare swear, would have been compelled to write: 'A queen unparallel'd.' But Shakespeare's daimon compels him otherwise; compels him not indeed consciously to remember, but instinctively to body forth in utterance, the Cleopatra who dreams, and is a girl; the Cleopatra who is super-human and human."

by the whole play. Charmian cries out, "O eastern star!"—
and we are reminded of the wide skies that have echoed the
rich Egyptian glory. But Cleopatra rebukes her, as she had
previously rebuked Iras:

> Peace, peace!
> Dost thou not see my baby at my breast,
> That sucks the nurse asleep?

CHAPTER VII

SHAKESPEARE'S LAST PLAYS

I

The play that Shakespeare wrote after *Antony and Cleopatra* is his last serious presentation of man in relation to the state. *Macbeth* is one kind of political play, in that it describes how a country suffers as its king grows evil; *Antony and Cleopatra* is another kind, in that it describes the conflict between passion and empire; *Coriolanus* is a third kind, in that it portrays the conflict between the two halves of a commonwealth: the leader who is too proud, and the people who are too foolish, to arrive at any orderly collaboration.

Coriolanus is an excellent piece of dramatic craftsmanship; the action is varied and exciting, the main characters are strongly drawn, the climax is made to seem inevitable, and unlike *Troilus and Cressida*, for example, the play is a single firm unity. But it has never been popular, and though we admire it, we admire it in cold blood. We feel that it is a *study* in human behavior, as Ben Jonson's plays are studies, and this is a feeling we never have when we think of *Hamlet* or of *Lear*. *Coriolanus* is the product of a remarkably vigorous and able mind, who sees what the dramatic problem is and solves it with remarkable distinction and success. But it is a tight play; it does not open vistas, like *Antony and Cleopatra;* it closes them. Coriolanus himself is forced, by the circumstances of the society in which he lives and by the faults of his own nature, into a series of inescapable positions, and this, combined with the fact that he is, as Bradley says, "what we call an impossible person," [1] makes

[1] "Coriolanus," British Academy Shakespeare Lecture, 1912, p. 10.

the play even more claustrophobic than *Macbeth*. Neither in situation nor in character is there any release, as there is in the other tragedies, as there notably is in *Antony and Cleopatra*.

Perhaps this should make *Coriolanus* the most tragic of all the plays, but in fact it does not. For *Coriolanus* lacks reverberations. Nothing that happens to the hero is reflected in external nature, as in *Macbeth* and *Lear;* there are no storms and tempests in the elements to reflect the tempest in man's soul. Coriolanus is not conceived as the kind of man whose behavior would cause sympathetic responses in any world outside of himself. He is too rigid. The play has no cosmology, and the gods who are referred to by the various characters are mentioned, we feel, for the sake of local color, not because they are part of a vision of things, as they are in *King Lear*. There is nothing here

> to shake our disposition
> With thoughts beyond the reaches of our souls.

The supernatural world, like the natural world, has no place in the political world of *Coriolanus*.

This limitation is clearly illustrated if we compare the speech about the members of the body made by Menenius near the beginning of the play with the speech on order by Ulysses near the beginning of *Troilus and Cressida*. Both speeches serve the same dramatic purpose; in their different ways they describe the proper kind of relationship, the pattern, which the action is later to violate. But Menenius' comparison of the senate to the belly and the other parts of the state to the members of the body, is limited to the physical and practical, whereas Ulysses' speech takes in everything: the cosmos, the elements, the realm of government and the hierarchy of the faculties of man. Furthermore, though the concepts elaborated by Ulysses are based on the common assumptions of Elizabethan thought, their application to the particular action of the Troy story is Shakespeare's own invention. But neither the analogy drawn by Menenius nor its application is an invention. The parallel between the human body and the state may be the central symbol of *Coriolanus,* yet, as Miss Spurgeon points out, "it is significant that this has not been born out of the creator's feeling of the tragedy; it has just been taken over by him wholesale, with much else, from North's *Plutarch.*"[2]

But with all its limitations, *Coriolanus* presents a very clear-sighted view of the relation between an individual and society. Both have their faults, and the tragedy is that they are irreconcilable in consequence. The proud individual will not stoop to the wavering multitude, and the wavering multitude is only too easily persuaded to bring down the proud individual. Each, as Shakespeare describes them, is to blame, and we misinterpret his intention if we imagine that his sympathies are more on one side than the other. For just as Menenius is an older variety of one of Shakespeare's favorite kinds of character, the man with no nonsense about him who has, like Berowne and Mercutio, a witty common sense that sees through anything false, so the whole play is another example of Shakespeare's main dramatic intention: not to prove a point or to preach, but to present things as they are. In every play the presentation is controlled, of course, by the angle of the vision and by the intensity of the gaze: in *Coriolanus* the vision is aloof, and the gaze insufficiently comprehensive to see the disruption of an individual as the disruption of a world.

2

But *Timon of Athens,* which was apparently written immediately after *Coriolanus* (the date is uncertain; it may have come immediately after *Lear*)—*Timon* is a very different affair. Here

[2] *Shakespeare's Imagery,* p. 347.

there is no controlled inevitability; all is rage and violence. From the point of view of Timon, every human being is bestial, and confusion is all that mankind deserves.

The play is by no means a satisfactory unity, and there are three possible explanations for the rough condition in which it has survived. It may be a re-working by Shakespeare of an incomplete play by somebody else, it may be a re-working by somebody else of an incomplete play by Shakespeare, or it may be entirely Shakespeare's, but left incomplete by him. Each theory has its strong advocates, but, though I am inclined to agree with Sir Edmund Chambers in believing that the last theory is correct and that the play as it stands is all Shakespeare's, it does not matter for our purpose which theory we accept. For what concerns us is how Timon speaks about mankind, and everyone agrees that his bitterest railings could have been written by Shakespeare alone.

The story of Timon, the open-hearted and over-generous spendthrift who turned into a violent misanthrope and fled from human society when he lost his money and found that none of the people who had profited by his generosity would come to his aid—this story, handed down from Lucian and Plutarch, was an Elizabethan commonplace, and as such was likely sooner or later to be dramatized. And it obviously called for a denunciation of mankind. But neither of these things completely accounts for the fact that Shakespeare decided to dramatize it toward the end of his tragic period, nor do they account for the kind of savage relish with which Shakespeare's Timon attacks human nature. It is difficult to resist the conclusion that the old misanthropic story was at this time sympathetic to Shakespeare, just as, if we accept the view that the play as we now have it is all his, it is difficult not to conclude that he abandoned it because he saw that the story could not, from its very nature, be turned into a first-class play.

As the play begins we see Timon at the height of his extravagant generosity, surrounded by artists, lords and senators, all of them busily absorbing as much money as Timon will give them. It is a scene of thoughtless luxury in the midst of which, in spite of his carelessness, Timon stands out as a fine human being. One of the lords observes,

> the noblest mind he carries
> That ever govern'd man.
>
> (i, 1, 292)

There is only one sour note, and that is the cynical figure of Apemantus who, as far as his view of mankind is concerned, is a first cousin, if not a blood brother, of Thersites. To Apemantus

> the strain of man's bred out
> Into baboon and monkey.
>
> (i, 1, 260)

He has already reached the stage at which Timon is to arrive later, though his snarling and spitting is a much smaller thing than the all-inclusive storm of cursing and denunciation which comes from the bitterness of Timon's disillusionment.

For when Timon discovers that all his apparent friends are hypocrites, are

> Most smiling, smooth, detested parasites,
> Courteous destroyers, affable wolves, meek bears,
>
> (iii, 6, 105)

he can only wish on all human society that chaos which Ulysses had seen as latent in the world, and which, in very similar terms to those used by Timon, Lear in his madness had described. Timon leaves Athens with a curse that all order be overturned:

> Maid, to my master's bed;
> Thy mistress is o' the brothel. Son of sixteen,
> Pluck the lin'd crutch from thy old limping sire,
> With it beat out his brains! Piety, and fear,
> Religion to the gods, peace, justice, truth,
> Domestic awe, night-rest and neighborhood,

> Instruction, manners, mysteries and trades,
> Degrees, observances, customs and laws,
> Decline to your confounding contraries,
> And let confusion live!

And after invoking every painful disease to come and afflict human beings, Timon, stripped to nakedness, plans to live with the beasts:

> Nothing I'll bear from thee
> But nakedness, thou detestable town! . . .
> Timon will to the woods; where he shall find
> The unkindest beast more kinder than mankind.
>
> (iv, 1, 12)

Timon's mind continually dwells on the animals; on man's resemblance to them, and on his inferiority to them. When Alcibiades comes upon Timon in the woods, Alcibiades asks, "What art thou there? Speak." And Timon replies, "A beast, as thou art." He adjures the earth:

> Ensear thy fertile and conceptious womb,
> Let it no more bring out ingrateful man!
> Go great with tigers, dragons, wolves, and bears;
> Teem with new monsters—
>
> (iv, 3, 188)

He talks at length with Apemantus:

Timon: What wouldst thou do with the world, Apemantus, if it lay in thy power?

Apemantus: Give it to the beasts, to be rid of the men.

Timon: Wouldst thou have thyself fall in the confusion of men, and remain a beast with the beasts?

Apemantus: Ay, Timon.

Timon: A beastly ambition, which the gods grant thee to attain to. . . .

Apemantus: . . . the commonwealth of Athens is become a forest of beasts.

(iv, 3, 321)

To the bitterly disillusioned Timon

all is oblique;
There's nothing level in our cursed natures
But direct villany. Therefore be abhorr'd
All feasts, societies, and throngs of men!
His semblable, yea, himself, Timon disdains:
Destruction fang mankind!

(iv, 3, 18)

3

In a sense *Timon* may be regarded as the climax of Shakespeare's presentation of the evil reality in human nature under the good appearance. We might say—with some danger of over-simplification—that his other tragedies had portrayed the situation in various personal relationships: Hamlet discovers the evil in his mother, Troilus in his mistress, Othello (as he thinks) in his wife, Lear in his daughters, Macbeth in the dusty fulfillment of his ambition—while Timon discovers evil in all mankind. And we might think, in consequence, that *Timon* should be more terrible than any of the other tragedies, since it presents evil in such universal terms.

But just as *Coriolanus,* in spite of the inevitability of its hero's downfall, is not the most tragic of Shakespeare's plays, so *Timon* is not the most universal. If *Coriolanus* is a *study* in human behavior, *Timon,* by the very nature of the story, illustrates a thesis: the thesis that all men are bad; and though Shakespeare could describe men's badness with great vigor and force by reversing the traditional distinction between men and beasts, that reversal, no matter how strongly felt, is not in itself enough to produce tragedy. It produces only railing, and we feel toward Timon no particularly tragic emotion. The universality, as it were, is its own enemy—it becomes mere generalization, and we may say that if *Coriolanus* has not *enough* universality to rank it with the great tragedies, *Timon* has too much; there is not, in the individual situation or character of Timon, any change, psychological or otherwise, that can really move us, as we are moved by Macbeth or Othello. There is no purgation, and we feel only an abstract kind of sympathy. Timon's angry disillusionment at what he sees under the new circumstances is so complete that Shakespeare's presentation of it can take only the form of a series of set pieces, of satiric tableaux, which may express a bitter arraignment of the reversal of Nature's order, but which have only a fortuitous dramatic coherence.

Perhaps it was because Shakespeare was aware that he had started down a dramatic blind alley that he left the play unfinished—in trying to account for what he did it is always wise, since we are dealing with so consummate a craftsman, to suggest technical explanations first. But few Shakespearean critics, and I confess I am not among them, have resisted the temptation to go further, and to see in the fact that Shakespeare left *Timon* unfinished an indication of a change in Shakespeare's attitude toward the nature of man. Sir Edmund Chambers, one of the most cautious of scholars, has even suggested that at this time in his career, Shakespeare had a nervous breakdown, and that thereafter the intensity of the tragic vision was physiologically impossible; it was more than Shakespeare could stand. This may or may not be so; at all events, if *Timon* was written after *Coriolanus*, it was the last of his tragedies. In the remaining four or five years of his active career he chose a new kind of subject matter, which he presented through a new technique and in the light of a new illumination.

4

We may think of *Timon* as bearing the same relation to the end of Shakespeare's tragic period as *Measure for Measure* does to the beginning. The last act of *Measure for Measure*, as we saw, is a kind of desperate attempt to give a "happy" ending to what is essentially a tragic theme; the reconciliations, which have no right to be reconciliations, are, as it were, plastered over the basically tragic material. The comic spirit, the voice that can speak with equanimity of human nature, is at its last gasp, and it can talk only in tones that are strained. *Timon* is just the reverse; for in *Timon* it is the tragic spirit that is strained, it is the *non*-reconciliation that is forced and desperate, and we are dissatisfied with the play for the opposite reason that we are dissatisfied with *Measure for Measure*. As we read both plays we say, "Life is not like that;" but we say it of *Timon* because we feel that *Timon* expounds a preposterous evil, whereas *Measure for Measure* creates an impossible good.

When we read Shakespeare's part in *Pericles*—only the last three acts are his—we are in another world from *Timon*. There is plenty of evil in the background: the apparent death of Thaisa, the murderous jealousy of Marina's foster-mother, the sufferings of Pericles—but at the end of the play all these things are redeemed. As Marina reveals herself to her father in the last act, we are in that enchanted atmosphere which is to be found in various places in all the last plays, and which is both an acceptance and an exaltation of normal reality.

> O Helicanus! . . .
> Give me a gash, put me to present pain,
> Lest this great sea of joys rushing upon me
> O'erbear the shores of my mortality,
> And drown me with their sweetness.
>> (v, 1, 192)

He calls for fresh garments; he hears supernatural music:

Pericles: Give me my robes. I am wild in my beholding.
    O heavens! bless my girl. But, hark! what music? . . .
Helicanus: My lord, I hear none.
Pericles: None!
    The music of the spheres! List, my Marina. . . .
        Most heavenly music:
    It nips me into listening, and thick slumber
    Hangs upon mine eyes.
>> (v, 1, 223)

And when, through a supernatural vision, Pericles rediscovers his lost wife as well as his lost daughter, he exclaims,

> no more, you gods! your present kindness
> Makes my past miseries sport.
>
> (v, 3, 40)

These are not the gods of *King Lear*, whose sport was of another kind. The world of *Pericles*, like the world of all the later plays, is the tragic world turned inside out. The Shepherd, in *The Winter's Tale*, as he picks up the infant Perdita, speaks to the clown who has just described the death of Antigonus: "Now bless thyself," he says: "thou mettest with things dying, I with things new born." And we, who look back to our experience of the tragedies, can say the same thing as we read the final plays.

At the tragic height of *King Lear*, when the mad king meets the blind Gloucester, Edgar comments:

> I would not take this from report; it is,
> And my heart breaks at it.

But in the final plays, that which *is*, the reality, does not break hearts; on the contrary, it is a cause for thanksgiving. As Theseus says, addressing the gods at the end of *The Two Noble Kinsmen*,

> Let us be thankful
> For that which is, and with you leave dispute
> That are above our question.

Rebirth through spring, through woman, acceptance of things as they are, but with a glory round them—that is what we find in all the plays from *Pericles* on. In the tragedies the appearance may be good, but the reality—the lust of Gertrude, the faithlessness of Cressida, the hypocrisy of Regan and Goneril, the crown of Scotland, and, to Timon, all mankind—is evil. In the last plays the appearance may be evil, but the reality is invariably good. Marina and Thaisa are alive, not dead, Imogen is faithful, Hermione and Perdita are restored to Leontes, and Miranda's view of man is the opposite of Timon's:

> How beauteous mankind is! O brave new world
> That has such people in't!

5

"Before a man studies Zen, to him mountains are mountains, and waters are waters; after he gets an insight into the truth of Zen through the instruction of a good master, mountains to him are not mountains and waters are not waters; but after this when he really attains to the abode of rest, mountains are once more mountains and waters are waters." [8]

Something like that must have happened to Shakespeare, as it has happened to other people who have contemplated, not only mountains and waters, but the nature of man.

For Shakespeare's later vision of man and his place in the scheme of things, the vision that grows out of an inner turmoil, is different from the first unthinking acceptance of youth. Rebirth is another thing than birth, since the memory of evil is behind it. In Shakespeare's last plays the memory and the possibility of evil are reflected in the belief of Posthumus, in *Cymbeline*, that Imogen has betrayed him, in Leontes' fury of jealousy at the beginning of *The Winter's Tale*, in the storm and shipwreck of *The Tempest*. And because the possibility of evil is still in the background, the theme of rebirth is often expressed in a tone of incredulous wonder, as if it could hardly be believed.

> O! Stop there a little.
> This is the rarest dream that e'er dull sleep
> Did mock sad fools withal; this cannot be. [4]

---

[8] Quoted D. T. Suzuki, *Essays in Zen Buddhism*, First Series, London, 1927, p. 12.
[4] *Pericles*, v, 1, 162.

                    O thou goddess!
Thou divine Nature, how thyself thou blazon'st
In these two princely boys.[5]

                    O queen Emilia,
Fresher than May, sweeter
Than her gold buttons on the boughs or all
Th' enamell'd knacks o' th' mead or garden! Yea,
We challenge too the bank of any nymph,
That makes the stream seem flowers! Thou, O jewel
O' th' wood, o' the world, hast likewise bless'd a place
With thy sole presence.[6]

The tone is that of incantation, not of dramatic action; the
"sensation," as Mr. Middleton Murry says, "belongs to a man
to whom the re-birth of spring has become intolerably tender."
And, Mr. Murry continues, "there is a connection, I am certain, between this . . . exquisite celebration of the miracle of
re-born Nature, which is uttered in so much of the loveliest
verse of the latest plays, and the imagination of a re-born humanity, which takes substance in the rare women, 'tender as
infancy and grace,' who are the chief figures of their drama." [7]

There is also a connection with the theme of reconciliation, of
union, and it is significant that the gods in these last plays are
repeatedly referred to as benevolent. "You gods, look down,"
says Hermione,

          And from your sacred vials pour your graces
          Upon my daughter's head.[8]

Gonzalo, in *The Tempest*, says the same thing:

          Look down, you gods,
          And on this couple drop a blessed crown.
                              (v, 1, 201)

"Laud we the gods," says Cymbeline,

---

[5] *Cymbeline*, iv, 2, 169.
[6] *Two Noble Kinsmen*, iii, 1, 4.
[7] *Shakespeare*, pp. 385, 386.
[8] *Winter's Tale*, v, 3, 121.

And let our crooked smokes climb to their nostrils
From our bless'd altars.

(v, 5, 478)

The gods seal the discovery, the rediscovery, of the good reality
underneath the apparent evil. The beneficence of their rule is
undoubted; they are "above our question," and their blessing is
a confirmation of the blessedness of the individual human life.[9]

6

Many Shakespeare scholars have suggested that the change in
tone, in attitude and in technique that occurs in Shakespeare's
last plays can be accounted for by the fact that Shakespeare (as
usual, according to them) was merely following a contemporary
literary fashion. It was not Shakespeare himself, they say, who
tired of tragedy—it was his age; and they point to the clever, unrealistic romances of Beaumont and Fletcher, which were beginning to be successful at the end of the first decade of the seventeenth century, and they point to the Jacobean fondness for the
masque, a form of entertainment that at its best was an abstraction from reality and at its worst was mere decoration; that was
not a probing into experience, but was merely an elaborate and
stately flourish, presenting, with a formalized rigidity, gods and
goddesses, virtues and vices, but never the passions of individual men and women. Shakespeare, these scholars say, was
anxious to keep in touch with popular taste, and *Cymbeline*,
The Winter's Tale and *The Tempest* are illustrations of how
he could adapt himself to current theatrical conditions by using
unrealistic stories and by inserting masques as substitutes for
psychological dénouements.

Such views are useful as a corrective to those of the critics who

[9] It may be significant that of the 279 occasions on which Shakespeare uses the
word "bless" and its derivatives, 72, or more than 25%, occur in the last five
plays—excluding *The Two Noble Kinsmen*; whereas these plays represent less than
15% of his total output.

think of the sequence of Shakespeare's plays as an autobiograph-
ical revelation, and there is no doubt that the romantic plots of
the last plays, together with the presence of masques or masque-
like scenes in all of them, are related to what the audiences of
1610 and 1611 expected to see when they went to the theater.
But such explanations, though they may partially account for
the original stimulus, do not account for the final results; if they
were entirely correct, Shakespeare's last plays would not be, as
they are, unique in Jacobean drama.

For we have only to read a play in which Shakespeare, at the
end of his career, collaborated with one of his contemporaries,
to see the striking difference between Shakespeare's final style
and that of anyone else. Shakespeare's part in *The Two Noble
Kinsmen*, a dramatization of Chaucer's *Knight's Tale* which he
composed with Fletcher in 1613, was his last piece of dramatic
writing, and though it does not show him at the height of his
powers, it is highly characteristic of his final period, differing
only in degree, not in kind, from *The Winter's Tale* and *The
Tempest*. Fletcher's share in the play, about three-fifths of the
whole, is an accomplished, suave, sentimental piece of craftsmanship; he manages his contrasts with his usual unscrupulous and
effective opportunism; there is no depth, there are no emotional
reverberations and there is no vision. Shakespeare treats his
part of the story very differently; his lines are slow, and dense,
compared with Fletcher's easy liquescence; they have a deliberate yet vague grandeur, a remote and half-exhausted exaltation; they are expressed through a rhetoric that is the poetry
of a man who has finished with action.

> O great corrector of enormous times,
> Shaker of o'er-rank states, thou grand decider
> Of dusty and old titles, that heal'st with blood
> The earth when it is sick, and cur'st the world
> O' th' plurisy of people!
>
> (v, 1, 63)

O queen Emilia,
Fresher than May, sweeter
Than her gold buttons on the boughs or all
Th' enamell'd knacks o' th' mead or garden! [10]
(iii, 1, 4)

The positive values throughout Shakespeare's share of the play are those of friendship, of loyalty, of union; the friendship of Theseus and Pirithous, of Arcite and Palamon, of Emilia and Flavina, the union of that which is, to the will of the beneficent gods. It is the writing of a man who has come out on the other side of human experience, and who, looking back, can no longer be interested in what he once saw so vividly and so passionately felt. The rhythms are the rhythms of acceptance and of incantation, and the figures still struggling in the *selva oscura* are the figures of a pageant or a dream.

There is nothing like this in Fletcher. The emotional tone of his share of the play is not that of a man who has been *through* experience; it is the tone of a man who has never got there. Nor is there anything like this in any of Shakespeare's other contemporaries. Though in his tragedies Shakespeare had used, perhaps more completely than anyone else, the traditional views of man's nature and the conflict contained in them, at the end of his life as a dramatist he went beyond those views, and, by developing what had been throughout his career one aspect of his picture of man, he wrote plays which have a character all their own. What that character is, we can best discover by examining, not *The Two Noble Kinsmen*, however revealing it may be, but *The Winter's Tale* and *The Tempest*, plays which show Shakespeare's creative energy still in full force.

[10] One characteristic feature of the Shakespearean part of the play is the large number of invocatory "O's." In the first scene, of 234 lines, there are 12 such "O's"—a minor indication of the general tone. In a typical Fletcher scene, ii, 2, of 277 lines, there are only 4 invocatory "O's." I have discussed this play in more detail in an article "*The Two Noble Kinsmen*," *Modern Philology*, XXXVI (1939), 255–276.

7

No play better illustrates the difference between Shakespeare's tragic period and his final period than *The Winter's Tale*. The story as originally told by Robert Greene in his *Pandosto* had a tragic ending; the queen, wrongly accused of unfaithfulness, dies of grief on hearing of the death of her son, and the king, after falling in love with his own daughter and discovering his mistake, kills himself from remorse. The king of Greene's tale loses everything. But Shakespeare changes the story completely. His king only *apparently* loses everything. He may not, to be sure, rediscover his dead son, but his son's death is, in terms of the play, entirely made up for by his rediscovery of the wife and daughter whom he had apparently lost forever. Shakespeare's Leontes does not lose everything: he finds it. Only the appearance is evil; the reality is good.

Yet the first part of the play is dark enough—deliberately so, perhaps (as Dowden suggested), in order to make the golden light of the last two acts shine more brightly by contrast. The sudden jealousy of Leontes comes over him like a storm, and he does not recover from it until his son is dead, his wife apparently killed by grief, and his baby daughter abandoned by his order on the sea-coast of Bohemia. By the time we reach the middle of the play, the evil passion of Leontes seems to have caused the destruction of everything that matters to him. Such, as any Elizabethan psychologist or moralist would have said, was passion's inevitable result. But sixteen years go by—an interval that nearly breaks the play in two—and afterwards, though difficulties may crop up now and then, all is delight, and the chastened Leontes comes finally back to happiness.

Leontes is the last of Shakespeare's characters to see the passion of lust as dominant in human beings. In earlier plays, in *Measure for Measure*, in *Troilus, Hamlet, Othello* and *King*

Lear, lust had been described as the key to the evil in man's nature, and we sometimes feel that Shakespeare, like his contemporary Marston, puts an exaggerated or even morbid emphasis
on it, as in the mad speeches in the fourth act of *King Lear.* The
last shreds of this emphasis appear in Leontes' unjustified suspicion of Hermione, and though what Leontes imagines is made
to sound convincing enough as he describes it to himself, the
audience, who has seen Hermione and heard her speak, knows
quite well that there is no foundation for Leontes' self-torturing
images. Lust is not the actuality, as it is in *Lear,* nor does the appearance of it cause destruction as in *Othello;* it is the illusion;
and the gods, speaking through their oracle, finally convince
Leontes that his view of human behavior is a calumny. His sixteen years of self-reprobation are for him a necessary purge—so
Shakespeare makes us feel (thus mastering, in psychological
terms, the literal incredibility of the situation); Leontes must
suffer through that period before he can be worthy of his re-
created joy. Lear's purgation came too late to bring about the
resurrection of the Cordelia whom he loved, and his deluded
belief in the living movement of her lips was a delusion that
killed him. Not so with Leontes. The resurrection of Hermione,
the rediscovery of Perdita ("Perdita"—that which was lost is
found), are not delusions; they are facts.

But Shakespeare, in *The Winter's Tale,* does not use the relatively crude method of presenting the beauty of rediscovered
life that he had used in *Pericles.* In *Pericles* Marina comes out
of a brothel. White is against black, the star shines against darkness with an almost too formal and theoretical obviousness.
The technique of *The Winter's Tale* is far more subtle and
moving. For the contrast between the first and second parts of
the play is a contrast between two worlds: "Thou mettest with
things dying; I with things new born," says the Shepherd in
the scene that connects them. We do not discover Perdita in a

brothel, we discover her at a sheep-shearing, in a world of pastoral innocence, where the only rogue is a rogue who carries in his pack a bundle of songs.

Nowhere else in Shakespeare is there poetry like the poetry in the fourth act of *The Winter's Tale:*

> *Perdita:*   O Proserpina!
> For the flowers now that frighted thou let'st fall
> From Dis's waggon! daffodils
> That come before the swallow dares, and take
> The winds of March with beauty; violets dim,
> But sweeter than the lids of Juno's eyes
> Or Cytherea's breath; pale prime-roses,
> That die unmarried, ere they can behold
> Bright Phoebus in his strength, a malady
> Most incident to maids; bold oxlips and
> The crown imperial; lilies of all kinds,
> The flower-de-luce being one. O! these I lack
> To make you garlands of, and my sweet friend,
> To strew him o'er and o'er!
> *Florizel:*   What! like a corse?
> *Perdita:* No, like a bank for love to lie and play on;
> Not like a corse; or if,—not to be buried,
> But quick and in mine arms.
>
> (iv, 3, 116)

In *Antony and Cleopatra,* under the guise of tragedy, there had been suggestions of an exaltation something like this, but Antony and Cleopatra had had to look forward to a world after death, where

> Dido and her Æneas shall want troops
> And all the haunt be ours.

Here the exaltation is in life.

And at the end, when Perdita and Florizel are rapturously united, Hermione is restored to Leontes. The illusion of death is a deceit, and Hermione steps down to her husband, no longer a statue as she had seemed, but a living woman:

Music, awake her: strike!
'Tis time; descend; be stone no more: approach;
Strike all that look upon with marvel. Come;
I'll fill your grave up: stir; nay, come away;
Bequeath to death your numbness, for from him
Dear life redeems you.

(v, 3, 98)

8

The Tempest carries the theme a step further, though *The Tempest* is a play with so many layers of meaning that no single interpretation can do it justice. Yet if, as our discussion of Shakespeare draws to a close, we come back to our starting point, and think of *The Tempest* not only in terms of the difference between appearance and reality, but also in terms of the three levels in Nature's hierarchy—the animal, the human and the intellectual—which were the bases of Shakespeare's view of man, we may have a central framework from which further and broader interpretations may radiate. For in this last of his complete plays, as in those he wrote at the beginning of his career, Shakespeare uses, however unconsciously, the common body of psychological assumption that was given him by his time.

And yet, like everything else in the last plays, that assumption is transfigured and transformed; it is presented in a different climate of reality from its presentation in the tragedies, and there is less need for either the background of kingship—the hierarchy of the state—or the background and hierarchy of the cosmos; the individual human life itself, in its finest manifestations, is enough. At the heart of *The Tempest* there is an incantation which accepts things as they are, a tone which has forgotten tragedy, an order melted at the edges into a new unity of acceptance and wonder.

The action of the play takes place on a deliberately unidentifiable island, the kind of place where transfiguration is possible.

> The isle is full of noises,
> Sounds and sweet airs, that give delight, and hurt not.
> Sometimes a thousand twangling instruments
> Will hum about mine ears; and sometimes voices,
> Will make me sleep again.
>
> (iii, 2, 147)

In such a place, it is fitting that the animal level should be presented half-symbolically, through Caliban. We are no longer in the climate of tragedy, where human beings themselves are seen as animals, like the Spartan dog Iago or the wolfish daughters of Lear. The "beast Caliban," as Prospero calls him, is a thing "not honor'd with human shape (i, 2, 283)"; he is set apart—as it were, abstracted, from human nature. Unlike human beings he is unimprovable; he cannot be tamed by reason, he is

> A devil, a born devil, on whose nature
> Nurture can never stick; on whom my pains,
> Humanely taken, are all lost, quite lost.
>
> (iv, 1, 188)

And it is characteristic of him that he should take Stephano, the lowest available specimen of human nature, for a god.

The human beings on the island are a various crew, perhaps almost deliberately chosen to present as wide a range as possible. Stephano and Trinculo are associated with Caliban; Alonzo and Sebastian are selfish schemers, though royal; there is the good Gonzalo, and there is Ferdinand, who, excellent young man as he is, must still pass through some difficulties before he marries Miranda, who is to him the "wonder" of the island, and like the other heroines of the last plays, is a symbol of humanity at its best. All these people, with the exception of Miranda, go through some kind of punishment or purgation. The low characters are merely punished, they get be-fouled and be-labored, as is appropriate—they are incapable of purgation. But the courtly figures, Alonzo, Antonio and Sebastian, lose their human faculties for a time, to emerge purified as rational beings. As we know, the theme of purgation occurs earlier in Shakespeare, especially in *Lear*, but Lear loses his reason through a human agency, through filial ingratitude. Alonzo and Sebastian are purged through a superhuman agency, through magic. They enter the charmed circle made by Prospero (v, 1, 55) and once there, their reason, their specifically human faculty, is temporarily taken away, as—in such very different circumstances—Lear's reason was taken away. Their brains are useless, "boiled" within their skulls; "ignorant fumes . . . mantle their clearer reason," until finally

> their understanding
> Begins to swell, and the approaching tide
> Will shortly fill the reasonable shores
> That now lie foul and muddy.
>
> (v, 1, 79)

As soon as he comes to himself, Alonzo resigns the dukedom, entreating Prospero to pardon his wrongs. Then Miranda and Ferdinand are discovered, and it is on a regenerated humanity that Miranda looks when she exclaims:

> How beauteous mankind is! O brave new world,
> That has such people in't!

Prospero—until he drowns his book—is clearly on a level above that of ordinary human nature. Yet though we may recognize him as a symbol of the third, the intellectual, level, Shakespeare's presentation of him is so shimmering with overtones and implications, that to think of him merely as a representative of pure intellect is an obvious falsification. Nevertheless we may say that his use of magic is a way of making his superiority dramatically effective, and the elves and demi-puppets that have been his agents were considered in certain contemporary circles of thought to be creatures above man in the hierarchy of Nature, between men and angels.[11] Prospero's

[11] See W. C. Curry, *Shakespeare's Philosophical Patterns*, Baton Rouge, 1937, p. 194.

command of them obviously involves a more than human power. Yet Prospero gives up this power, and returns to the human level again. I do not agree with those critics who say that Prospero, at the end of the play, "finds himself immeasurably nearer than before to the impassivity of the gods." "His theurgical operations," says Mr. Curry, "have accomplished their purpose. He wishes now to take the final step and to consummate the assimilation of his soul to the gods. And this step is to be accomplished through prayer." [12]

But this is clearly a misinterpretation of Shakespeare's meaning. Prospero abjures his magic not to become like the gods, but to return to humanity:

> I will discase me, and myself present,
> As I was sometime Milan.

He compares (v, 1, 170) Alonzo's "content" at his rediscovery of Ferdinand to his own content at being restored to his dukedom, and in fact much of the point of the play is lost if we do not see Prospero returning to worldly responsibility. He must be restored to his position in the state, as he must be restored to his position as a human being. In a sense his temporary control of the spirit world has also been a purgation; he has come to

---

[12] *Op. cit.*, p. 196. In support of this view, Mr. Curry, like Mr. Middleton Murry, interprets Prospero's epilogue in religious terms:

> Now I want
> Spirits to enforce, art to enchant;
> And my ending is despair,
> Unless I be reliev'd by prayer,
> Which pierces so that it assaults
> Mercy itself and frees all faults.
> As you from crimes would pardon'd be,
> Let your indulgence set me free.

But the prayer is obviously merely a prayer to the audience. It is conventional for an actor to step half out of character in an epilogue, and that is what Prospero is doing here. His "prayer" consists of the last two lines, and has no metaphysical connotations.

the conclusion that, though he can wreak supernatural havoc on his enemies,

> the rarer action is
> In virtue than in vengeance,

and, his domination of the spirits having been outside the limits of human nature, his wisdom makes him return to his rightful place as a governor of himself, and as a governor, through his dukedom, of other human beings as well. Prospero, on his enchanted island, has been like a god, controlling the world of nature and the elements:

> I have bedimm'd
> The noontide sun, call'd forth the mutinous winds,
> And 'twixt the green sea and the azur'd vault
> Set roaring war: to the dread-rattling thunder
> Have I given fire and rifted Jove's stout oak
> With his own bolt: the strong-bas'd promontory
> Have I made shake; and by the spurs pluck'd up
> The pine and cedar: graves at my command
> Have wak'd their sleepers, op'd, and let them forth
> By my so potent art.
>
> (v, 1, 41)

But he abjures his magic, and having "required Some heavenly music" so that the courtiers may be restored to their senses—in Shakespeare's theater the music would have come from above, from the "heavens"—he breaks his staff and plans to drown his book of magic "deeper than did ever plummet sound." In the company of his fellow men, Prospero returns to Milan.

9

This is Shakespeare's conclusion, the conclusion of the dramatist, some of whose most normal and likeable characters—Berowne, Hotspur, Mercutio—had been, from the beginning, men with a strong sense of everyday reality. There is something of these men in Prospero, though Prospero is of course infinitely wiser than they are, since he has surveyed everything, and has risen to a control of the supernatural before returning to the normal human life which they exemplified so much more naively than he. But in one way they are closer to Prospero, to Shakespeare's final vision of man's nature, than the wracked and tortured heroes of the great tragedies. For those heroes were split by an internal conflict, a conflict that was expressed in terms of the conflict about man's nature that was so deeply embedded in the consciousness of the age: whereas in Prospero there is no conflict; in his control of his world, internal conflict has no place.

And yet the view of man's nature that is so profoundly and movingly illustrated in the great tragic heroes has, after all, a relation to the view of life that is illustrated by *The Tempest*. Evil does exist—in the plotting of the courtiers, in the untameable animal nature of Caliban. And it may not be too far-fetched to see, in the very different ways by which Hamlet, Othello, Lear and Macbeth become, at the end of the action, resigned to the situations in which they find themselves, some relation to the theme of acceptance and reconciliation which is dominant in *The Tempest*.

Theirs, however, was a tragic reconciliation, and though it ennobles our conception of their characters, it does not redeem the evil in man's nature which has brought about their downfall. In *The Tempest* the evil *is* redeemed. Here, as in all the last plays, there is a re-birth, a return to life, a heightened, almost symbolic, awareness of the beauty of normal humanity after it has been purged of evil—a blessed reality under the evil appearance. It is not merely a literal reality; the mountains and waters, the human beings, have changed since Shakespeare first looked at them in the early 1590's. The tragic period has intervened; the conflict has given the assurance a richer and deeper meaning. But the literal reality is there just the same, in a garland of flowers, in a harmony of music, as the basis for the acceptance and the vision.

10

When we try to distil from the craftsmanship of the last plays Shakespeare's final word on the difference between seeming and truth, and try to determine whether his final emphasis is on the good or on the evil in man's nature, the result is, apparently, such as I have tried to describe. It is not, to be sure, a "philosophy," and we must not imagine that Shakespeare was directly teaching a lesson. The tone, the overtone, the poetic meaning, is what counts, and it is of this, not of any philosophical system, that we must think when we speak of Shakespeare's vision or of his answer to the problems of reality.

But in describing this final vision—and we should beware of describing it too subjectively—we must not forget the craftsmanship which embodied it and without which it could not have been expressed. Again and again, as we review Shakespeare's completed career, we are reminded of the dramatic tradition which lay behind all Elizabethan drama, and which helped to give it its form. The sixteenth-century morality play and interlude almost invariably followed a tripartite pattern; as we saw, there is first "an account of the optimistic picture of what man ought to be, we then are shown how man is led astray by the lower part of his nature, and finally we have a reconciliation between man and the ruler of the universe." And if we think of Shakespeare's plays in their most elementary terms, we can see this same pattern recurring again and again. In one form it is the pattern of *Hamlet,* where the hero starts as an optimist, discovers evil, and at the end is reconciled, however sadly, to his world. In another form it is the pattern of *Othello,* where the hero begins grandly and self-confidently, then discovers evil and violence—is led astray by the lower part of his nature—

and ends with some measure of reconciliation to the terrible situation in which he finds himself. In another form it is the pattern of the last plays:—but in the last plays the emphasis is different. The emphasis in the tragedies is on evil and the struggle with evil, and the reconciliation, such as it is, occupies only a small part of the action and the thought. In the last plays the evil and the struggle—the jealousy of Leontes in *The Winter's Tale,* the plots of the court party in *The Tempest*— take up a relatively short space; it is the reconciliation that is emphasized and dwelt on, not the violence that precedes it.

In other words when we consider the last plays in relation to dramatic convention, we reach the same conclusion about them that we reach when we consider them in relation to the Renaissance conflict about man's nature. The amount of time that is spent on the reconciliation scenes is a technical and structural reflection of their poetic content, their vision of acceptance and rebirth. The craft and the meaning are one.

CHAPTER VIII

LITERATURE AND THE NATURE OF MAN

I

In the second chapter we saw that in Shakespeare's age the universal problem of the difference between man as he should be and man as he is, between the theoretically good appearance and the actually evil reality, was being felt by many people besides Shakespeare himself. Many circumstances, intellectual and otherwise, at the end of the sixteenth century combined to produce one of those periods when, with a sudden shock, men see themselves in new relationships and become aware that the new lights they have discovered only make the surrounding darkness more portentous and profound. The consequences of such a situation can be various. Some people may try to retreat into the comforting limits of the old concepts that have been overthrown; others may excitedly pursue, regardless of order, the fresh illumination; others may invent new formulae to include the new facts; others may escape into irrelevancies or fictions; others may extend their comprehension to say, "Yes; this is true; this is how things are; let us be thankful for that which is." Religion, science, philosophy, romance and art—each (though of course none can be entirely separated from the others) has its answer, as each had its apparent answer at the beginning of the seventeenth century, the century that formed, as we can see in looking back at it, our own civilization and our own concept of the nature of man.

It is a striking fact that the three chief satirists of the 1590's, Donne, Hall and Marston, men who used literature to expose the evil in human nature, all ended in the Anglican Church.

Hall became a clergyman about 1600, Marston in 1608, and
Donne in 1614. And though we know nothing of Marston's
ecclesiastical views, it is significant that both Hall and Donne
occupied a religious position that was the logical consequence
of the skeptical attitude taken toward man by Montaigne in
his "Apology for Raymond Sebond." It was the position
known, in its extreme form, as fideism, which said that man
could know nothing in himself, that faith, not reason, was the
primary form of human knowledge, and that only through
God's grace could he be saved.[1] The tradition of Augustine,
re-stated by Calvin and unexpectedly fortified by Montaigne,
made man, in the rhetorical prose of Donne, less than the lowest of God's creatures. "How poor and inconsiderable a thing,"
he says, "is man. Man, whom Paracelsus would have undertaken
to have made, in a Limbeck, in a furnace: man, who, if they were
all together, all the men that ever were, and are, and shall be,
would not have the power of one angel in them all, whereas all
the angels, who in the school are conceived to be more in number, than not only all the species, but all the individuals of this
lower world, have not in them all, the power of one finger of
God's hand: man, of whom when David has said (as the lowest
diminution that he could put upon him), *I am a worm and no
man,* he might have gone lower and said, I am a man, and not
a worm; for man is so much less than a worm, as that worms
of his own production shall feed upon his dead body in the
grave, and an immortal worm gnaw his conscience in the tor-
ments of hell."[2]

<hr>

[1] Fideism has always been condemned by the Roman Church, which maintains
the emphasis on reason which I described in the first chapter. The Vatican Council
teaches as a dogma of Catholic faith that "one true God and Lord can be known
with certainty by the natural light of human reason by means of the things that
are made." (*Catholic Encyclopedia,* s.v. "Fideism.") I do not mean to imply that
Donne deliberately became a fideist—his views merely tended strongly in that
direction.

[2] LXXX *Sermons,* London, 1640, No. vii, pp. 64–65.

And yet, though this may be man's condition considered in itself, all is not lost. For, Donne goes on to say, "to this man comes this God, God that is infinitely more than all, to man that is infinitely less than nothing." [3] By something outside himself man could be, and had been, restored to the dignity of his original position. And there can be no question that many other people beside Donne, who, like Marston, had themselves passed through a period in which they wrote only of the evil in man's nature, felt the truth of the old doctrines with a new and consoling belief.[4]

The fideistic view toward which Donne tended was only an extreme example of how many men in the first half of the seventeenth century returned to religion with new seriousness. Donne tells us that he met with seven dejected souls for one that was over-confident; such people must have found, like Donne himself, their consolation in religion. The universal intensity of thought and feeling about religion in the first half of the seventeenth century, culminating in what Sir George Trevelyan has called a "metaphysical war," was the natural consequence of the earlier metaphysical and emotional conflict between the two views of man's nature. An awareness of evil, a kind of passionate disillusionment, became a passionate desire for certainty, which found its expression in passionate action. The first stage was expressed through popular literature, Elizabethan and Jacobean drama; the second through popular religion.

[3] *Ibid.*, p. 65.

[4] Our ignorance of the last twenty-eight years of Marston's life is particularly to be regretted, since in the short period of his literary career, 1598–1606, he reflects, in a much cruder way, the same kind of interests and preoccupations that concerned Shakespeare. *Antonio and Mellida* and *Antonio's Revenge*, a revenge play and its sequel which he wrote just before *Hamlet*, show him concerned with lust as the key to evil in human nature, as does *The Dutch Courtezan*. Marston also borrowed extensively from Montaigne (see Charles Crawford, *Collectanea*, Second Series, Stratford, 1907, and my article, "John Marston," *Criterion*, XIII [1934], 581 ff.). Presumably when he became a clergyman his views were similar to Donne's.

Another seventeenth-century answer to the problem of the evil in man's nature was not so much an answer as a denial of the existence of the problem. And though at first it did not seem to have the immediate importance of religion, in the long run it was to dominate man's view of himself and the order of things. I refer, of course, to the theories of Bacon. Bacon implied that man should turn, not inward upon himself, but outward to external nature, and that the problems of the soul, with which drama and religion had been concerned, should be put in a separate compartment, a compartment that to his followers became eventually meaningless. To the disciple of Bacon, trying to master the external world by inventing for man's use the internal combustion engine and mustard gas, of what relevance are the questions of good and evil, of the difference between appearance and reality? Bacon, taking, as he thought, all knowledge for his province, was the fore-runner of those people who, down to our own day, have proclaimed the importance of knowledge for the sake of knowledge alone—people who have at the same time unconsciously sanctioned the irresponsible development of practical machinery and invention. Bacon was one of the first representatives of that split between knowledge and morality which has had such enormous consequences for our civilization.

There were other attempts, in the early seventeenth century, at solving the problem and evading despair: Chapman, for example, tried to use Stoicism as a bulwark against disorder, and in the person of Clermont d'Ambois, in the *Revenge of Bussy D'Ambois* (1610), he presented an ideal hero who solved the familiar struggle between "passion and reason, self-division's cause" by means of a strict following of Stoic philosophy. But Chapman was a solitary figure as far as the drama was concerned, and the dramatists came more and more to abandon the subject; after 1615 or so their characters and situations very rarely include an awareness of the universal problem of the

LITERATURE AND THE NATURE OF MAN   207

nature of man. They rely more and more on the effectiveness of the individual scene, on surprise, on superficial contrasts. In the history of Elizabethan drama, as in the Greek, emotional opportunism succeeded integrity of vision.

We may say then, with some danger of over-simplification, that there were four chief ways in which the early seventeenth century answered the essential humanistic problem of the Renaissance. Religion, science, Stoicism or frivolity (the work of Beaumont and Fletcher, like that of the Restoration dramatists who admired it, is essentially frivolous)—each in its different way seemed to take the burden from men's minds.

Shakespeare's picture of man's nature, as I have tried to describe it in this book, is a fifth way of regarding the situation. If we think of it as a whole, we can see that his work embodies, more completely than that of any other artist, the primarily artistic vision. To see it as a whole is essential. As T. S. Eliot remarks, "the standard set by Shakespeare is that of a continuous development from first to last, a development in which the choice both of theme and of dramatic and verse technique in each play seems to be determined by Shakespeare's state of feeling, by the particular stage of his emotional maturity at the time. What is 'the whole man' is not simply his greatest or maturest achievement, but the whole pattern formed by the sequence of plays; so that we may say confidently that the full meaning of any one of his plays is not in itself alone, but in that play in the order in which it was written, in its relation to all of Shakespeare's other plays, earlier and later: we must know all of Shakespeare's work in order to know any of it." [5]

And as we look at all of Shakespeare's work, and try to derive from it his view of the nature of man, two facts emerge. In the first place there is the "continuous development" of which Eliot speaks, the development that begins with a period of experimentation—what we might call Shakespeare's

[5] *Selected Essays*, New York, 1932, p. 170.

"external" period—a development that continues with an enormous increase in dramatic scope and that presents the evil in man's nature with tragic force, a development that ends with acceptance, with regeneration, with a vision that sees human life as it is and sees it redeemed.

The second fact that emerges from our picture of Shakespeare's work as a whole—and this is something at which I have previously only hinted—is that though he drew very largely on what he inherited of the conventional concepts of man, and though his picture of man's nature would have been very different without them, nevertheless Shakespeare's vision of human life transcends anything given him by his time. The inherited concepts represent, of course, one particular codification of what is permanently true about humanity, and when a civilization lacks such codification, that civilization is in danger. But Shakespeare's presentation of Hamlet, of Lear, of Cleopatra, of Imogen and Miranda goes deeper than any codification: it is the individual human life, the thing itself underlying codification that Shakespeare gives us, and which makes him, in Ben Jonson's familiar phrase, "not of an age but for all time."

2

If we keep these two aspects of Shakespeare's vision of man in mind we may perhaps be able to accomplish the last of the three aims with which this discussion began. We have so far tried to see Shakespeare in relation to his time, and we have tried to see how his craftsmanship enabled him to use what his time gave him. The final problem remains: we must try to judge Shakespeare's work in relation to what we believe to be true of human experience as a whole. For the conflict between order and chaos, in the world, the state and the individual, the difference between appearance and truth, the search for what is most natural to man—these central problems of human thought; they were as pressing in the age of Aeschylus as they were in the age of Shakespeare and as they are today. The greatest writers have, directly or indirectly, always been concerned with them, and though these problems may take on different forms in different periods, it is only their accidents that change; the essence remains the same.

Since art, as Aristotle says, is an imitation of life, the individual artist is necessarily compelled to imitate the life of his own period, and it is clear enough that certain periods are more favorable to good art than others. It is also clear that there are different kinds of imitation, even in the same period, and that a writer like Ben Jonson, who is concerned with the surface of experience, who describes social vice rather than spiritual evil, whose characters, unlike Shakespeare's, never look inward or experience an inner division—it is clear that a writer like Jonson will give us a different picture of his period from that of a man who probes more deeply and resolves more conflicts. It is not with Ben Jonson, or others like him—admirable in their own sphere though they may be—that Shakespeare should be compared. He should rather be compared with those writers, and they are not many, who used the views of their time to see human nature in its broadest terms, and whose imitation of life is an imitation not only of man in relation to society, but also in relation to himself and to the larger forces by which he feels himself controlled.

The periods in which the greatest writers have flourished have been those which, like Shakespeare's, have enabled the writer to use all three relationships; and this means that they have been periods when the writer's medium has been close to the life of the people. In such periods the artistic form has been traditional in the sense that it has been taken for granted, as the drama was taken for granted in the time of Aeschylus and Shakespeare, the allegorical vision in the time of Dante, and the novel in the nineteenth century. And in each of these periods there seems to have been a heightened consciousness of the precarious balance in human affairs between order and chaos, with varying emphasis on religion, the state and the individual.

3

The *Oresteia* of Aeschylus, more than any other dramatic unity, represents a completely fused relationship between literature and society. As Professor Thomson has recently shown,[6] it was produced at a time when the drama had an intimate connection with religious and with social forms, and hence we find in its magnificent conception an interweaving, a fusion, of the three realms of man's being, the religious, the social and the individual; in the *Oresteia* an essential problem of man's nature is solved in relation to the gods, to the state and to himself. Orestes, the central figure of the trilogy, has killed his mother Clytemnestra because she had previously killed his father Agamemnon, and the moral problem he faces is whether or not he should be punished for having tried to avenge one crime by committing another. The situation is similar in many respects to that of Hamlet,[7] but it is treated very differently. The play of *Hamlet* is equivalent, as far as the action is concerned, only to the second part of the trilogy of Aeschylus, and if Shakespeare had wanted to treat Hamlet's story as Aeschylus treated that of Orestes, he would have had to write an introductory play about the murder of Hamlet's father and a concluding one which would have assumed that Hamlet's revenge had been successful, but that he was now himself on trial before a court of supernatural powers. We can imagine the first play easily enough, but the last one is inconceivable in terms of

[6] George Thomson, *Aeschylus and Athens*, London, 1941. Mr. Thomson writes (p. 297): "The great plays of Shakespeare were not immediately and consciously related to the social movement of his time; in the *Oresteia* the citizens of Athens witnessed the history of their civilization, culminating in a festival in which all of them annually took part."

[7] See Gilbert Murray, *The Classical Tradition in Poetry*, Cambridge (Mass.), 1930, pp. 205 ff.

Elizabethan drama. In the *Oresteia* of Aeschylus, on the other hand, the last play, the *Eumenides,* is the essential culmination of the whole story. When Athena solves the problem of Orestes' individual guilt she at the same time solves the problem of man's relation to the supernatural by appeasing the Furies, and she solves the problem of justice in the state by establishing the court of the Areopagus. The three realms of ethics, religion and government are all brought together in one solution, in one reconciliation. The intimate relation between drama and the life of the people in fifth-century Athens, combined with his own extraordinary genius, enabled Aeschylus to create a work which fused into a single unity the three essential aspects of the nature of man.

The other Greek dramatists accomplished nothing so grand as this. Yet if we think of the plays of Sophocles in chronological order—though general speculation about them, since only a small percentage of them has survived, cannot be very securely based—we can see that the view of human life which they present also ends in a reconciliation, like the end of the *Oresteia* and like the last plays of Shakespeare. *Oedipus at Colonus,* the play of Sophocles' old age, shows us Oedipus after his terrible ordeal, exiled and blind, stern and awe-inspiring, but no longer the proud and self-willed man whom Fate had so dreadfully punished. His death is miraculously calm:

> It was a messenger from heaven, or else
> Some gentle, painless cleaving of earth's base;
> For without wailing or disease or pain
> He passed away—an end most marvelous.[8]

His death also is surrounded by wider implications, for it is heralded by a thunderstorm sent by Zeus, and, because he dies on Athenian soil, Athens will be forever preserved from her enemies. The death of the individual hero is related to the gods and to the state.

[8] Ll. 1661 ff., trans. F. Storr, Loeb Classics.

The use of the *deus ex machina* by Sophocles in the *Philoctetes* and by Euripides in nearly all his plays may be seen as another method of giving universality to the individual action, and of relating human concerns to the supernatural powers that control them. But in the hands of Euripides this device becomes only too often merely a mechanical trick, and we feel that Euripides, here as elsewhere, is unscrupulously manipulating his plot in order to give his audience a false satisfaction that has no basic relation to a view of human experience in general; he is striving for results that will surprise his audience rather than fulfill their expectations. There is a great difference between the Athena of Aeschylus, who solves the moral problem of Orestes with such rich social and religious connotations, and the Castor and Pollux of Euripides who appear at the end of Euripides' version of the story. The *dei ex machina* of Euripides merely describe what will happen to Orestes as a result of the murder, there is no weight of social implication; the effect, as usual with Euripides, is not an effect of grandeur but of pathos, and we think chiefly of Orestes himself, not of a world restored to order.

There is a striking parallel between Euripides and the dramatists, such as Webster, and—on a lower level—Fletcher, who immediately followed Shakespeare. In each case we find a kind of irresponsibility, an emphasis on the unusual, a fondness for solving the problems of plot by some external means, like a *deus ex machina*—all of them characteristics which may be immediately successful on the stage, but which illustrate a view of man's nature that tends to disintegration, to a divorce between literature and the essential concerns of man. In each case we feel that individualism is glorified, instead of being made, as it is in Shakespeare, one of the attributes of villainy, and when this happens in the thought and literature of an age, that age is on the road to decadence. For it means that one of the three realms in which man lives is being emphasized at the expense of the others, and that the proper balance between the individual, the state and the forces behind Nature has been lost. The part—and the same thing is true of all romantic literature—becomes more important than the whole, as it never does in Aeschylus, Sophocles or Shakespeare.

Nor does it, of course, in Dante. *The Divine Comedy* is the most perfectly ordered poem ever written, and the chief element in its order is Dante's use of the medieval view of life to present man in relation to the three realms of his being. In fact it would be possible to use the poem as an illustration, perhaps the best illustration, of the orderly view of the cosmos, the state and the individual which I described in the first chapter as so important a part of Shakespeare's intellectual and emotional inheritance. In *The Divine Comedy* the spheres of the Ptolemaic heavens correspond to various states of intellectual being and of moral purity; they control everything on earth, and, in Dante's words, "direct every seed to some end according as the stars are its companions" (*Purgatorio* xxx). To Dante man's worst sins are those by which his special faculty of reason has been corrupted, and throughout the poem man's function as a citizen receives equal emphasis with his function as a rational animal; his duty to the state is as much a part of his nature as his duty to God. And after Dante has described the whole orderly universe, disordered only by man's wrong use of his free will (and even that disorder is taken care of by the ordered punishments of Hell and Purgatory), at the end of the poem he finds beneath the order the unity that is its soul, and in the final vision he sees all the individual accidents and substances which are scattered in leaves through the universe "bound up by love in one volume."

In its final emphasis nothing could be more different from Shakespeare than this; though to Dante man's behavior in time may determine his place in eternity, Dante is primarily concerned with the eternal rather than the temporal world. His subject matter is as different from Shakespeare's as the form of the allegorical vision is different from the form of the drama. Yet though Dante may describe order and the life that begins with death, while Shakespeare in his tragedies describes chaos and the life that *ends* with death, nevertheless Dante and Shakespeare have one thing in common, for both use the same views of man's nature for their very different purposes, and like the greatest of the Greek dramatists, see man's situation in relation to the three realms in which his thought and action move.

The greatest novelists treat human experience in the same way; we have only to think of Tolstoi's *War and Peace* to realize that if the nature of man is to be fully presented in literature, the same fundamental relationships must inevitably be included. Tolstoi's account of Prince Andrew and of Pierre, of their relation to peace and war, includes a description of their relation to the external forces that move them and to the society in which they live, as well as a description of the various ways in which they try to find a moral basis for action. It is because *War and Peace* contains all these things, these central relationships in which man sees himself, that it is a touchstone by which other fiction can be judged. By its side the work of Dickens, even the work of Flaubert, takes on a smaller dimension, for Dickens and Flaubert do not describe so *much* of what we believe to be true of human nature. In the long run the criterion of literary greatness must be not only qualitative but quantitative as well; quantity, or scope, as far as the vision of human life is concerned, being itself the final quality.

Tolstoi's description of man's nature differs, however, from those of Aeschylus, of Dante and of Shakespeare. For in the earlier periods of human history it was much easier than it was in the nineteenth century to take a positive attitude toward man's primary relationships; in fifth-century Athens, in the Middle Ages and in the Renaissance, thought on the subject was far more clearly formulated than in Tolstoi's day. The earlier periods gave the writer a set of beliefs, the nineteenth century gave him a set of questions, and in no respect does Tolstoi more clearly reflect his time than in the way he presents Pierre Bezukhof, his main character, as *seeking* for answers to the meaning of life. Aeschylus, to be sure, is more original, more a creator of his own belief, than either Dante or Shakespeare, but Aeschylus could rely much more firmly than Tolstoi was able to do on a community of belief, just as he could relate his dramas much more closely to the social concerns of his audience, grouped together in a theater, than Tolstoi could relate his novels to his nineteenth-century readers, miles away from each other, scattered in a thousand arm-chairs.

Yet Tolstoi's questioning, so far as *War and Peace* is concerned, does produce an answer; an answer that is closer to Shakespeare's, perhaps, than those of Aeschylus and Dante. He also comes back to the individual experience, to the simplicity of the facts, to the marriage of Pierre and Natasha, to their life in their children, to that which is. The end of *War and Peace* lacks the exaltation of Shakespeare's last plays, because the medium is not poetry, but the meaning is the same. It is richer than the conclusion of Voltaire's *Candide,* whose hero shrivels into the restricted conviction that the only thing to do is to cultivate one's garden; it has a warmer human truth than the end of Goethe's *Faust,* whose hero self-consciously reclaims a swamp for the impersonal benefit of mankind.

4

When we think of the literature of the past in such general terms as those which I have been using, and which are universally applicable both to the life of action and to the art which interprets it, we are bound to have in our minds the thought of our own literature and our own lives. What strikes us at first is the contrast between the past and ourselves.

At the height of the Italian Renaissance, when, toward the

end of the fifteenth century, the tradition of humanism was being felt with a new vigor and man's crucial position in the world of created nature was being re-stated with new force, Pico della Mirandola summed up the traditional thought of his time in his famous *Oration on the Dignity of Man*. To Pico, as to his contemporaries, man was in the center of things, since by the right use of his reason and his will, he could choose whether he would live the life of the angelic intellect or the life of the brutish senses. Heaven and hell were on either side of him, and, as the chief inhabitant of an ordered universe, his responsibility was to see that he played a conscious and rational part in the marvelous structure which the divine architect had created for him, so that he could praise the God who made him. Out of that view, that dramatic tension of responsibility, grew the drama of Shakespeare.

What has our own time to say that would be as typical of the twentieth-century view of man's nature as Pico's view was typical of the Renaissance? What can we say of the dignity of man?

At first sight it would seem that we could say very little. We see ourselves today as living on a minute satellite of a tiny solar system that is of an almost infinitesimal size compared to the hugeness of the galaxy to which it belongs, a galaxy that is itself only a small part of the material universe. We can comprehend our universe only in terms of mathematical formulae, we cannot see it. And our existence on this unthinkably small planet seems to have come about by accident. A set of apparently chance events started the peculiar biological process called life of which we are the temporary products. Both the space and the time which have produced us are incomprehensibly huge. And, to shift the focus, we owe what we are, not to our wills, but to a set of predetermined forces, the accidents of birth and environment, which decide what sort of beings we will be long before we are conscious of being. Our unconscious desires turn us this way and that, like weathervanes, and if we are to be happy, we are told, we must let the wind blow us where it pleases. "I think I could turn and live with animals," says Walt Whitman, "they do not make me sick discussing their duty to God." We pay a kind of lip-service to reason, but we trust our instincts more than we do our brains. We have lost any real belief in the capacity of intellect to dictate our actions, and our prevalent theory of education persuades us to adopt as our principle of behavior the motto which Rabelais put over the entrance to his Abbey of Thélème, "Fais ce que voudras"— Do what you please—without any of the Stoic principles of order which Rabelais had assumed the inmates of his Abbey to possess before they went there.

Believing ourselves to have no necessary relation to the cosmos, and to be at the mercy of our unconscious impulses, and hence finding ourselves in an unsatisfactory relation to two of the three aspects of our situation as human beings, we are in danger of over-emphasizing the importance of the third aspect, and of seeking in our relation to the state a compensation for the impersonality of the universe and the impotence of our wills. In some countries this over-emphasis has already gone almost as far as it can go, and the countries that remain are being forced into temporary imitation in order to destroy their rivals so that the balance may be restored.

In other words, as we look today at man's relation to the three aspects of his world, we seem to be facing a depressing and belittling situation, and our concept of the insignificant nature of man seems unlikely to produce any permanent expression of human life, in literature or elsewhere, that can compare with the expressions of the past.

And yet, if we consider more deeply, and take into account the possibilities of the future, this gloomy picture, which was given in such different terms at the beginning of the seventeenth century,[9] represents only a partial truth. Though some aspects of science—which bears the same relation to the thought of our day as religion did to the thought of the sixteenth century—seem to make man hopelessly insignificant, other aspects present him as occupying a more favorable and important position. From one point of view contemporary scientific thought about man is even parallel to the religious thought of Shakespeare's day. For example Mr. Julian Huxley, in his essay on "The Uniqueness of Man," after discussing the differences that science observes between man and animals, remarks that "biology . . . reinstates man in a position analogous to that conferred on him as Lord of Creation by theology. There are, however, differences," he continues, "and differences of some importance for our general outlook. In the biological view, the other animals have not been created to serve man's needs, but man has evolved in such a way that he has been able to eliminate some competing types, to enslave others by domestication, and to modify physical and biological conditions over the larger part of the earth's area. The theological view was not true in detail or in many of its implications; but it had a solid biological basis." [10]

If man's importance can thus be formulated by the impersonal and long-range view of science, can we derive similar convictions by examining the more immediate and local situation? Biological science describes man in relation to Nature; is there any evidence at the present time that man's relation to his own consciousness and to the state promises anything more satisfactory than psychological or economic determinism would pessimistically describe?

---

[9] For example the early seventeenth century, as represented by Godfrey Goodman (above, p. 26), thought of the decay of Nature as caused by original sin; we describe it by the second law of thermo-dynamics.

[10] *The Uniqueness of Man*, London, 1941, p. 5.

If an awareness of the problem indicates the possibility of a more hopeful answer, we can, I believe, say "Yes." Of course it is far more difficult in our own time than it was in Shakespeare's to say that any one view is typical of the age or predominant in it, for variety of opinion is much greater with us, but there can be little question that serious thought about man's nature is at the present time moving away from determinism to a view that re-establishes some psychological hierarchy in man's structure. The old emphasis on reason and will, the division of man's mind into faculties, is not likely to be re-accepted, any more than what Mr. Huxley calls the theological view of man's relation to the other animals is likely to be re-accepted. But just as that theological view is recognized to have had "a solid biological basis," so the old concept of an element in man's nature which can know and can direct is recognized as having a solid psychological basis. "There is nothing in the intellect which was not first in the senses," said Locke. To which Leibniz replied, "Only the intellect itself." And modern psychology, returning to the central problems of man's nature, is trying to describe that "intellect" in terms consistent with scientific knowledge. "Mental life at its best," says one of the most distinguished of contemporary psychologists, "exhibits a consistency, a coherence, and a hierarchy of values." [11] And it is on this fact that emphasis is now being laid with increasing force; the higher, rather than the lower aspects of man's nature, are being re-examined and re-defined.[12] What is chiefly lacking (and it is a very large lack indeed) is an intellectual and emotional sanction—a conviction of truth like that which the Christian system

[11] Wolfgang Köhler, *The Place of Value in a World of Facts*, New York, 1938, p. 411.

[12] I refer, not merely to the professional psychologists, but to those writers who are reconsidering the whole problem of man's nature. See W. Macneile Dixon, *The Human Situation*, New York, 1937; Sir Charles Sherrington, *Man on His Nature*, Cambridge (England), 1940; F. T. Stace, *The Destiny of Western Man*, New York, 1942.

gave in the sixteenth century—which will make the higher impulses of the mind seem the right ones to obey.

Certain people, as we know too well, have found a sanction
in the state, but the sanction they have found is evidently not
the kind that demands the use of man's highest faculties. And
that is why, in government as in psychology and in science, fresh
thought is being given to the old problems; necessity is forcing
us to re-define our concept of the relation of the individual to
the state. Here, as in natural science and in psychology, a change
is taking place, and just as materialism and determinism have
had to be abandoned because they do not fit the facts, so our
unthinking acceptance of the nominal form of democracy, where
the average citizen has had little or no relation or responsibility
to the state—this also has had to be abandoned because it does
not fit the facts. Upon the new order that may result, all our
lives depend.

In other words the gloomy picture of man's present relation
to the three aspects of his world, the picture which seems so
easy to paint, need not, and, if our civilization is to survive,
must not, be the right one. It gives only half the truth, just as
the pessimism of the early seventeenth century gave only half
the truth. And if we think of ourselves in relation to that period,
and in relation to the two different views of man's nature which
that period expressed, it would seem, as I suggested in the
preface to this book, as if a three-hundred-year cycle were coming to a close. What brought about the essential conflict in Shakespeare's day was the fact that the old views of man were being
broken by new discoveries which widened the split between
what man should be and what he was, and which made the
reality seem evil under the appearance of good. Order was
breaking into chaos. And in the course of the three-hundred-
odd years between that time and our own, the consequences of
those new discoveries have been pushed, it appears, as far as
they will go. Galileo's confirmation of Copernicus has become

the cosmology of Einstein, Montaigne's comparison of man to animals has become psycho-analysis and behaviorism, Machiavelli has become Hitler. Those once disruptive forces have mastered men's minds and the world; they have created a new world of their own. But, as I have tried to indicate, their mastery is perhaps only an appearance, and when the first half of the twentieth century is regarded three hundred years from now, as in this discussion we have regarded the early seventeenth century, our situation may perhaps be seen as the reverse of Shakespeare's, and our time may be described as a time when the new forces were not disruptive but collective, and when man's orderly relations to the three facets of his world were not broken, but restored in a new and vital shape.

If this is to happen—and enormous resources of thought and activity will have to be used to make it happen—literature will inevitably reflect the situation. Prophecy is, in such matters, rash, but we can safely say that if a first-class writer is to appear in our century he will have to present, in an artistic form that is taken for granted by his audience, the individual experiences of human beings in relation to themselves, to society, and to the larger forces that control them. The best writers of our generation have already recognized this responsibility, and any future historian of our time, in considering the work of Thomas Mann, of Proust, of Eliot, Yeats and Joyce (and there are others besides these), will see that each of them, in various ways, has been seeking for that ordered pattern of relationships which is the only true universality. Perhaps, for a complete expression of our age, we shall need a writer greater than any of these. Or we may, as seems likely, find that our time will be expressed in another form than that of the merely written word; the movies and the radio are closer to our lives than anything on a page. But whatever medium he may use, it is clear enough that the great interpreter of human life in our century, if he appears, will have to be in as intimate touch with the central problems of

our thought and emotions as was the dramatic art of Shakespeare with the Renaissance conflict about man's nature.

5

But Shakespeare was in touch with something more than his
age, and if we are to come back to our starting-point and try to
arrive at a final view of his work as a whole, we must see it as a
reflection of deeper truths than any that can be described by a
local and temporary picture of the cosmos, of psychology, or of
the state. Beneath any view of man's nature, at the very basis of
human experience, are the elementary facts of birth, of life and
of death. The rhythm of their sequence and renewal lies behind all our knowledge and emotions, and it is the rhythm that
we share with all of living nature, with animals and grass. The
earliest known religions are based on it, and so is the earliest
literature. Birth, struggle, death, and that which is beyond death
—these, as Gilbert Murray says, are the subjects of that primi-
tive dance and song "which is the fountainhead of ancient classical poetry." [18] They have been the essential subjects of all
great literature ever since, as they were the subject of the morality plays which were so important a part of Shakespeare's technical background. And if we think of Shakespeare's work in relation to this essential pattern, this fundamental rhythm, we
shall have, perhaps, a view of the sequence of his plays that will
both underlie and transcend any view that we can obtain by
thinking of his work merely in relation to the ideas of his time.
"Shakespeare," said Keats, "led a life of allegory; his works
are the comment on it," and we may interpret this somewhat
puzzling remark by remembering that Shakespeare's career was
divided into three stages: a period of experiment and adapta-
tion, a period of tragic vision, and a period of affirmation. Birth,
struggle, death, and renewal; these are not only the themes of
the individual final plays, they are the themes which describe

[18] *Op. cit.*, p. 51.

the course of Shakespeare's work as a whole, from his earliest plays through *King Lear* to *The Tempest*. Such, we may say —as we think of art and life together, so that historical description and technical analysis merge into an understanding of the symbolism of all men's lives—such was the allegory of Shakespeare's life: to have illustrated in his own work more richly than any other writer, that rhythm, that sequence, that vision, which all human beings must recognize and accept as fundamental to the nature of man.

INDEX

NOTE: Except under "Shakespeare," entries are listed under each head according to the order of their occurrence in the text. Under "Shakespeare," the headings are listed alphabetically.

Pico della Mirandola, Giovanni, 9n, 48, 216

Plants, created for man's use, 6; souls of, 11

Plato, 1, 4n, 87

Pliny, the Elder, 35n, 8on

Plutarch, state compared to body, 18; on man and animals, 35n, 36n; in relation to *Antony and Cleopatra*, 164n, 165, 168, 172; to *Coriolanus*, 179; to *Timon*, 180

Pole, Reginald, Cardinal, 44

Praz, Mario, 44

Proust, Marcel, 221

Primum Mobile, 8, 19

Prince; *See* King

Protestantism, 46

Psychological hierarchy, description of, 10-14, 24; compared to state, 18; Raleigh on, 19; destroyed by Montaigne, 34-40; Marston, on, 48; morality plays on, 54-58; twentieth-century views of, 217, 219; *See also* Shakespeare, treatment of

Ptolemaic cosmology, 5, 7, 30; importance of astrology in, 10; pessimistic interpretations of, 26; questioned by Copernicus, 29; elaborateness of, 30; persistence of belief in, 31f; implications questioned by Montaigne, 33; Dante on, 213; *See also* Shakespeare, treatment of astronomy

Purgation; *See* Shakespeare, dramatic technique, use of purgation

QUILLER-COUCH, SIR ARTHUR, 77n

RABELAIS, 217

Rastell, John, 58

Raleigh, Sir Walter, 2, 12f, 19

Realism, late sixteenth-century, 47

Reason, degrees of, 12; function of, 12f, 24; distinguished from understanding, 13; weakened by fall of man, 23; Sabunde on, 33; weakness of, Montaigne on, 34, 39; personified in morality plays, 55, 57; in fideism, 204; Chapman on, 206; Dante on,

Reason (*continued*)
213; *See also* Shakespeare, treatment of reason

Recorde, Robert, 4n, 5n

Republic; *See* Commonwealth

Respublica, 59

Richard II, 74-77, 132n

Richard III, 70-73

Robinson, Henry Crabb, 66n

Roman Catholic Church, 46, 204n

Romei, Annibale, 3n, 4, 14n, 19

Romeo and Juliet, 90-92, 115

SABUNDE, RAMÓN, on book of nature, 2n; on God as architect, 3n; on position of man, 5; on macrocosm-microcosm, 18; on psychological hierarchy, 24n; Montaigne on, 33f, 38

Satire, late sixteenth-century, 47f

Satire of the Three Estates, The, 59

Schrager, Victoria, 105n

Scriptures; *See* Bible

Senses, 24, 40, 48; personified in morality plays, 55, 57

Senecan tragedy, conventions of, 61

Shakespeare
  background, intellectual, 1-50
  background, technical, 51-69
  dramatic technique, general: development of, 93, 207; early plays, characteristics of, 85; influence of dramatic tradition on, 201; tragic period, 124; *Antony*, 166; *Lear*, 136; *Lear* and *Macbeth* contrasted, 153; *Measure for Measure*, 123; *Troilus*, 111
  dramatic technique, special: choric characters, *Antony*, 170; *Lear*, 137; *Macbeth*, 157; *Othello*, 137; *Timon*, 181; *Troilus*, 111, 114, 118: hero, ideal of, 81; Hamlet as, 106-109: generalization, chronicle plays, 71; *Antony*, 166; *Hamlet*, 96-100, 107; *Othello*, 129; *Timon*, 183: ideal standard, 79: morality technique, *Henry IV*, 77; *Henry*